What's Your Plan?

How to turn your business and life around
with heart, vision and purpose

Suzzanne Laidlaw

First Published in 2020 by Dalmeny Group Pty Ltd.

National Library of Australia Cataloguing-in-Publication data:

ISBN: 978-0-6485923-1-0 (paperback edition)
ISBN: 978-0-6485923-0-3 (e book)
ISBN: 978-0-6485923-2-7 (audio)

Editor in chief: Renee Jongsma.

Cover design: Jef da Silva, Web Wizards.

Cover photography: Erick Regnard, Ian & Erick Photography.

Diagrams: Fauzan Sahri Ramadhan, Freelancer, and Jef da Silva, Web Wizards.

Dedication

This book is dedicated to you, the courageous people who own their own business or are thinking about going into business.

Particularly, if you:

- Want more out of your life and business
- Are ready to learn and grow
- Need to follow through with your actions and goals
- Are looking for greater inspiration and insight
- Have reached your breaking point and need a better way to move forward

My aim is to inspire, motivate and educate you about *all of the things you don't know that you don't know about running a business.*

Through my own story and experiences, I have broken things down into simple, easy-to-understand concepts that you can learn along the way, and apply to your own business and life.

With this information, my hope is that you can overcome your challenges, reach your potential and live out your wildest dreams.

Acknowledgements

To David, my biggest hero, husband, life partner and inspiration. You have shown me that anything is possible, change is a constant and that we can always improve.

To my children, Hamish and Eve, my god-daughter Caley, my son-in-law Dylan and my beautiful grandson Chet. I'm incredibly honoured to be your number one supporter as well as have your ongoing love and support in return.

To my incredible Mum, for always believing in me and being my guiding light. You instilled in me the values of acting with love, thinking with my heart, practising gratitude for the privilege of being born in this beautiful country and that making a difference in the lives of those less fortunate than ourselves is our responsibility in life.

To Renee Jongsma, for being instrumental in creatively transforming my words and bringing my story to life, whole-heartedly dedicating your time and energy into this project and giving me 100% of your belief throughout the process. I couldn't have achieved my dream of writing this book without your talent and support.

To Lisa O'Neill, for your unwavering encouragement from the very beginning. Your amazing energy and positivity has pulled me through this journey when I couldn't see an end in sight; from our Sunday morning writing sessions, to attending multiple writing courses together, and our many hours critiquing and holding each other accountable. It wouldn't have been the same without you, my writing buddy and wonderful friend.

To Jennifer Marr, for giving us so much direction with the draft and final stages of this book, and teaching us *all the things we didn't know we didn't know about publishing a book*. I'm thankful our paths crossed again, from first meeting at your delightful book store decades ago.

To Brett Odgers, for welcoming me with open arms into your book writing group and encouraging me to share my story. Thank you for your never-ending abundance mentality and openly sharing your knowledge, time and experience.

To Clare McAlaney, for your wonderful writer's retreat in Bali where I was able to first gain clarity and prepare for my book writing voyage ahead, and for first publishing part of my story in your book, "*16 Inspirational WA Women*."[1]

To my dear family and friends who have shared life's journey with me, especially those who have *been there* through my lowest lows and remained pillars of strength in my darkest hours, thank you from the bottom of my heart.

Last but not least, to my many clients, mentors and supporters, there are too many of you to acknowledge here. However, it has been your belief in me that has been paramount to keeping my dreams alive.

Contents

Foreword – by Brad Sugars

Suzzanne has created a refreshingly different business book which hits the mark. This book insightfully navigates the challenges that life throws at us; unlike any other story I've read. It covers many facets of business and life; the theory is in depth, yet simply explained. Perhaps most importantly this book provides practical, actionable and proven insights on how you can change your business for the better, navigating adversity to create a life that some business owners can only dream about.

I know Suzzanne to be a dedicated, passionate and knowledgeable leader who, among many of her achievements, has been recognised multiple times as a global leader in Business Planning. In fact, I have had the privilege of personally handing over many of those awards to her year after year in recognition of her success. After reading her book, I now have an even deeper admiration for Suzzanne and the journey she has travelled to reach where she is today. In spite of her challenges, she has demonstrated how following her vision and plans has enabled her to keep getting back up, proving that you can build and create a successful business that withstands any challenge thrown at you.

Since founding the business coaching industry and ActionCOACH over 25 years ago, my vision has been to create, "World abundance through business re-education." Over the years, I have seen Suzzanne passionately and diligently work towards this vision. Since joining forces with my team one decade ago, she has helped hundreds of her clients to change their lives by teaching them to leverage their efforts to reach their goals and build sustainable future success. I'm proud to call Suzzanne a colleague, and am honoured that she chose to be an ActionCOACH Business Coach to better the lives of business owners worldwide.

Suzzanne can help you to connect with the true essence of who you are and what you want to achieve in your business; an invaluable lesson that you will carry with you through each step of your business and life. Running a business can be a rollercoaster of highs and lows – I urge you to learn from the ups and downs of Suzzanne's story, to grow, learn and develop your knowledge to take your business to the next level.

In reading this book I have no doubt you will laugh, you will want to cry, and you will learn; but my greatest hope is that you will change the way you see and act in your business forever.

To your success.

Sincerely,

Brad Sugars
CEO and Founder of ActionCOACH Global

"Don't let the fear of what could happen, make nothing happen."

Kelly Wiles

CHAPTER ONE

The Day it All Changed

Wednesday evening, 18th of May 1988, was where it all started. It was nearing midnight and I was half asleep as David drove us home from the theatre. In my drowsy state, I was thinking how perfect life was for me in that moment. In many ways, I finally felt like a real adult. Married for just over two years to the love of my life, we had moved into our new home only a few months earlier. Even though it was an old 1950's house, I loved it – especially the smell of fresh paint, new carpets and curtains that hit my senses every day as I awoke. Each time I walked through the door after work, my heart gave a little jump for joy at the excitement of actually buying our own home. I had never felt so happy.

I was also unbelievably contented with my job. Finally, I was not working in *commission only* sales positions and had what I saw was a real job, one of which I was proud. I was working for the Australian Medical Association (AMA), and loved my role of running an employment agency for doctors. I felt I was making a difference in the world.

Perhaps it was the combination of tiredness, two gin and tonics or the warm hum and rock of the car that created this feeling of euphoria within me, but whatever it was, I didn't care. I was blissfully at peace. I was not used to this feeling. It was actually a bit scary to think how perfect everything seemed. It was almost so perfect that it felt like the calm before the storm.

After a long day, I fell into bed as soon as we arrived home, but David wasn't feeling sleepy so decided to stay up for a night cap. I drifted off to sleep, happily dreaming of our blissful life together.

In a matter of what seemed like only minutes later, I was woken by the sound of David screaming in panic, "Suzzie, Suzzie! Save me, save me!"

I jumped out of bed instantly, sleepy and disoriented, wondering what on earth was going on. The room was pitch black. We had only been sleeping in this bedroom for a few days after renovating our home, room-by-room, so I still had no idea where anything was and just couldn't find the light switch.

I became increasingly frustrated as I franticly fumbled around trying to find my way out of the dark room, thinking maybe I had just heard David's cries in my dreams.

But then, I heard the screams even louder, "Suzzie, help me, please!"

Seconds passed as panic began to rise within me; I couldn't comprehend what was happening.

I eventually found the switch and flicked it on, but nothing happened. I tried the switch back and forth a few times, but still no lights. My heart was beating faster now; it felt like I was stuck in a bad dream. David's shrieks were now eerie and frantic.

Finally, I felt the door handle, turned the knob and pushed the door open. From my vantage point, standing at our bedroom doorway, I could see straight across the narrow hallway and into our bathroom, as the door was open.

What I was faced with was beyond my comprehension. I stood frozen in disbelief as I saw David, my beautiful young husband, on fire, his whole body engulfed in flames, burning from head to toe. This was not a bad dream; it was a living nightmare!

The smell of burning skin and fat mixed with melting plastic paint was disgusting. I wanted to be sick, my gut wretched with a pain from deep within the pit of my stomach.

I raced into the bathroom. David was standing in the bath with the shower above turned on full pressure, water spraying everywhere but not making the slightest difference to the flames. Even with the water pouring over him, they wouldn't wane. David's body was black and charred under the flames; bits of skin were falling off and other parts were melting and bubbling with the intense heat. The skin from both his hands hung off him loosely, as if he was halfway through taking off a pair of long rubber gloves.

The smoke was getting thicker and I suddenly realised that my house was on fire! The severity of the situation hit me in that instant; I needed to get us out of there straight away.

My immediate instinct was to smother the flames with a towel. After doing so, I carefully, yet quickly, guided David out of the smoke-filled bathroom and dragged him through our house. I noticed, in horror, that each time his body touched the walls, he left a trail of melted skin in his wake. It was almost too much to take in.

We stumbled outside the burning house and into the cool night air. At least now we were in the relative safety of the backyard. I was even more relieved when we reached the edge of our below ground, saltwater pool. Somehow, I managed to get David into the water to cool his skin down.

He stood there screaming, "My wee house! My wee house is burning down. Save my wee house!"

He was in shock and I was totally confused at this stage, not even knowing how the fire started. I felt strangely alert, but also half asleep. Everything had happened so quickly, yet time seemed to have slowed down. I realised I needed to get help, fast.

I took no more than ten seconds to sprint out of our back gate, next to the pool, and up to the neighbours' front verandah.

I banged on their front door, and screamed for help as loudly as I could, "Fire! Ambulance! Help! Come quickly!"

I didn't wait for an answer before hurrying back to David, who was still standing in our pool screaming pitifully. I switched into automatic mode and followed my instincts. I hopped back into the pool and cradled David, gently guiding his head in and out of the water. The skin on his head was melting and I knew it needed to be cooled down immediately. This was the only thing I could think of to do. His mouth was also burnt, so I assumed he must have breathed in some of the flames. I encouraged him to swallow water between each breath and in between his screams. Logic told me that if I kept putting his head underwater, hopefully his throat would not swell-up and obstruct his breathing.

As I waited for help, time stood still. I remember shivering uncontrollably, either from shock or cold or both, because the water was freezing and the whole of our pool was covered in melted, charred skin. David's ears were hanging off, almost touching his shoulders, and more and more skin was shedding from his hands.

I shook my head in disbelief as I thought to myself, "I am in a horror movie."

Every time David's head came out of the water, he screamed the same thing over and over again, "My wee house is burning down. Save my wee house."

It was like a song playing on repeat and something that I have never forgotten. As I looked past the pool to our house, the smoke and flames had gathered momentum. No longer than a minute after I'd banged on our neighbours' door, the whole family was at the poolside to help. The Mum, Dad and all four children had run through the back gate with buckets and hoses. They reassured me that the emergency services were on their way.

All I could think of was, "Where are they? Why are they taking so long?" I also prayed that our beautiful home wouldn't burn down completely.

I finally heard the faint sound of sirens in the distance. As I breathed a huge sigh of relief, I realised that I was standing stark naked in the pool. I hadn't given a second thought about the implications of sleeping naked before; but there I was, naked and vulnerable, in the middle of the night.

I raced back into our home, managing to crawl under the level of the smoke which had now almost filled the house. I pulled the first piece of familiar clothing out of my wardrobe, my dressing gown, then reached for my handbag and crawled back out of the burning house as quickly as I could. There was no time to rescue photo albums, passports or anything else. It was too late for that.

Back at David's side, I could still hear the sirens as they approached. It was one of those deathly quiet, still nights in Perth where you could hear for miles. Time felt like an eternity and my thoughts kept racing, "How far away are they? I need help! Why are they taking so long? Where are they?"

When the ambulance finally arrived, the paramedics rushed David off on a stretcher as he began to fall in and out of consciousness.

On arrival at emergency, I sat in a tiny waiting room. A nurse approached me and gently asked, "Do you need to call anyone?"

All I could think of was my mum and dad. I dialled their number over and over again, but couldn't get through. With each failed attempt, I became more upset. I was in such a state of shock that I had forgotten the only home phone number I had ever known.

I turned to the nurse and pleaded, "Why is the phone not working?"

Understanding the situation, the nurse tried a different approach and asked me, "What are your parents' names and address? I will find their number for you."

She came back with their number written on a piece of paper, which I dialled, and finally reached Mum. It was around 1.30am and after I shared the shocking news with them, they raced straight to the hospital to be by my side.

Once David was cleaned up, assessed and settled into the Intensive Care Unit (ICU), the Doctor warily explained the situation to me.

"Your husband is in a critical condition. He has third degree burns to 30% of his body, with the rest of his body covered in first and second degree burns. Most of the flesh has gone from his hands; we can see the bones and he may need to have some of his fingers amputated. We do not know how much internal burning has occurred."

I couldn't believe what I was hearing. Then I thought of David. He was emotionally volatile at the best of times, so I could not begin to imagine how he would cope if he had some of his fingers amputated. I anxiously walked through to the ICU to see him. I still could not believe what was happening was real. I felt a sick, numb sensation in my stomach.

David was in an isolated glass room; he was unconscious and did not look like himself at all. My mind questioned, "Maybe they got it wrong. Maybe this is not him. Maybe he's sitting up in another ward with just a few minor burns."

But my heart sank when I noticed David's beautiful, delicate feet sticking out below the sea of bandages which covered him. This seemed to be the only part of him which was left untouched by the flames because his feet were protected by the woollen socks and leather shoes he had been wearing. They were such neat, perfectly proportioned feet (almost feminine) and far more attractive than my huge bloke-like feet.

I stood and stared at my husband wrapped in countless bandages, with a multitude of noisy machines and tubes attached to him. I knew we were both in a state of the unknown, and the only thing keeping me going was adrenaline.

Morning finally arrived and after having had no sleep, I felt totally wrecked. I received a message to say that the Coroner would like to see me back at our house.

When I arrived home, it was surrounded by 'Do Not Enter' tape, which made it look like a crime scene, sending my anxiety into overdrive.

A police forensics team and the arson squad were everywhere trawling through our burnt out home. I was relieved that Mum was with me, but the whole experience was traumatic. After many discussions with the police and forensics, we were finally able to piece together what had happened.

After I had gone to bed, David had decided he wanted to have his night cap in front of a warm fire before coming to bed. However, the fireplace was cold, and the fire would have taken a while to get properly established.

David's next idea, quite literally, changed the face of his and my life forever.

He had obviously remembered that my dad had recently lent us a lawn-mower and a can of petrol, so he had made his way to the back room to get the petrol can. He had decided that the best way to start the fire quickly was to put a tiny drop of petrol onto the wood. He had taken the petrol can into the lounge to do this, but as the investigators and I looked at the untouched, cold fireplace, we could see that he didn't even get close to the hearth. It turned out, the can of petrol exploded before he even reached the wood, igniting him with fumes as soon as he opened the can.

David had been wearing a coat with nylon lining, with a woollen jumper underneath. This combination had created sparks of static electricity so intense that the fire was ablaze within milliseconds.

As I walked through our house, it felt cold and eerie. The smell of melted paint was overpowering, so toxic that I could taste it. I couldn't believe how our first home had instantly changed from a freshly painted, bright, newly renovated property into *this*, in only a few hours. The whole front lounge room was burnt from the floor to ceiling. The rest of the house wasn't structurally damaged, but black soot covered everything. Nothing had been spared. Everything, in every drawer and every cupboard, was covered in thick, black ash.

I could smell the sickening stench of burnt flesh lingering in the air and wondered if anyone else could smell it. As I walked out to the back patio to get my handbag, I saw the trail of David's burnt skin stuck to the walls. I felt close to vomiting; it was like a morbid murder scene.

I had no idea what lay ahead for us; the thought made me dizzy. I stood outside and looked at our pool, which only 12 hours ago was a sparkling turquoise blue, but had now transformed into a deathly, grey soup of ash and melted skin. I searched every chair and corner of our outdoor setting looking for my bag. I was certain I had thrown it onto one of the chairs the previous night, but it was nowhere to be seen. I figured Mum must have picked it up, so I gave up my search.

Through all the sadness, a spark of happiness shone through the darkness, when I heard the tiny cry of our three-month-old kitten, Ginger. She was stuck up in a tree, covered in black soot; she was frightened. I was so happy to see her and cuddled her gently in my arms. At least our darling kitten was safe amidst the devastation.

Over the next couple of days, all our friends visited David in ICU, even though he was unconscious the whole time. It had been three days since the fire, and it had not occurred to me that he might not survive. In my heart, I had assumed he would somehow pull through. Yet, at the same time, David's face had swollen up so much that he was not only unrecognisable as 'David', but he was almost at the point of being unrecognisable as a human being. His head was the size of a large medicine ball. His eyes, nose and mouth bulged outward, split and weeping in places, so charred black that no glimpse of their original shape remained. The only tell-tale sign of his nose was the tiny breathing tube which came out of a hole in the huge swollen mass of flesh which was now his face. The nurses even asked me to bring in a photo of him to hang on the wall, so they knew who David was and to help make him appear more human.

As I sat with him, I gently spoke words of encouragement over and over again, in the hope that he could hear me.

"It's OK, darling. It's OK; I'm here. I love you."

I stayed by his side for three days straight in the ICU, but there was still no sign of life or consciousness. Instead, his whole body seemed to be swelling and weeping more each day. It was surreal to look at this burnt, foreign body in front of me, knowing that my darling David was in there, buried somewhere deep inside.

All of a sudden I was jolted from my thoughts. There was a loud beeping sound which rang through the room. The machines hooked to David were all going off at once, the piercing sound echoing through my head.

What was going on? Everyone started frantically running around and I was pushed out of the path of the doctors and nurses, away from his side. Oh no, I thought, David was in deep trouble. My heart sank.

"Please God, no!" I prayed. "You can make it, David. You can't die now!"

Unbelievably, in that same moment I heard a radio somewhere in the distance playing a familiar tune by Talking Heads, "*Burning Down the House*."[2] A weird sensation came over me as I listened to the words. The irony was paralysing. David and I had danced to this song together so many times. Now the song had such a different meaning. I could only hope this was a sign that David would pull through.

Seconds ticked by; there were still no signs of breath or life. I couldn't help but wonder if this was the end of our short journey together, but I wouldn't believe it. I was numb and did not yet comprehend the enormity of this moment.

I started praying that David had the strength to fight for his life. I pleaded internally to him, hoping he would somehow hear me.

"I know the road ahead will be hard and I know there will be lots of pain, but I will be beside you and carry you for however long this journey takes. Don't give up, darling."

Our wedding vows spoken only a couple of short years earlier rang in my mind, "*Till death do we part, in sickness and health.*" Every cell in my body hoped this was not the end for him. I sent every bit of energy I could muster to him as I prayed for what seemed like forever.

"Come on David, you can come back. You can do it."

The machines continued with their noises. *Beep, beep, bbbeeeeeepppp.* My prayers halted, as I prepared for the worst.

"How could he die on me now? How dare he! How can this be happening?"

Our life together had only just begun. But for the first time since the accident days earlier, I pondered, *this might just be the end*.

The Power of Dreams

You may be wondering what this story has to do with owning (or starting) a business?

Let me explain.

Not long after David and I were first married, we went to a business entrepreneur's seminar in Melbourne presented by Zig Ziglar, the great American motivational speaker. One of the exercises in his seminar was to create our vision of what our ideal future would look like together. We could dream as wildly and as expansively as we wanted and include things in the short, medium and long-term future.

David and I started dreaming big, instantly energised and excited about planning our future life together. At the time, we had no idea just how life changing this exercise would be for us, nor how it would change the course of our lives. We came to learn that the power of dreams had a profound impact on determining whether you give up, or keep fighting.

In fact, whether in life or in business, the clearer you are on what success and happiness looks like for you, the more conscious you become of the choices you make. This awareness will inevitably lead you to creating the life you want to live. The truth is that dreams and plans are extremely powerful.

As a Business Coach, clients often ask me, "How long will it take to become successful?" or "What is the best business strategy?" or "What's the difference between a successful business owner and one who fails?"

My answer is that it's completely up to you and it depends how much you want success. However, if you have a positive growth mindset, with laser focus on your goals and purpose; if you test and measure everything that matters with tenacity, grit and determination, you will increase your chances of success and give yourself the best chance to reach your goals.

On the other hand, if you give up, have a fixed mindset or don't give it your best, you can't expect success or positive change to happen. Planning for success is critical, because if things get a little rough, you will be able to weather the storm and stay focused on your plan in the face of adversity.

So, if you're ready to make a difference in your business and life, buckle up and join me as I share my journey of triumphs and tribulations, death and new life, wealth and financial crisis, alcoholism and transformation as well as how I picked myself up from rock bottom to create a magical, successful life.

There is always a way forward for you to follow and if I did it, you can too.

"Tell me, what is it you plan to do with your one wild and precious life?"

Mary Oliver

CHAPTER TWO

Bring Your Dreams to Life

I waited with bated breath in the ICU room as David's life hung in the balance. As I sat and watched the nurses and doctors trying desperately to keep him alive, I began to replay snippets of our short life together over in my mind.

I remembered the moment we started dating. We had known each other for around a year and became close friends during that time. We loved having fun and dancing with each other at night clubs after our long work days, often sitting up until the early hours of the morning chatting about life. We laughed and cried together, feeling totally at ease with one other. David had become my new best friend, someone who I could trust with my hopes, fears, celebrations and tears. He also bared his soul with me and seemed just as comfortable listening and learning about my life as sharing the details of his own.

We were not focused on the surface stuff of life; we were so much more than that. In fact, other than my brother, I had never before spoken so deeply with a man. I could see that David was different. He was not just trying to get me into bed, he was there for me and our hearts connected on a deep level. David was a 26-year-old, red haired Scotsman, with bright blue eyes and I certainly wasn't expecting to fall in love with him. I also never imagined that he would be interested in me, a 17-year-old, 6-foot-tall Aussie chick with long brown hair and legs to match, who was fresh out of a private Catholic girl's school. However, somehow it seemed that we were meant to be.

We met on the first business day of 1983 after all the usual Christmas festivities had come to an end. My final high school exam results had just come through, but I had not applied for a university course as I already knew that I wanted to get a job that would help me see more of the world. I was eagerly looking for the chance to create a new life for myself.

It was at this time that I found an advertisement for a job which offered "Free Travel Around Australia." To me, it sounded like my ticket to freedom, so I submitted an application. Meanwhile, David had recently migrated to Australia and was seeking adventure, so when he saw the same advertisement, he applied for the position too.

We both landed the job and it turned out that our new career was selling encyclopaedias door to door. It was a far cry from what we had expected, but neither of us cared as we just wanted to have fun and see Australia. We were to be based in the state of Victoria, which meant that I would be living and working over 3,000 km away from my family on the other side of the country. I was excited at the thought of this new life.

David and I started our jobs within a few weeks of each other, properly meeting for the first time during a sales training session in Melbourne. When I first saw him, he looked so mature and stylish. I remember thinking to myself how markedly different European guys were from Australian guys; David wore a white long-sleeved shirt with white long pants and shoes to match in mid-summer. This was such a contrast to Aussie blokes whose summer uniform consisted of singlets, board shorts and flip flops. Even though we each worked in different sales crews, our sales teams would meet up to socialise any time our crews were nearby each other.

Unbeknown to me, during that first year of our working friendship, David had fallen in love with me. One day he casually asked, "Suzzie, can you please fall in love with me?"

I was quite shocked by the idea because I thought we were just good mates. Additionally, he was nine years older than me which seemed way too grown up for an 18-year-old girl who was still relatively naïve, fresh out of home and high school. I saw him more as a trusted older brother and had never thought of him in that way, but (after giving it some thought) I realised we were more than just friends. Within a few days, we were officially a couple.

On our first night out to dinner together, we cheerily explained to our waitress that it was a very special night because we had just announced our engagement. Of course, we hadn't, but it was fun to pretend that we were engaged. Weirdly enough, we had already spoken about having children together and discussed our future plans for years to come. In fact, our relationship developed so quickly that it seemed totally natural to 'fake' our engagement.

A few months later, we were engaged to be married. At the time, I was only 19-years-old, in awe of him and our potential new life ahead. We were so excited to be planning our wedding and imagining how we would spend the rest of our lives together. We were creating our dream future.

My focus returned to reality. I was back in the glass isolation room in the corner of the Intensive Care Unit at Royal Perth Hospital. David was still not breathing or showing any sign of life. Sitting beside each other on the opposite side of the glass wall, I could see Noreen and Robin, David's parents, who had flown in from Scotland. They were holding each other tightly and not moving an inch. I witnessed the terror clearly etched upon their faces at the thought of losing David. I could only imagine that to watch your child die in front of you must be every parent's worst nightmare. I wished I could go out, give them a hug and tell them that everything would be OK, but I couldn't. Everything wasn't OK, and I knew with certainty it wouldn't be any time soon.

Poor Noreen and Robin had not even been allowed to enter the isolation room to let David know they were there with him. They had flown in from Scotland as soon as possible after the accident but, because Noreen had recently been in hospital in the UK, they were not allowed to go near him until her blood tests were given the all clear for staph infection. I was heart-broken for them. I looked across to where David was lying lifeless on the bed and wondered if he would come back to us?

Time seemed to be going so incredibly slowly. I told myself over and over, almost to convince myself it was true, "It's not the end of our road; it's just not. It can't be."

As if someone had heard my inner thoughts, at that very moment, there was a change in the sound of the machines as David's vital signs returned. Like the rising phoenix, David had come back to life.

"Oh, thank you, thank you," I wept, feeling immense, heartfelt gratitude that our story wasn't over, just yet.

David's breath and heartbeat continued to build, slowly getting stronger and stronger as life returned to his body. I breathed a deep sigh of relief, not realising how much tension I had stored in my body until that moment of release. He had made it, he was alive. At the same time, chills coursed down my spine at the thought of what had just happened. I'd watched my husband die, and then come back to life. The 'surreal-ness' of this new world was breaking me into pieces.

The doctor looked at me and could see that I was shaken and exhausted. He suggested that I get some fresh air, but I was frozen by all of the 'what ifs' rushing through my head.

"What if David died again while I was outside?"

"What if I never saw him alive again?"

I couldn't bear the thought of losing him and becoming a widow. Eventually, the doctor reassured me that his vital signs were stable and convinced me to take a break.

I walked outside the hospital and stood at the entrance where a huddle of smokers had gathered. Dazed and without thinking, I accepted a cigarette from one of them. After inhaling one puff, I threw it to the ground before I momentarily fainted in exhaustion.

"What was I doing? I didn't smoke!" I was not thinking clearly. I quickly regained consciousness; I was clammy and pale, but OK. My smoker friends had no idea what I had just been through only minutes earlier.

My thoughts wandered as I considered how all the 'difficult' decisions David and I had made in the previous few weeks, seemed inconsequential now. We were recently trying to decide on which pub to go to on the weekend and what colour to paint the walls of each room in our house. In our new reality, our choices were about life and death.

When I returned to ICU, the attending doctor explained to me that no-one was allowed to visit David in the isolation room anymore, except me; not even close family or friends. From that point onward, I had to scrub down and change into a special gown before I visited David. I also couldn't have the slightest hint of a cold or sniffle if I wanted to enter the room.

Unfortunately, this also meant that even though Noreen was finally given an all clear on the staph infection test, she and Robin were still not allowed to enter their son's room. They could only watch on from behind the glass wall. I could see that Noreen's heart was shattered; that she couldn't even tell her son she was there, by his side, and that she loved him.

I pondered why everyone had been allowed to go into the isolation room to see David when he was initially admitted during those first three days? Looking back, it all made sense. The doctors had thought David wasn't going to make it before this point. That's why they had allowed almost everyone in to see him, so they could say their 'goodbyes.' Now they thought he had a chance of pulling through, so they considered the risk of infection too high. After all, he had won a huge battle to survive this far, so they could not risk any further complications.

I wondered what David must have been feeling and thinking as he lay motionless on the bed. Did he know what was going on?

I spent the next few weeks sitting beside David in the ICU unit, talking to him with general chit-chat and positive encouragement. He was unresponsive and I had no idea if he could hear me or even knew if I was by his side. As difficult and painful as it was, the nurses assured me that it was critical for him to have me there with him.

Every night I drove back home to sleep in our charred house. It was still covered in black soot, and by this stage, the front corner of the house was sectioned off with black plastic. A burnt-out shell of what it once was, our happy home now felt like a void. It smelt disgusting and the pool was still blackened and dirty with smoke and ash. I cringed to think that David's burnt skin was still stuck in the skimmer box of the pool filter; it made me nauseous.

To compound matters, I had no money. My handbag never did turn up; Mum had not collected it as I'd thought earlier, and it was never handed into the police. I realised that someone must have stolen it from our backyard. It was sickening to think that anyone could have done that.

So, on top of having a burnt house and a husband hanging between life and death, I had no access to my cash. I had cancelled all my cards as soon as I realised my bag had been stolen, and a visit to the bank was not high on my list of priorities. To add to this dilemma, I had almost no appetite and physically couldn't tolerate eating. I was weak, my sleep was restless, and I was having disturbing dreams, due to the trauma I'd experienced. I asked myself why I was even sleeping in this wreck of a home. I was a mess.

After over three weeks in the intensive care unit, David was finally taken off the critical list and transferred to an isolated room in the burns unit. He still hadn't regained consciousness, so it didn't feel that much had changed, yet this was at least a small sign of progress. For me, my days began to blur into one. I would drive the 15-minute journey along the freeway to and from the hospital each day in a trance. I could see everyone else in their cars bustling around in their busy lives, but it all meant nothing to me. They had normal days ahead of them, as I used to, including going to work, the shops, to see a friend or driving home to loved ones at the end of the day.

How could life go on so normally for everyone else, whilst our lives had been completely turned upside down?

This was the longest time David and I had spent apart since we met. I missed talking to him and being with him so much that my soul felt depleted. I missed my dancing partner, my drinking buddy, my confidant and my soul mate. I missed the man who was always there for me, who gently held me in his arms when I woke up from a nightmare and told me, "It's all OK; it's just a bad dream."

My heart ached as I thought of my beautiful husband, so broken and burnt, clinging onto life. Often, my eyes filled with tears at the pain of it all, but I was so numb that I held them in and continued on, as if on auto pilot. I was in a state of limbo, and knew I couldn't just fall in a heap. I had to keep going.

The time soon came to bid a sad farewell to Noreen and Robin as they needed to go home to Scotland. I couldn't imagine how harrowing it must have been for them to leave their only son in this condition. They hadn't even spoken to him or held him during their entire stay, and the body they had been staring at for three weeks held no resemblance to their son. As the three of us stood there in the hospital corridors to say our goodbyes, my heart felt as if it was being ripped out; they didn't even know if they would ever see David alive again.

I will never forget the smell of death in the air. For the first time since the accident, I started retching as the enormity of the previous three weeks came tumbling in on me. The floodgates opened within me and tears poured down my face in torrents. My whole body shook uncontrollably, and I heaved as I sobbed inconsolably between goodbye hugs. I felt distraught and alone as I went back to sit beside my husband's hospital bed once again.

Within a couple of days, David finally regained consciousness, if only for a brief moment. I elatedly sent thanks to the heavens, the universe and the fantastic medical team. I had never felt so grateful in all my life. Unbelievably, through a swollen and charred throat, David attempted to slowly and carefully speak to me for the first time since that fateful night.

He said he loved me and how happy he was to be alive, before he drifted back to sleep. Just hearing his voice was enough to give me a much-needed boost of strength. The relief was overwhelming and the determination I saw in his eyes was enough to move a mountain, filling me with the first sense of joy in over three weeks.

When David woke for the second time, he had a little more strength and was eager to tell me about the weird dreams he'd had. I still remember this conversation vividly.

He spoke softly to me, "Suzzie, some of my dreams were so bizarre. In one of them, I was in a different hospital room, one with glass walls. You were sitting next to me and my mum and dad were sitting outside the glass wall and couldn't come in. It was as if I was floating, looking down on my body and it looked like a real mess. The doctors were running around trying to look after me and I remember having a choice to stay or go. I remember it was a real decision. I knew I had seriously stuffed up and I could see how much hard work it was going to be to get my body working again, but I could feel an intense amount of love radiating from you. I could see all the dreams and plans we had laid out for our life together and I didn't want to let you down. We had only just started on our 50 year plus journey together. It was at that moment that I decided to stay. I knew the pain would be horrific, but I simply couldn't let you down."

As I listened intently to what David was telling me, I felt goose-bumps ripple across my skin and tears blur my vision. I was speechless. There was no way that David could have seen any of what he had described to me. His eyes were never open at any stage whilst he was in ICU; he wasn't even conscious during his stay there either.

The tears streamed down my face; my voice was shaky with emotion. I just couldn't believe what 'Mr Sceptical' (my nickname for David) had just shared with me.

I explained, "What you have just described is the exact setting of the Intensive Care Unit when your body gave up on day three. You were gone for what seemed like forever, but it was probably only a few minutes. Your parents and I were sitting exactly as you described."

I found it difficult to make sense of what David had just said, but it was real and true. I felt full of wonder, love and appreciation for life and all the things beyond our explanation and control. All I knew was that this man loved me enough to choose to stay alive and the picture we had painted of our life together was a key reason why he had decided to come back. Doctors later confirmed that David had indeed died for a short time on that unforgettable day. It was after that incident they realised his desire to live was so strong that his mind convinced his body not to give up.

I gave David a quick update on what had happened over the last three weeks and the extent of his injuries. As he fell in and out of consciousness through the quagmire of drugs, pain and emotion, we explored what our future looked like now.

"I love you so much. No matter what happens, I am here for you; we will get through this," I promised.

What Underpins Success?

It's quite amazing what potential lies hidden dormant in all of us, until we are called upon to use it. In business, I often remind myself and clients that your L-plates to *earning is learning*. By that I mean, if you want to earn more and achieve more in life or business, you have to learn more about it first. No new skill is taken up or endeavour overcome without learning about it first. When our storm came in the form of a house fire accident, we had to research, ask, test and measure everything to see what worked and what didn't. We also had to ask for, and accept, loads of help from people who had more experience and knowledge than us in this area.

In the 1970s, a model known as "The Conscious Competence Ladder" was developed by Noel Burch of Gordon Training International.[3] This landmark model has since been adapted and used by many scholars and educators globally as a tool to explain the learning process. Sometimes referred to as the 'Ladder of Learning' or 'Four Stages of Learning', it describes the four quadrants of competence:

- Unconscious Incompetence
- Conscious Incompetence

- Conscious Competence
- Unconscious Competence

The premise behind the theory is that for every new skill or activity we learn, we experience competency awareness during each stage of the learning process. This is important to understand because whenever you are learning, you will be able to acknowledge which stage you are in and therefore know how you can move from quadrant to quadrant as you improve your skills and knowledge.

Diagram 2.1 shows the four Quadrants of Learning which we all progress through, starting from unconscious incompetence through to unconscious competence.

Quadrants of Learning

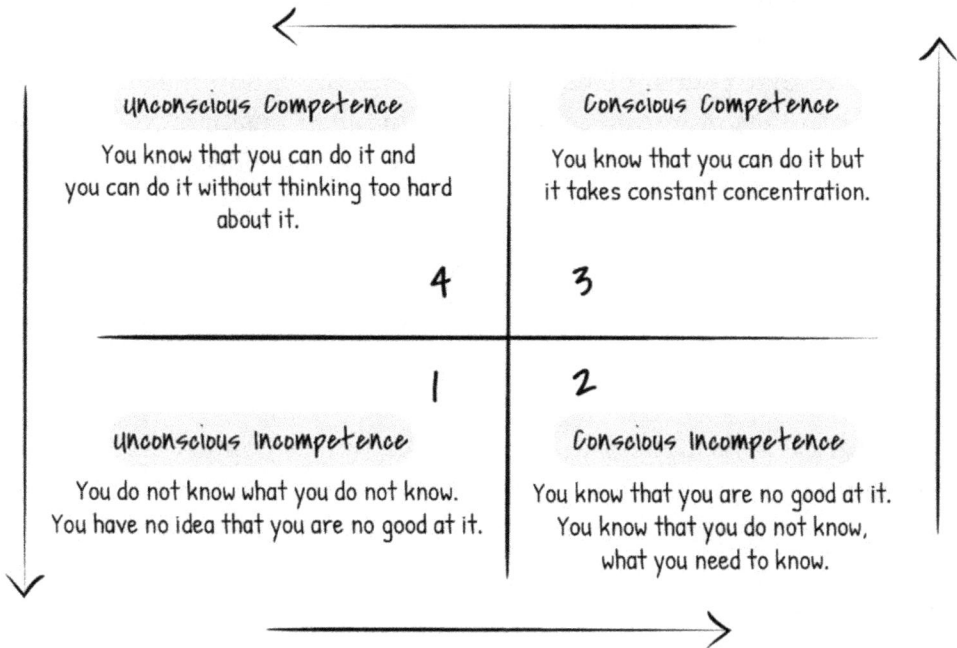

Unconscious Competence	Conscious Competence
You know that you can do it and you can do it without thinking too hard about it.	You know that you can do it but it takes constant concentration.
4	3
1	2
Unconscious Incompetence	Conscious Incompetence
You do not know what you do not know. You have no idea that you are no good at it.	You know that you are no good at it. You know that you do not know, what you need to know.

Diagram 2.1

Ladder of Learning

In business, most of us without formal training will be sitting in quadrant one or two to begin with. That is, we don't know what we don't know (unconscious incompetence) or we know what we don't know, but haven't started learning yet (conscious incompetence). This is completely normal, but the difference comes when we become aware of all the things we can learn as well as the ways we can develop our skills. We simply cannot be expected to know something that we have never been taught or exposed to, so it's important to always be open to learning new skills and ideas. Therefore, if you've never owned and operated a business, there will be many areas where you'll sit in the first quadrant of subconscious incompetence.

When I first started in business, I didn't know then what I know now about running a business. David and I also didn't know a thing about burns before the accident, just like a newborn baby knows nothing about how to drive a car. We each had to learn about these new areas of skill when the time came where we needed to expand our knowledge.

Correspondingly, don't expect that just because you are highly experienced in your trade or profession that you will know how to run a business. This is one of the fundamental errors people make when they start a business, and one which can have major repercussions.

The second step of learning is conscious incompetence. A whole new door opens here, as now you know what you don't know. For example, if you've never learnt much about starting or operating a business before, as you read this book you may realise that there are many concepts and ideas that you now know you don't know. You may also have had a conversation with someone recently or read an article online or come across an area of expertise which you didn't know was something you needed to know.

It's in these moments that you start to realise that there is much you don't know about running a business, but more importantly, also many things you now have the opportunity to learn. It can be a little challenging once the door of your awareness is open to all the concepts you weren't previously aware of. However, the key difference between those who progress and those who don't, is in being willing to say, "OK, now I know what I don't know, and I've decided I'm going to learn."

If we look at the analogy of driving a car, when a child is around four or five-years-old, they know that they can't drive a car. But they can understand that when they are older, they can learn how.

Once you start to make learning, research and development an ongoing part of the way you and your business operate, you have stepped into the third quadrant, conscious competence. This is where you know what you know and are working on a continual learning process. You are alert and totally aware of what you know and how it works for you; it is a very conscious process. Just as when you first learn to drive a car, you know the steps involved to being able to drive a car, but still need to remain alert and focused at all times. Being aware is the key.

The third quadrant is the doing or action quadrant where the learning actually takes place. This is where you have the ability to make a transformation. What have you learned that may transform the way your business operates? What can you do differently to work smarter, not harder? What is no longer serving you in your business? Take the time to learn deeply from your history, take a look at your business model, identify where your strengths lie and where you can develop your learning further. Your opportunities here are endless; your learning is never complete. Importantly, if you absorb new information and continually learn from everything you do, you will become more capable than the majority of business owners who stay stagnant in their personal and business development and don't push their boundaries to expand their knowledge.

The last stage of learning is when you reach the unconscious competence space, where you take action and complete tasks without even consciously thinking about them. Using the driving analogy, this is where you drive your car without even thinking, you listen to the radio, take in the scenery and then arrive at work without even remembering how you got there. This can be advantageous but, on the other hand, it can also be a danger zone in business where you become so complacent that you don't consciously think or learn anymore. This is when accidents can happen because you are not fully aware. Don't let this zone become a threat to your business.

It's critical that you aren't lulled into a false sense of security, where you're so confident in your abilities that you stop doing any further learning, research and professional development. This is the point where you think you know everything about your business, then something changes and before you know it, this isn't the case. Suddenly, there's a shift in your industry or world innovation and you and your business are left behind. The industries around you are always changing, new competitors are entering the market, new technologies are launched and it's important to keep up if you want to be successful. Stay aware of what you don't know and strive to bridge those gaps in your learning.

Unfortunately, I often see business owners who may have been *operating* their business for 20 years, but in reality have only *been in business* for five years. At year five, they reached the ceiling of their knowledge and stopped learning and growing so simply repeated year five, another fifteen times over.

Being on auto-pilot can be the start of a slippery downwards slope, because sometimes when we don't think, we make mistakes. So, if you are running your business on auto pilot and think you know everything there is to know about your industry, I urge you to think again. Being fully alive is a continuous journey of learning and change until the day we die. There's actually a Japanese philosophy that sums this up well named, "*Kaizen*", meaning constant and continuous improvement.

When I found myself faced with the journey David and I had to endure after he was burnt, we were in the first quadrant of learning, as 'we didn't know what we didn't know.' We had never experienced anything like this before and had to rely on the stories, advice and triumphs of those who had already been through what we were going through. To do this, we listened to doctors, read books and spoke to others who had travelled a similar path. This was the only way we could get the inspiration and knowledge required to continue, as the journey was totally foreign to us. If it hadn't been for the support of those around us, I don't think David and I would have climbed the massive mountains we had to overcome, as well as we did.

To apply this to your business, if people have already been on your path before, why not learn from them? If the concept of learning new things is scary for you, luckily there are many different ways of learning new information available to you. If you're not great at reading and prefer to watch a screen, try learning from YouTube videos, documentaries or TED talks. If you don't have time to watch a screen, try listening to audiobooks or podcasts when you're in the car or out walking, exercising or just getting some fresh air. There are literally hundreds of thousands of inspiring business owners out there and different resources that can help you. The first step is to find an inspiring authority which you can connect with in the area you most need to improve.

It All Starts with Your Mind

Having a growth mindset, and being open to learning from people who ignite inspiration in your heart, can make all the difference. A growth mindset shifts your perception of challenges into being opportunities. With a growth mindset, you can acknowledge your weaknesses and learn to mitigate them.

Always seek to learn new things as you develop as a person, and you will persist in the face of setbacks. The great thing is we can *choose* to have a growth mindset and by opening our minds more consistently, we will naturally adopt a growth mindset in future scenarios. The concept of a *growth mindset* was developed by psychologist Carol Dweck.[4] In recent years, many have used Dweck's theories to teach the philosophy.

Diagram 2.2 shows a wonderful depiction of Dweck's theory, demonstrating the contrast between a fixed and a growth mindset.[5]

Fixed Mindset Vs Growth Mindset

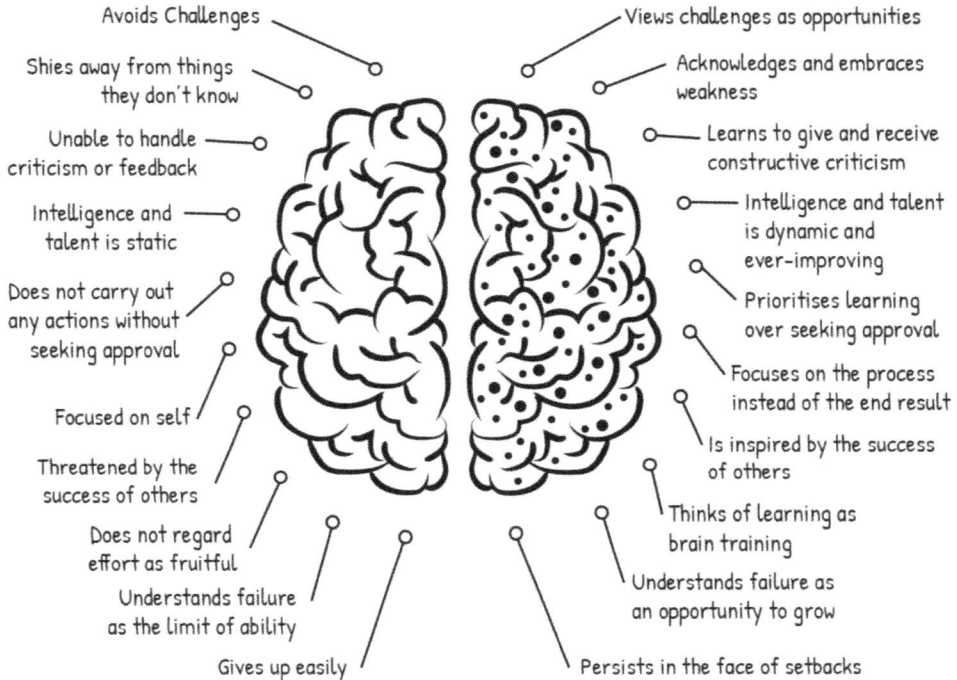

Avoids Challenges

Shies away from things they don't know

Unable to handle criticism or feedback

Intelligence and talent is static

Does not carry out any actions without seeking approval

Focused on self

Threatened by the success of others

Does not regard effort as fruitful

Understands failure as the limit of ability

Gives up easily

Views challenges as opportunities

Acknowledges and embraces weakness

Learns to give and receive constructive criticism

Intelligence and talent is dynamic and ever-improving

Prioritises learning over seeking approval

Focuses on the process instead of the end result

Is inspired by the success of others

Thinks of learning as brain training

Understands failure as an opportunity to grow

Persists in the face of setbacks

Diagram 2.2

What Do You Want Out of Your Life?

Life's too short to not get clear on what you want out of it. Wouldn't it be great to make your time on earth as worthwhile and meaningful as possible?

Through my life, I have seen the huge impact that dreaming, visioning and believing can have on one's life. After all, if you don't have any vision or plans for the future, how are you going to remain inspired when the road of life becomes bumpy? Whenever you have something important you want to achieve, it all starts with your vision and a plan for achieving it. It doesn't matter if it is a sporting achievement, your perfect life partner, house or business – the vision is where it all starts. It is the magnet that draws you towards achieving it.

Whether you are starting out in your business and still in the dreaming phase, or if you have been running a business for a long time, it's so important to have a clear vision. Write it down for all your team, suppliers and clients to be excited about. Everyone involved in making your vision turn into reality, should know and feel the vision in their heart and behave in sync with it.

Gemma

Gemma had a retail store which operated seven days a week. She was working 12 hours a day just to keep it going and had a huge financial debt hanging over her head. When Gemma came to me, she had a yearning to change her life. She wanted to get married, have children and get rid of her debt. She was 'in a rut', as she called it, and didn't know how to make the change to break free. She had capped out her business knowledge and reached breaking point due to the amount of time and energy she was putting into the business.

Gemma and I sat down and became crystal clear on what it was that she truly wanted in her life. From there, we put together a comprehensive three-year plan to help her achieve her dreams. She knew what she didn't like about her life and she was determined to change the situation. We depicted exactly what needed to happen to reach the business sales targets, to generate enough revenue to start paying off her debt. Gemma also wanted to stop working such ludicrously long hours and have her business run without her there, so she could have children in the future without being tied to the business.

Over the three year period that followed (with Gemma's vision, mission and plans clearly outlined, and regularly assessing and adjusting milestones along the way), she promoted a suitable manager from within her business and trained her to run it. Gemma was then able to step away whilst still receiving an income from the business. She married the man of her dreams, they bought a nice house together and had a couple of children, all while paying down their debts.

By the end of Gemma's initial three-year plan, her vision and plans allowed her to irrefutably change her entire life. Gemma's business ran successfully without her and she only went into the office once a week to meet her trusted business manager to make sure everything was on track. Her business paid off all her debts and still afforded her the lifestyle to be out of the business and doing what she was most passionate about in life – being a mother to her children.

Chapter 2
Blue Ocean Thinking

☐ **What do you need to learn?**

If you can identify the gaps in your learning that will impact your business, scheduling time to increase knowledge in those areas will be instrumental to your business success.

☐ **Do you have a fixed or growth mindset?**

Start to listen to your thoughts and words, to determine if your mindset is fixed or if you are open for learning and growth.

☐ **Business Vision**

What is the vision of your business in the future that is so powerful it inspires you, your team, your clients and suppliers?

"The only impossible journey is the one you never begin."

Anthony Robbins

CHAPTER THREE

The Big Picture

After months of visiting David in hospital, the day finally came for him to come home. It was a goal we had dreamed of so many times since that nightmare evening; it was both an exciting and scary prospect. The idea of getting some kind of normality back into our lives was far from a reality, but we had achieved such a huge milestone that we felt we were taking a major leap forward.

My excitement quickly dampened when I looked at David's body and reminded myself that it was far from functioning as it once did. The drive home from hospital was torture. I had not considered the severity of David's skin sensitivity, where every single bump, pothole and corrugation in the road sent rushes of pain through his whole body. Worse still, when a little girl in the car next to us got a glimpse of David's face and quickly turned away with fright, my heart ached. Was this our new normal?

With David home, it was still a life of total dependency for him. He could not use his hands so he couldn't eat, dress, go to the toilet, walk or even talk on the phone without assistance. David needed a full-time carer. He also had to wear pressure garments for a minimum of one year, fitted extremely tight to minimise the scarring of his skin but this meant they were as uncomfortable as a straight-jacket. He hated the full face mask most of all, but also had full-length pants, gloves and a pressure garment for his torso, too. All of them were so tightly fitted, he couldn't get them on and off by himself.

Luckily, David's best friends from Scotland, Stuart and Moreen, had just moved to Australia and were staying with us for their first few weeks in the country. Moreen was a nurse, so when I was not around she washed, dressed and fed David, and helped with anything else he needed. These two friends were a godsend. I have no idea how I would have coped without them.

Unfortunately, sometimes mishaps happened. One day while I was at work, David managed to ring me via speed dial using his elbow as Stuart and Moreen were not home.

"Suzzie, come home quick! I need to go to the toilet; I need help now!"

I rushed home as quickly as I could, but I was too late. Poor David was frustrated, sweating and humiliated when I found him, unable to pull down his own pants to go to the toilet. To add to this, due to his lack of movement and the many drugs prescribed, constipation was a daily companion. Just another part of David's dignity gone out the window. To try to ease the issue, my daily 'to do' list now included inserting David's suppositories, taking trust and intimacy to a whole new level.

My heart was sad and heavy to see David so desperate for his freedom. Although he couldn't use his hands, he started driving the car using his knees and elbows to steer just so he could get out of the house. Luckily, it was an automatic car. I was not happy about this at all, but there was little I could do when I was at work during the day and he was home alone. He was going stir crazy without his independence. He stopped wearing his face mask in public because it was so uncomfortable, and he hated it. However, seeing the reaction on others' faces was also particularly distressing when unsuspecting people were confronted with a disfigured, reddish-purple raw face, still weeping and scabby as it healed. Not to mention, unsettling for the people who got a fright when seeing him again for the first time since the accident. I wished they wouldn't always jump, but no matter how many times I warned family, friends and workmates, they always jumped, even gasped, open-mouthed with shock when they saw him.

David's mental health also started to show signs of wear and tear. He wasn't in a good place and seemed to go in and out of depression. The pain was never-ending, so David resorted to painkillers mixed with alcohol and marijuana to take the edge off his constant discomfort. I could not imagine how difficult it must have been for him to go from a healthy, good-looking, 33 year old bloke one day, with a great job, new wife and home, to being a totally dependent burns survivor and Freddy Kruger look-alike the next. It must have been a never-ending nightmare for him to endure.

Prior to the accident, David had been working as a sales consultant for a company named GBC. They had been amazing in their support for us, and continued to pay David's wages for the whole time he was unable to work. Although he still couldn't use his hands properly, after months stuck at home he decided to return to work for just a few hours per day with the intention of slowly increasing his hours as he recovered.

This was another step forward and he was even okay with visiting his old clients as they were keen to say 'hello' after hearing about his horrible accident. However, to see new prospects was very difficult for him, as most people found it a challenge to look at him without thinking about what had happened, instead of concentrating on the meeting. Nevertheless, he worked hard between hospital visits to get back into the swing of things, as a gesture of gratitude and in an attempt to get his life back to normal as soon as possible.

Our days were spent going back and forth to the hospital physiotherapy department, mostly working on David's hands. I watched him courageously doing his exercises every day, never missing a session. He mustered every inch of effort he could find to move his fingers a couple of millimetres, grimacing and shaking as the sweat dripped down his face in an attempt to get the message from his brain to his mangled fingers. It was torture to watch.

Always practical and keen to know the truth, David asked every professional involved in his treatment, "Will I ever be able to use my hands again? Are these torturous exercises and all this pain worth it?"

The answer was always the same, "I don't know, but if you give up, you will definitely never use them. If you keep working on them and never give up, there is a chance." This made him even more determined.

Once or twice a month we found ourselves back in hospital for further surgery. David had to stay a few nights at a time for further skin grafts. Each time healthy skin grew back on the top of his legs in the areas where he wasn't burnt, they would get out the instrument which we called the 'potato peeler' to slice a layer of healthy skin off his leg and place it onto a burn site somewhere else on his body. This was extremely painful for David and something which he dreaded with every fibre of his being.

However, to have him looked after in hospital for a few days was often a welcome respite for me. I felt guilty for feeling that way, but this was the reality of the situation. The roller coast ride of deeply depressing moments of life with a burns survivor, dotted with only the occasional bright moment of excitement, such as progress in his hand occupational therapy or the realisation that I saved my husband's life, was exhausting. I was still working in my full-time job running the employment agency for the doctors at the AMA, so when David was in hospital, I would only see him at lunch time and in the evenings.

On one visit to hospital for another round of skin grafts, we wanted to do things a little differently. The usual procedure was for him to check-in and stay overnight, so he had a bed allocated to him and was fasted correctly. We arrived at the ward at around 9.00pm and a grumpy duty nurse filled out the usual forms, then asked me to leave.

Instead, David asked, "Now that we have completed all the paperwork, can I please go home to my own bed for a good night's sleep? I promise I will fast from eating and be back at 6.00am tomorrow morning."

The nurse had obviously never heard such a silly idea and was quite angry with us for suggesting such a thing. The three of us stood and argued for some time until we decided to give up and walk out of the hospital anyway. She was annoyed because if an emergency came in overnight, the bed for David would be taken and the operating list would be disrupted, resulting in more work for her. We figured that if an emergency came in, then it would be a priority, and more urgent than our needs, so it wouldn't be a problem. David's procedures weren't seen as an emergency now, so it was totally fine with us.

Once we were happily tucked up in our own bed at home, we decided that it was time to see if David's 'man bits' were in working order. This was one of David's biggest concerns; it was important to find out if he was still okay down below. He was so focused on getting back to living the life we had planned, that he was insistent on knowing if we'd still be able to have children. We had always talked of having children together and the thought of losing that dream played on our minds ever since the accident. This was the first time since that day in May that we had even thought of trying to be intimate. It was a delicate, emotional, slow dance of love, but somehow we managed okay. Our love and gratitude for life was so strong, that the physical challenges we had to overcome to get there were worth it.

When we walked back into the hospital bright and early the next morning we had an extra spring in our step. We were overjoyed that we'd followed our hearts instead of hospital procedures and managed our first intimate encounter together since the accident. We didn't know or even care if the hospital bed was still available. We'd made a huge leap in David's recovery, his manhood and our marriage. Our spirits were soaring. It had been the one question we were too scared to ask, and it was finally ticked off the list. We had reached another milestone on the road to recovery.

My heart exploded with joy when I discovered only a few weeks later that I was pregnant. As I shared the news with David, it was as if a newfound hope was given to us both. He was elated and all the physical and mental pain we had both been through was forgotten in a moment. This new life inside me was worth fighting for. Better still, at the time, David's parents had been with us for a few weeks on holidays, so we had booked a table at a fancy restaurant to bid them farewell. Finding out the great news only hours earlier, we spent the entire evening grinning from ear to ear. No other piece of information could have been as good as the confirmation of our pregnancy. It was a magical feeling and I had never before been as elated as I was in that moment.

The atmosphere at dinner overflowed with love, joy and excitement. David's parents were ecstatic. David and I had never lost hope of our dream to have children together and, despite the lifelong struggles which still lay ahead, it was the most wonderful news ever. After everything we'd been through, we could not have ended the year on a higher note.

The nine months of my pregnancy were an absolute dream. I felt super excited, filled with energy and joy the whole time. I was definitely one of those glowing pregnant ladies who blossomed whilst expecting. Sadly, on the other hand, I found my relationship with David becoming increasingly strained. As I was carrying our precious child, I no longer drank alcohol, but David continued to drink heavily. He was either drunk or hungover most days.

In my sober state, it felt as if we were living two different realities and I began to feel a distance between us. Loneliness set in as I became more and more aware of the way David was using alcohol as a pathway to escape his pain. Yet I knew how challenging his life had become and hung on to the hope that once I gave birth, he would experience a renewed sense of purpose. With this in mind, I was optimistic that we would reconnect as soulmates again.

Eight months into my pregnancy, I finished work and was excited to spend some time nesting at home in preparation for our little baby's arrival. In that first week at home, I visited the doctor for a check-up on how things were progressing. He casually asked me what I was doing the next day.

I can't remember what I had planned, but whatever it was he replied, "Sorry, Suzzanne. You can't do that as you'll be having a baby."

He went on to say that my blood pressure was through the roof and I had developed toxaemia. This prognosis meant that our little baby was in grave danger, so they had to induce the birth the following morning.

Other than the anxiety of what lay ahead in giving birth for the first time, as well as the choice of giving birth naturally being taken out of my hands, the birth was pain free for me. I was given an epidural and Pethidine, so I felt nothing except anticipation.

However, David, who was so familiar with pain, found the whole experience quite distressing and almost unbearable. I think a combination of pent-up emotion, seeing my body in an emergency procedure, legs in stirrups, tubes, monitors and needles right in front of him was all too close to home. He also felt unable to help me and did not cope well through the whole procedure. Overwhelmed with tears of fear and helplessness, he looked away in pain many times, but did not leave my side. We would do this together, no matter what.

Delighted to finally see the first of a new generation come into the world, we had a beautiful baby boy who we named Hamish. He was big and healthy, and other than a little cone on the top of his head from the suction equipment used during his birth, he was just perfect. David couldn't believe his eyes. In awe, he wondered how he had been part of creating such a perfect little human being, when he was so scarred, damaged and, in his eyes, ugly.

My parents, who had waited patiently outside the maternity suite for almost an hour after the delivery, were keen to meet baby Hamish. I must say they were splitting at the sides with excitement when they came in to see their first grandchild. I had never seen my dad more in love than the moment he first set eyes on Hamish; it was like he'd seen an angel. He confidently scooped him up with his big arms, staring intensely with overwhelming love and awe at meeting his first grandson. Hamish's birth started a new beginning for us to get back on track to the path of our dreams.

How Strong is Your Vision?

Due to my personal and business experiences, I cannot emphasise highly enough the importance of having a clear vision for your life and your business. If our vision for the future saved my husband's life, then perhaps it could help save yours and your business when the going gets tough? Yet this profoundly transformative tool is commonly undervalued. In fact, I will say that being crystal clear on your vision is vital to your success and your plans will be the glue that hold your dream together.

When David and I pictured our future life, back at the Zig Ziglar seminar all those years ago, we decided we would buy a house, have children, backpack around the world, start a business, have a family, buy a holiday house, grow our own vegetables, send our kids to private schools, help disadvantaged people, find a sport that was fun, make some wonderful friends, own a Jaguar car and a fast motorbike, run a marathon and climb a mountain – the list went on and on!

It was exciting to picture our life's journey together and it felt like anything was possible, because it was. David and I were convinced that whatever we did would be wonderful, as long as we were together. When we created our vision, I felt the same feeling I still get when I plan an amazing holiday with someone I love; that euphoric, butterflies-in-the-tummy excitement. We enjoyed listing our dreams and turning them into our own personal road map for our lives. It was a fun and powerful experience; the cornerstone of what has pulled us through life's ups and downs.

Your *personal vision* is different from your *company vision*. Your personal vision might be to eventually sell your business, retire and spend your days fishing, but this isn't your business vision. This won't ignite the hearts of the people working in your business. However, feel free to have that picture of you in your fishing boat hanging up on the wall at home to remind you of that personal dream. In fact, creating a vision board with a collage of pictures, quotes and images which inspire you and are aligned to what you want to achieve in your life (also referred to as a *dream board*), is a great visual way to motivate yourself. It will also act as a constant reminder and draw you closer towards achieving your dreams.

The Visioning Process in Business

If you're in business, the power of having a vision works using the same principles. Ask yourself:

- What do you want for your business?
- What is the long-term goal that you're working towards?
- Is it powerful and moving for yourself and others?
- Does it inspire you, your team and your clients?

The Oxford *Learner's Dictionary* describes having a vision as, "The ability to think about or plan the future with great imagination and intelligence."[6]

Having a business vision is the guiding light in the long-term future of what you would like your company to become or to achieve. It's a short, positive, easy-to-understand statement describing the picture of what your company will look like in the future. Additionally, it is a public declaration of your outcomes, whether it's your team, clients, suppliers or the general public who read your business vision. It ought to be clear to everyone *where* your company is heading and *when* you would like to achieve your dream outcome. Some people have a five or ten year vision, some even shoot for 100 years into the future. How far in advance can you see your business achieving its goal? It's totally up to you.

A powerful business vision statement will engage your team's hearts and minds, just like my husband's heart and mind were seriously committed to achieving our life's vision. It's a written description of the end point of your business plan that can be understood by everyone. In this way, your team know where they are going and can work together towards the same goal. Think about your business five, ten or twenty years in the future. If your company was the best in the industry, what would it look like? Sometimes it can take a little time and soul searching to get clear on your company vision. It's great to get your team involved in creating an awesome vision statement too. This way, they can be part of creating the future and they will be more passionate about helping you achieve the company vision.

The long-term benefits of going through this clarification within your business are substantial. In fact, a Deloitte study in 2016 determined that you will become eight times more successful over a ten year period when you work on the heart and soul of your business.[7]

In life, we all go through ups and downs, and businesses are no different. If you have a clear vision of where you are heading, it's much easier to stay on track. As a team pulling together in one direction, you are far more powerful than many people going in different directions. A common misconception is that the majority of people are motivated by money first, but this is far from true. Being part of a team, and something bigger than ourselves, is far more rewarding for most. In his book, *"Great by Choice,"* the author, Jim Collins, talks about level five leadership, where people are motivated by things above their own ego; wanting to leave a legacy that may last longer than themselves.[8]

In a nutshell, visioning in business is the process of imagining how a business will develop into the future and planning for this in a suitable way. These examples of business vision statements might help you to get creative when thinking about your own vision:

"Empower every person and every organization on the planet to achieve more." – Microsoft

"A just world without poverty." – Oxfam

"Be one of the World's Leading Providers of Entertainment and Information." – Disney

"To create a better everyday life for the many people." – IKEA

"Bring inspiration and innovation to every athlete* in the world." (**If you have a body, you are an athlete.*) – Nike

If you would like to create an awesome vision statement with your team, I recommend leaving your normal working environment and going somewhere away from your normal day-to-day business routine that inspires and activates the right side of your brain. Simon Sinek, a leadership guru, once tweeted, "Customers will never love a company until the employees love it first."[9]

The clearer you and your team are on the future picture of the best possible business, the simpler it will be to achieve it. Everyone can then start to be the people they need to be and do the things they need to do to achieve it.

Your Business Mission

Once you have created a crystal clear vision of what your business looks like in the future, the next step is to think about the mission of your business. The mission statement is the backbone statement which joins together what your business is made up of, what it does and how it does it. It explains which products and/or services you provide, who your target market is and where and how you will deliver them. It gives your clients, prospects, suppliers and team members a clear picture of what you are all about as a business.

Imagine you are an electrician servicing the mining sector of the North-West region of Australia, think about how you could quickly and clearly let your prospects know what you do, how and where you do it. This is where your mission statement comes into play. People who visit your website, see an advertisement, a business card, brochure or signage should be able to fully understand who you are and what your company does. In this way, your mission statement provides a simple snap shot of your business. A clear mission statement for this company could be 'Experts in serving the electrical needs of the mining sector of the North West region of Western Australia.' If you require further clarity or examples, conduct some online research to see how other companies describe themselves and which mission statements are most effective.

Your Purpose

What is the greater purpose of your business? What difference do you want your business to make? Your life is about your place in the world and the difference you make to people and society. If you have a business, you have the power to use it to make a difference to the lives of others. Interestingly enough, I have noticed that the closer people's personal values are aligned to the purpose of their business, the more passionate they are about their business. They seem more invested, with their whole heart and soul. If you are looking to buy a business, thinking about starting a business or have an existing business, it is very empowering to have a clear purpose of what you are actually there to do in the bigger picture. Simon Sinek explains in his TED talk, *"How Great Leaders Inspire Action"* that "People don't care what you do, they care why you do it."[10]

If your business purpose is aligned with your own personal values, it creates far more enthusiasm and inspiration within the business. But perhaps you haven't actually considered what your core values are? Maybe it's time to look within and identify which values are most important to you, both personally and professionally? Remembering that your personal values may be different from your business values, but if they can be aligned, then your chances of success in all areas of your business and life will be greater.

Your Business Values

When you're talking about the values and behaviours that your company stands for (some companies call them the 'Rules of the Game', a 'Culture Statement' or 'House Rules'), each team member should know up front what you stand for and what your company behaviour expectations are, with no assumptions. Just as a child needs guidelines on how to behave, as they navigate what they do, your team have agreed rules and behaviours by which they abide – with each other, your customers, your suppliers and your clients.

Diagram 3.1 shows an example of some organisational rules to get you started.

> # Rules of the Game
>
> 1. We are honest with ourselves and others
>
> 2. We value who we are as individuals and a team
>
> 3. We work as a team to achieve common goals
>
> 4. Our clients are our top priority
>
> 5. We take pride in our work environment
>
> 6. We own up to our mistakes
>
> 7. We trust and respect each other
>
> 8. We commit to our personal and professional growth

Diagram 3.1

Your Brand Promise

When you have a clear picture of your vision, mission, purpose and values, you can start to develop your *brand promise*. Determining what your brand promises are, is a very powerful aspect of your branding and is something which is vital to share with your team, customers and suppliers. In your brand promise, you get to decide *what* you will deliver to your customers and *what* standard of service you will be known for. In a nutshell, your brand promise is what is non-negotiable when it comes to the delivery of your products and services. Your brand promise ties your vision, mission and purpose together by displaying to your customers what your integral values are, and what your business is all about. To determine your business's brand promise, ask yourself the following questions:

- What do you want your business to be known for?
- What do you promise to deliver to your customers?

Your promises should be reflected in your service standards and clearly inform your customers exactly who they are dealing with when they do business with your company. Your brand promise should also be aligned with your company values and be represented in everything you do in your organisation. The importance of this is demonstrated when you deal with companies which do not deliver on their promise. For example, if one of your brand promises is to only use top quality raw materials in all products you make, then you definitely shouldn't use cheap or inferior quality products. Otherwise, your promises will be tainted, and your company values of 'trust' and 'truth' will not be aligned. Remember that distrust and broken promises are a quick way for an organisation to develop a bad reputation – and this spells disaster.

Key Performance Indicators

Once the core of your business is clear – your vision, mission, values and promises – it's time to delve deeper and think about what you'd like to achieve with your business. This is where your *Key Performance Indicators* (KPIs) come into play and form a vital part of your business targets and measurements. The definition of a Key Performance Indicator is '*A quantifiable measure used to evaluate the success of an organisation, employee, etc. in meeting objectives for performance.*'[11] To identify and formulate your KPIs, consider the following:

- What outcomes and standards do you want to see achieved within your business?
- What goals or milestones will you reach along the way to let you know that you are on the right track to achieving those results?

The importance of your KPIs cannot be overstated because it's difficult to have clarity on the day-to-day operations of your business if you don't have clear goals, milestones and outcomes that you are working towards and can measure to assess how you are performing. KPIs also work to keep you on course. Imagine hopping into an Uber car and saying, "I want to go on a journey but I'm not actually sure of the destination." It sounds crazy, doesn't it? Yet, 95% of business owners I speak with have no clear goals or plans, neither written nor verbal.

Furthermore, imagine how difficult it would be for your team members to achieve targets if they are not clear on what you actually want them to achieve. This is always the case where there are no clear goals or KPIs in place within a business. In fact, I often ask business owners about their team members and what the goals are for them over the next year or into the future. Most owners simply say, "I don't really know".

If you don't know what the goals are for your team, they certainly won't know what they are either. How do you think this lack of clarity and goals affects performance in the workplace? It is not good. On the other hand, it's a great deal more rewarding if both you and your team members are clear on expected results, so you each know exactly what to do to achieve these, as well as understand how they are measured.

Your Business Outcomes

The next step towards clarity and focus across your business is in determining what your *business outcomes* actually are. When thinking about these, I find it helpful to separate them into four main areas – Marketing and Sales, Operations, Management and Financial. Ask yourself:

- What outcomes do you want to see in each of these areas in your business?
- More specifically, what are the desired results over the next 12 to 24 months?

Writing these answers down will help you to get clear, so you can share them with your team. If they are not aware of these outcomes, how will they help you to achieve them? Following are some examples of outcomes in each of those areas.

Your *Marketing and Sales* outcomes could be focusing on building quality leads which will convert into higher paying clients. This, in turn, could build long-term relationships with clients who are using products with larger margins. Or you may look to build your brand throughout your geographic location so the business can fulfil its sales goals over the next five years. Through your marketing activities, you might want to push your message and brand promise of being 'the premier supplier' in your industry and as a result attract a higher quantity and quality of client. Your marketing activities should inevitably focus on generating enough quantity and quality of leads so that you can convert these at a reasonable rate. Generating a repeat business culture could also be a focus of your marketing outcomes so your business can gain higher sales revenues.

Your *Operational* outcomes might involve developing more robust systems to increase the capabilities and productivity of your team (i.e. systemising the routine aspects of your business and humanising the exceptions to these, so your customers experience a consistent level of service). An operational strategy may be reviewing a sales process or system in your customer relationship management (CRM) system, so the procedure is clear; the same process is applied to all customers. By prioritising your customers and their fulfilment, you will build a more substantial repeat business culture and increase your average dollar sale.

When you're formulating the *Management* outcomes of your organisation, perhaps your focus over the next 12 months could be to build a stable, high quality team with capabilities in the areas of marketing, sales and client fulfilment. Additionally, most business owners know they need to find good quality prospective clients in order to convert them into paying clients and to ultimately build long-term relationships with them. Thus, your management outcomes might involve employing a General Manager (GM) to take over some of the responsibilities from the owners. The GM can then support further revenue and profit growth through the implementation of all your business strategies.

Last but certainly not least, are your *Financial* outcomes. These are the actual dollar value figures of your business and each preceding area of outcomes, reflected in your financials. If you need to improve cashflow, perhaps consider increasing your prices, reducing the number of discounts given or reducing your cost of goods. Another financial outcome may be to adjust your debtor policies so you can receive a greater portion of cash in advance, or at point of sale, or ensure that your accounts are paid in a shorter amount of time. You may also improve your supplier relations, so you gain better trading terms or have the ability to increase your credit limit and payment terms.

As your business outcomes are so vital to your success, I will be covering each area at a more in-depth level as this book progresses.

Your Goals

Now that you have the overall outcomes clear in the four main areas of your business, it's time to look at the specific goals you would like to achieve within each of these. I recommend having twelve-month goals in each key area and then breaking these down to smaller quarterly and monthly goals. Using this process, you will end up with a plan with clear month-by-month goals in each area, so you can develop strategies to achieve them.

To increase your chances of success, I create SMART goals.[12] A good way of doing this is to remember the acronym S.M.A.R.T, which refers to a framework of writing management goals and objectives that are:

- *Specific* in that they are quantifiable
- *Measurable,* in that you can determine if they are accomplished or not
- *Achievable,* in that the goals are attainable
- *Realistic,* in that they are not outside the realms of possibility
- *Timely,* in that the goals can be achieved in a reasonable or agreed upon time frame.

As an example, one goal around income generated might be, "By the 31st of December this year, my gross turnover for the calendar year will be one million dollars." From this annual goal, you can break this up into quarterly goals such as, "Between the 1st of January and 31st of March, I will generate $250,000 in gross sales revenue." Continue this for the remaining quarters of the year. Based on your past invoiced sales, you will know whether that is a realistic goal to achieve within each period and at that time of year. If not, how could you adjust your goals to be more realistic or what actions would be required to make those goals possible? The more detailed your goals can be, the easier it is to achieve them.

Your goals should clearly and specifically state what you are trying to achieve and generally relate to your business vision. Being as specific as possible, you will be able to see, feel and believe your goals as a reality. As I've already mentioned, if your goals are particularly large, break them down into smaller, more specific goals with appropriate incremental deadlines. I can honestly say that the power of having firm, SMART goals will help you achieve results you never thought possible.

As Tony Robbins, a well-known author, philanthropist and life coach, says, "Setting goals is the first step from the invisible to the visible." Research has proven that setting and writing down goals will improve your chances of success. In a study on the impact of goals by Dr Gail Matthews, a psychology professor, it was discovered that the more committed and focused people were on their goals, the more likely they were to achieve them. In fact, just by thinking about your goals, you are more than four times more likely to achieve them. This increases by 42% if you write your goals down and a further 77.6% if you have written goals that you schedule time to work on and review.[13]

Diagram 3.2 shows the mean goal achievement scores out of 10 that were rated by participants in the study.

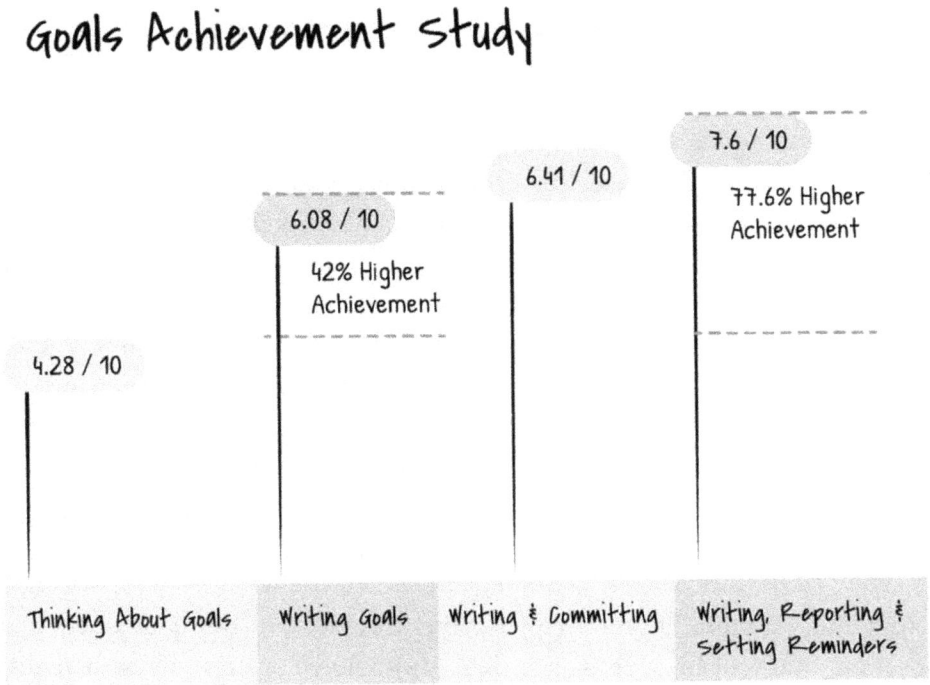

Goals Achievement Study

4.28 / 10 — Thinking About Goals

6.08 / 10 — 42% Higher Achievement — Writing Goals

6.41 / 10 — Writing & Committing

7.6 / 10 — 77.6% Higher Achievement — Writing, Reporting & Setting Reminders

Diagram 3.2

Once you have your goals set, I encourage you to make sure they are visible so that you can see them regularly to remind yourself of where your focus should be. With your business goals, it is critical that you share them with other people in your team because communicating them with others is an extremely powerful tool and adds the aspect of accountability; which again, dramatically increases your chances of success. When you achieve a goal, it is also a good reason to celebrate with your team because you have reached a small milestone along the way. It is also confirmation that you are moving towards your dreams and doing well. On the other hand, if you don't have any goals, you won't get any feedback that you're doing a good job and you won't have as many reasons to celebrate.

When I think back to my darkest moments, watching my husband crumble to a shell of his former self after our house fire, I think about how vital it was for us to continue setting little goals along the way. To achieve these goals, I also asked for help from others and kept working towards one goal, one step at a time. So often when people face life threatening challenges or traumatic events, they find strength and clarity that they never knew existed. But sadly, it is also this vulnerability that can force people into desperation.

If I can impart some small seed of wisdom from my experiences, it is for you to start setting goals and making changes in your life *now*, before your choices are taken away. Take the time to think about what it is that is truly important to you. Learn to open up, accept your challenges and be honest with yourself. It will change your life.

Sarah

Sarah took over the family business from her mum, it was somewhat thrust upon her and not exactly in her life plan. She felt a responsibility to take over the business so that her mum could transition into retirement. Sarah simply operated the business with the attitude of just, 'getting the work done.' She had no bright purpose for the business and no desire to do more than what was absolutely necessary.

After many years of feeling bogged down and tied to the business, working up to 60 hours per week and struggling to get the business to the next level, Sarah's life had been dramatically impacted. Even her family relationships were suffering. When we met, I asked Sarah "What makes your heart sing?" She replied, "Spending time with my children while they're young." At this point, she broke down in tears. It was clear that her business purpose was not supporting her ambitions – and it had to change.

By identifying her vision, purpose and mission for the business and setting clearly defined business outcomes and goals, we were able to gauge what was needed to create a viable and successful model that worked for Sarah. Over a period of 12 months, significant changes were made in systems, processes and the team, which ultimately created a happier work-life balance for Sarah. She leveraged her business to provide a lifestyle of no longer working 60 hours per week, while still being in full control of her business. Not only did she free up her time, but she also started drawing a consistent wage from the business for the first time. With clear benchmarks now in place, Sarah had strategies in place to sustain the business for the long-term.

Sarah's aspirations were never to grow an empire; she just wanted a happy team and a business which supported her family. She now has the freedom of making choices that work for her and says, "My jaw has literally stopped aching from all the tension I felt." Sarah has taken two months away from the business in the last year; she also takes every Friday off work. The business manages just fine without her, something she never thought was possible. Most importantly, Sarah has regained invaluable time with her family and is loving life again.

Chapter 3
Blue Ocean Thinking

☐ **Business Mission and Purpose**

What does your business do and what is the greater purpose of your business?

☐ **What are the brand promises that you stand by?**

What are you promising to deliver to your customers?

☐ **What are your business outcomes and goals?**

What are the overarching outcomes for your business in the next 12 months, and what KPI measures do you have in place to track the performance of your strategies?

"Building a good customer experience does not happen by accident. It happens by design."

Clare Muscutt

CHAPTER FOUR

Shine Your Own Way

A year and a half after David's accident, he was still working with his old company, GBC. They sold a specialised line of products called word finishing equipment, which included paper binding, drilling, stapling, collating and folding machinery. However, they didn't provide wire binding equipment or supplies. The demand for wire binding in Western Australia was not being met because no one was supplying the equipment at the quality the market required. With this knowledge, David had recognised there was a significant gap in the product range GBC supplied, leaving a hole (and missed opportunities) in their business model.

David started to lose his passion at work, which was only amplified by the daily discomfort he suffered from the burns. Almost two years after the accident, the burns still wept through his clothes. He had to constantly wear the pressure garments and continued to have skin graft operations and treatment. In addition to this, he had not come to terms with how he looked, and his self-confidence had hit rock bottom.

With the combination of work sales pressures and his own internal battles, the stress became too great for him. Something had to change. As the second Christmas since the accident approached, David was feeling increasingly dissatisfied. In fact, my usually motivated and practically minded husband said he'd much rather be at home with me and Hamish than at the office working a job with no future prospect of growth. Hamish was a bright and contented little baby, who made life so much more worth living for David. I, on the other hand, was finding that being at home alone as a full time mum for the first time was not really meant for me.

Looking back now, I think I may have had some post-natal depression or even post-traumatic stress syndrome from the accident. Through that whole nightmare year of seeing my house on fire, my husband burning alive, looking after him and working full time, I had just 'kept going' and never really took stock of how I felt. Instead, I had stood strong so I could be a rock for David to lean on through all the ordeals he had to face. To compound this situation, neither David nor I had sought professional psychological treatment after these traumatic events. So, whilst we were 'coping', in hindsight I wish we had done more to take care of our mental health. Even though we knew we had both been affected by it, we had never really talked about our inner thoughts to anyone.

Perhaps it was the hormones of child birth which were the key to releasing all the emotions I had kept hidden inside for so long, but in those first six weeks after I gave birth, I didn't go a day without sobbing or having paralysing anxiety. If I couldn't get a stain out of the cloth nappies, I would cry. If I didn't get all the housework done, I'd cry. If the evening meal wasn't perfect, I'd cry. Sometimes I'd even break down in tears and I wouldn't have any idea why I was crying. My beautiful friend Fran, who I'd worked with at the AMA, would ring me most days to cheer me up and check on me. However, I was in such a dark place that it was hard to break free of the low emotions I was feeling.

David and I were not happy. It was time for a change, but we weren't sure what exactly that meant for us.

Hamish was only a couple of months old when my Dad came to us with an idea. He knew I was struggling and so I think he was listening out for any possible opportunity to make his daughter happy; his idea was one that got David and me very excited. Dad had been offered the chance to take on the exclusive distributorship for wire binding equipment produced by a German manufacturer named Renz. These high quality products were not available in Western Australia and he presented us with the opportunity to start our own business with this distributorship.

This was precisely the gap in the market that David had already identified. He had known that this equipment was missing from the product line at GBC for many years but, as Renz was one of GBC's global competitors, GBC couldn't supply this product line. David and I could both see this business opportunity opening up so many doors for us; it was compelling us to jump right in. At the same time, for David and me, it was difficult to walk away from a company that had been so good to us and had supported him through his recovery.

With a great deal of consideration, a tremendous amount of fear and my dad's business reputation on the line, we took the plunge. We made the decision to start our own business. My father was also kind enough to offer us a room at his business premises, rent free for our first year in business, to give us a helping hand.

In January 1990, we commenced our sole distributorship of Renz Binding Equipment and Supplies, setting up our office in the tiny back room at my dad's business in Subiaco. We had two phones, two second-hand desks and typewriters as well as a borrowed filing cabinet. With a three month old baby to care for, Dad kindly let us use the old bathroom next door to our office as a little nursery where Hamish could sleep.

We were excited and grateful for this wonderful opportunity and knew we would give it our best shot to make it work. Each day, David and I focused on getting on the phones and calling as many prospects as we could. It was tough calling people for hours and hours on end and experiencing many rejections, but David was much happier working together as a family. He also didn't have the pressure to achieve huge corporate sales targets each month. Perhaps most importantly, he was hidden from view; close only to people who loved him, and avoiding having to interact with those who judged or stared at him.

An added bonus was that Dad's office was air conditioned, so David was able to escape the heat of a second summer after being burned. The thought of being a sales rep on the road or in a hot office for another scorching West Australian summer was just horrible. Though only 30% of his body had sustained third degree burns, the rest of his body was covered with second or first degree burns or donor sites, so very little of him was left unaffected. This meant that he didn't sweat because most of his skin pores were burnt over, so he was constantly overheating. All in all, this opportunity of starting our new business was turning out to be a miracle in more ways than one.

We still faced the pressures that start-up businesses need to contend with, and the fact that it was *our* business meant we had to be successful. With a large mortgage and now a young baby to care for, this was our only source of income. Also, interest rates were at around 18% and Australia had just embarked upon the recession that Paul Keating (the Prime Minister at the time) said we had to have. Under these circumstances, the interest rates kept sky rocketing so it was a challenging economic climate in which to start a business. On the upside, although we had the pressure of making sales, it was a lot less than David was used to and with me and my father helping, it made a huge difference.

With all we had been through, we knew that any help we could get, we would take. Fortunately, from the beginning, we were introduced to people who were of influence in large organisations; Dad had many clients and contacts in the city who trusted him. This gave us a huge advantage at the start of our business career.

The benefits for me were also considerable as I was no longer at home alone with my emotions. When Hamish was awake, we all took turns in entertaining him and taking him for a walk. My mum came into the office twice a week to do the banking and accounts for the business, so she would take Hamish for a walk during her business errands. She particularly enjoyed this special bonding time with him. Every second lunch time, Dad took Hamish for a walk on his usual round to the dry cleaners, post office, bank and lunch bar, stopping to chat with anyone who would listen. To him, his grandson was the best grandchild in the whole world.

We felt blessed with family support, much happier working together and David was out of a male dominated sales environment where many egos were involved. Our new arrangement worked well for us, it made our family stronger and brought us together as an unshakable team.

First Steps

Without a doubt, in those early days of our business, the most essential component for David and me, was regularly planning and assessing our goals (and we still do so to this day). We always had a plan and worked towards realising that plan – no matter what.

In reality, if you are not planning and running the direction of your business, the business may be planning and running the direction of your life. I commonly hear business owners saying after a few years in business, *"What life? We don't have a life anymore; the business runs our life. All we do is sort out problems and put out bushfires all day long. We never seem to get time to relax. We couldn't possibly think about going on a holiday."*

This is typical of a business that is not being planned and it saddens me deeply. Having your own business can provide you with joy and purpose, giving you the freedom of choice. If your business isn't giving this to you and is, in fact, taking more away from you, it's never too late to make the necessary changes. No matter what stage of business you're at – start up, growing or an established business – it is always a good time to plan your future and adjust your business model to make it work *for you*, if it's not giving you want you want.

Another lesson learned from the experience of starting our own business was that if you are offered help, take it. There is no shame in that. If you can save money by sharing an office with a friend who might be under-utilising their premises, snap up that opportunity and be grateful for it. It might be a small thing to them, but a huge advantage for you. Often people rush into buying or leasing a premises much larger than they require to begin with. Yes, it may allow you room to grow in the future, but the huge cost of rent or repayments in the early days might just be the difference between making it, or not, in the first few years of business.

Where accepting support is concerned, the power of referrals are invaluable. Ask your friends and network to share your details or give introductions to the people who trust them. Referrals are the most powerful introductions you can get, and your chances of converting those prospects into a sale are so much higher than when you deal with a cold lead. People are generally happy to help their friends and colleagues, especially when they're starting something new. In fact, many love knowing that they can be part of your success. Referrals are a huge benefit for any company and they certainly made a tremendous difference to David and me in our new business venture.

An additional advantage that David and I had in the beginning of our business journey was that we conducted in-depth research of the industry into which we were launching, to increase our knowledge and better prepare ourselves. Yet, when I ask some business owners detailed questions about their products, competitors and target market, sometimes it's almost as if I'm speaking a foreign language. I understand that these owners may be in the first quadrant of learning – unconscious incompetence, where they don't know what they don't know – but after going through the process with them, I can see their eyes growing wide as they sadly lament, "I wish I had found this out at the start ... things may be a whole lot different." But it doesn't have to be this way.

There is not an endeavour in life that I can think of where you can reach long-term success by taking a short-cut. Business is no exception, but you *can* achieve consistent sales by creating a proactive plan, by testing and measuring the effectiveness of the strategies you implement and by continuously researching, learning and innovating. As 'success leaves clues', you can look at what is happening in other countries as well as understand as much as you can about the competitors in your own backyard. It's important to know how your product differs from theirs. Research your industry and your benchmarks, and understand as much as you can about your clients.

Understanding your product and your market will assist you to answer these key questions:

- Have you considered whether the amazing product or service you sell is new to the market or if it has been around for a long time?
- Is there a current market for your product?

- How many other suppliers or outlets are supplying the same product?
- If there are many other suppliers, what is so special about your product?
- Why would someone buy it from you instead of someone else?

Let's look a little deeper.

Unique Selling Point

What makes your product and your company unique? Knowing your unique selling point (USP) will set you apart from your competitors. You and your team need to know why you are different and fully understand what this means; and your website needs to reflect it as well. If you don't know, find out! Ask some clients what they think is special about your business compared to others, or take a look at some competitors to see what you are doing that sets you apart from them. Your USP must be truthful so that you are congruent with your actions and behaviours.

Being the first to promote a USP is important, as companies known to have copied USPs are not effective. If you can't think of one, it simply might be the certain way you do things in your processes. For example, I have seen companies develop their own USP such as, "We have a unique five step fitting process." Sometimes, it may be stating the obvious, but if you are the first to say it, then it is unique to you and you can own it. So often the key ingredient of a very successful marketing campaign is a powerful USP.

I remember a beer brand advertisement that was super successful. They explained in their television commercial that their special process of making the beer involved filtering the product through ice. Apparently, this process was standard for other beers too, but because they were the first to explain the process, it made them seem unique and they were hugely successful. In another example: Within Western Australia, we have a common challenge of tradespeople booking a job with a client and then not even turning up for the job (hard to believe, I know!). So, one enterprising tradesperson decided their USP would be, "We guarantee to turn up." It was very effective!

Your USP can be articulated as a single, unique benefit, appeal or big promise that you hold out to your prospects and customers, or a benefit or promise that no other competitor offers. The key here is to identify the one distinctive, attractive selling advantage that you are best suited to provide. Don't try to be all things to all people, just focus on one thing and do it extremely well. This builds loyalty and consistency with your team and your customers. Your unique difference may be that you sell a higher quality product or service, offer better customer service, offer a better or longer guarantee, or have a larger selection of products or options for your customers. You might have a trade-in program or generous points system that your competitors don't offer, or you may provide your customers with better value for money. At the end of the day, the best USPs are the ones that target a key frustration or angst your customers are facing.

Some well-known examples of a clear USP:

"Lowest Prices are Just the Beginning." – Bunnings

"Melt in your mouth, not in your hand." – M&M's

"When your package absolutely, positively has to get there overnight." – FedEx

"Quality Food Costs Less." – Coles

"The Fresh Food People." – Woolworths

Deliver What Your Customers Want

If you have not yet selected your products or services or if you are choosing between two products, my suggestion is that you firstly fill a gap in the market. Another key point to look for is the potential for your product to have your clients keep coming back to purchase more from you. That is the ideal business model and will allow your business to always have recurring income. It will mean that once you get a new customer, you can keep them for many years by looking after them with your amazing service or regularly supplying them with products and services they require. In contrast, it is far more difficult if you have a 'once off' product purchase, where each time you have finished delivering to a client you will have to rely on referrals or go out and find a brand new client, which is both a tiring and expensive way of doing business.

If you already have a product or service, there are ways to create ongoing business. For example, a pool company has a product which many people only buy once or twice in a lifetime – a swimming pool. Therefore, every month they start off having to find new customers again, costing valuable time, energy and money. Alternatively, a car repair shop, which is systemised and looks after its clients well, will have all their clients' cars pre-booked in for their regular service maintenance, bringing them back time and time again. With this model in place, they will already know how much business is booked in for the month, which takes away the monthly stress of, "Where am I going to get the business from this month?" or "Will I be able to pay all the monthly wages and bills?"

If you were the pool supplier, perhaps you could expand your products by also servicing, cleaning and repairing your customers' pools. You could also sell all the ongoing chemicals and equipment required to keep the pools in top condition and thereby keep your clients for a much longer period of time. I have yet to come across a pool company that offers all those services. Perhaps they are too busy trying to get new customers each month to think of adding on a service that will keep their customers coming back?

Business is so much easier if you have the opportunity to keep your clients for a long time. There are a few simple ways to help clients coming back for more. One way is to implement an online or phone app purchasing system, where clients have their log-in and can re-order their products directly from you when they run out. Another way is offering something to your customers that complements your main product or service (often called upselling) and that would increase your average dollar sale also. With multiple clients coming back more often and spending more with you, the compounding effect will dramatically impact your bottom line. If you can't think of anything additional to provide to your client, go back to researching your competitors and see what they are offering as an add-on at the checkout or finalisation of the sale. This is a great source of market research.

In considering changes in your business, you may also like to think about ways you can recoup part of the acquisition cost of each client (being, how much it costs in marketing, money and time to acquire a new client). The goal for any business is decreasing the acquisition cost of a client and increasing the lifetime value of the client; that is, how long a company keeps its average client. These are all elements of your business to understand and measure.

Reach Your Customers

Once you are clear on your USP, it's a great idea to look at how you reach your customers. You can do this by first considering how you get your product or service into the hands of your clients. Ask yourself, what is the most effective distribution plan for your product or service? Is it possible for it to be up-scaled so that it can be leveraged by other people or systems, making each and every sale not totally dependent upon you? Could you consider options for distribution such as agents, commission sales people, catalogue/direct mail, distributors, franchisees, licensees, multi-level marketing, party planners, promotors, referral groups, resellers, retail outlets, sales forces, telemarketers, vending machines or wholesalers? This way, your sales may be limitless.

Imagine if sales could happen, regardless of whether you were at work or not, and imagine if sales occurred while you were asleep? One way of achieving this could be by introducing a simple online booking system or purchasing facility which will make you and your clients' lives so much easier. For example, Justine sells children's after school classes and she told me they often get orders at very odd times throughout the night. We all have different time schedules; by introducing an online ordering option, it will give your clients 24 hour access to purchase from you, rather than being limited to ordinary business hours. *Easy and simple* is the key; the fewer steps to the checkout, the better. The more online shopping sites you interact with, the more you will see how simple and easy some are to buy from, whilst others just give you a pounding headache and make you close the site, wondering how they make any sales at all.

Know Your Customers

Knowing who your customers are and which target market/s they belong to will have major benefits to your business. To identify your perfect client or gain greater clarity on existing clients, think about the following: If you imagine your ideal client, how would you describe them as an *avatar*? Do you know how old they are, whether they're male or female, what their occupation is, what their interests are, where they hang out, what they watch on TV, what they read, what social media they use, what's important to them, and so on? The more you know about your ideal client, the easier it will be to build a marketing plan to attract them and then to build a customer service plan to service and retain these clients.

You might be thinking, "My business is different; everyone is a potential client for me." But in business, *anybody* can equal *nobody*. As an example, if you are a car mechanic or an architect, you may be mistaken for thinking anyone with a car or wanting to build a house is a prospect in your target market. However, if you look at who your best clients are to deal with, who you enjoy serving the most, who gives you the best margin when they buy from you, who gives you the most referrals and who comes back more often, you will begin to uncover some similarities amongst these clients. In fact, by doing this exercise, you will discover that you *do* have a desired type of client and will discover your *ideal* target market. You may also discover you have more than one type of ideal customer. In fact, some businesses have three or four target markets and each target market will have a different marketing strategy.

How big is the market you are targeting? Is it local, national or international? Do you have one target market or multiple target markets? Where does the highest concentration of your target market demographic live? Are the needs being met for your target market or is there an under or over supply in a particular area? Focus your marketing activities on the specific target market you would like to attract. For further clarity on your target market, you can find more information from your local councils, market research companies and online sources.

Solve Problems

Once you are clear on each of your ideal clients and target markets, start by identifying the challenges they might be facing and the problems you will solve by selling your product or service to them. You can then decide how to best communicate that message to them. Another way to look at this is by learning about where your potential clients' thoughts are *focused*. You may have heard of the phrase, "Setting your RAS?" Your RAS is the *reticular activating system* of your brain which steers the compass in your brain to identify things that you pre-determine as important. This reticular formation in your brain is, "A diffuse network of nerve pathways in the brainstem connecting the spinal cord, cerebrum, and cerebellum, and mediating the overall level of consciousness."[14] In layman's terms, it's the place in your brain that connects unconscious and conscious thoughts and directs your attention.

As an example, have you ever decided to buy a new car and once you have decided on the make and model of the car, you start to see them everywhere? The same is true when you decide on a holiday location; holidays for that destination start popping up everywhere you look. Or when you fall pregnant, all of a sudden you notice how many pregnant women there are around you. Of course, these things have always been present in your environment, but you have only just started to notice them because your RAS has been set to do so.

Another example can be seen if you look at a car tyre company advertising *safe tyres*. If their target market is Mums who drive children around, then their RAS will be set on keeping their children safe and anything safety related. They may not consciously be looking for new tyres for their car. However, by advertising children's safety, instead of just boring old tyres, the tyre company will automatically start appealing to this target market. So, the question is, do you know where your target market's RAS is set?

Marketing is fundamentally about communicating and educating. If your target market doesn't know who you are, then you can't communicate with them and they won't be able to buy from you. Once you discover how to reach them, it's about educating them on how you can solve their problem. I have found that it usually takes between seven to nine points of contact before someone buys from a new supplier. This equates to you being visible between seven and nine times to your target market before they will generally make the decision to buy from you.

So often I have prospective clients who come to me saying they have no sales and that it is causing all kinds of cashflow problems. I do a little research of their business on the internet to look at the main product they supply, and they are nowhere to be seen. It is critically important that you have online visibility when people look up the product or service you supply. If your business is not visible on internet searches (because you have no website, or it is so outdated that Google doesn't rank it), your marketing strategies are hugely diminished.

Hang Out Where Your Customers Do

How do you let your target market know that you exist? There are so many ways for you to communicate with your market. Getting clear on your ideal target and their needs will help you brainstorm ways to reach them.

Once you are visible to your target market, for them to take the next step, you'll need to build some credibility. This could be via a free offer, posting a variety of interesting articles or YouTube videos giving out valuable information, or via credible testimonials. Traditionally, once a potential client has enough trust in you through all the credibility you have built, only then will they move to the next phase and make their first purchase from you. Before they buy, it's a good idea to think of a way to capture the details of the people looking at your business or website. What can you offer your prospective clients that is so attractive they have to swap it for their email address? The reason for choosing your target market first is because you would use different channels of communication depending on the target market. It may be a combination of a few methods that could include social media platforms, newsletters, TV or radio advertisements, etc.

Diagram 4.1 shows a quick brainstorming session of the many different ways you could connect with a prospect.

Brainstorm Ways To Communicate

Sales People

Speaking

Newspapers / Magazines

Radio

Emails

Mail Drops — Target Market — Events

Phone Calls

PR

Signage

Social Media
Facebook, Instagram, Linkedin, etc.

Sponsorships

Networking

Expos

Diagram 4.1

The content you share should inform them of the fact that you can solve a problem they have, with a call to action so they are urged to contact you. When you put information out to educate your target market on who you are and how you can help them (via social media, website, emails and physical presence, to name a few), keeping the message consistent across all channels will help you gain better traction with your prospective buyers. If you're confused and don't plan your messages, your prospective clients will also be confused. To avoid this, carefully consider your overarching message, then choose the types of images, colours and theme you wish to use across your messages. The key to remember here is that your branding ought to be constant throughout your business messaging, including everything in the public eye.

For example, I went into a printing shop which was very keen to explain on their website how efficient and high tech their printing processes were. I was shocked when I visited their actual premises; I couldn't believe it was the same business. I'd even say the people who built their website had obviously never visited their premises either; the office and printing areas were dirty, messy and disorganised. Plus, the business was filled with old, outdated printing equipment. This was so incongruent to the pictures of the equipment and office space on their website; it was a total disappointment.

Test and Measure

One of the paramount things to remember with any marketing plan is to test and measure all your activities and document the results so you know whether your strategies are effective. If you put up a Facebook post, check how many people liked it, how many people commented and if it generated any sales. Sometimes it takes time for a strategy to build momentum, so don't just try something once and decide that it doesn't work. Instead, decide upfront how much time and money you are going to invest into each strategy, and measure the results carefully within that period.

The Google analytics reports from your website are another valuable tool which will help you learn where the visitors to your website come from. It will also allow you to see which section of your website they visited and how long they stayed in certain places on your site. Looking up your competitors' marketing will also give you some clues too. However, don't be fooled into thinking that just because a competitor invests in a large marketing budget, that their efforts must be working. This is not always the case, so don't let the blind lead the blind.

I recall a client thinking of investing in cinema advertising, so we went along one evening to a cinema promo night to see how it worked. We wrote down the names of all the local businesses that were advertising on the big movie screen. In pursuit of our research, soon after I called each one of those businesses to ask how many leads or sales they had received from their cinema advertising. I was shocked to discover that none of them had any idea. None of them had tracked or measured where their leads were coming from; they had no idea if they were wasting their money or not. The lesson here is to measure your marketing campaigns, so you know if you're making a return on your investments.

When a sale is processed, wouldn't it be beneficial if there was a way of finding out where the sale was originally generated? Setting up a system to track which of your marketing efforts are working and which aren't, is a great way you can measure the acquisition cost of a client and ultimately where to focus your marketing energy. A customer relations management system (CRM) is an application which can often be linked to an accounting program. This is a useful way to track a client's purchase history and to automate the process of keeping in touch with them. Acquiring a new client is just one focus, but the other part of marketing is keeping existing clients coming back time and time again. Imagine if you kept every single client you ever had? Wouldn't that be valuable to your business?

Show You Care

In a piece written about, "The 5 Reasons Customers Leave," it was shown that the top reasons clients leave their suppliers are:

- Poor attitude or perceived indifference (68%)
- Product, price or service dissatisfaction (14%)
- Lured away by a competitor (14%)
- Moving location (3%)
- Death (1%)[15]

Most clients leave and buy from someone else because they think you don't care! If you're not in touch with your clients regularly and doing something to show them that you care, then someone else will be – and that someone will undoubtedly be your competitor. Having a proactive systemised way of keeping in touch with your customers often produces referrals, too, because people share with others when people care about them. As I have said earlier, in most instances the conversion rate of a referral to a sale is much higher than a normal lead.

What do you currently have in place to regularly communicate with your clients, so they know you care? How can you provide such a level of care that they would not think of going anywhere else? If you have put many deposits into the emotional bank account of the relationship with your customer – and something was to ever go wrong with an order or if there was an alternative for your client – there should be no way they would think of changing supplier. Are you doing everything possible in your power to nurture the relationship with your clients?

When David and I decided to start our own business, a few areas were crystal clear to us. We knew our competitors well. We knew what they looked like, who their clients were, what products they sold and for how much. We were clear on the gap in the market that we were filling and what was unique about us. Our profit margins were healthy, and our expenses were low. Doing our homework thoroughly was also a massive advantage for us, and of utmost importance to anyone in business who wants an edge over their competitors, and to better connect with their customers.

Before you make any life-changing decisions in your home or business, always put your hand up to seek help and advice; and do research so you know clearly what lies ahead on whatever road you are taking.

Phil and Cathy

Phil and Cathy had been running their fencing business for many years at a loss and they were at their wits' end when they came to me for help. They said that things needed to change, or they would be forced to close their business. We identified their biggest challenge was inconsistent cashflow, due to their clients not paying on time (or not paying at all). To add to this situation, they were in an industry which was 'on its knees'.

With no marketing plan in place, or website, they were not even sure of their target market. Their answer was simply, "We don't care who our clients are, as long as they pay on time." We looked deeper into the customers they already had and found a pattern that some clients were better to deal with than others. We identified the similarities between those clients and started actively focusing on that target market and built a website to attract those types of clients.

Getting clear on the problems their target market was facing, we then depicted how Phil and Cathy's business could fix those problems and described this clearly on their website and on other marketing platforms. Once we knew what this target market wanted, we researched what else we could supply to the same market and found there were other products that could easily be added to give Phil and Cathy an edge over their competitors.

Based on the credibility Phil and Cathy already had with their existing customers, it wasn't hard to increase their product range, and it even reduced the administration required, as they started buying from just one supplier instead of two. Twelve months later, their sales and cashflow increased dramatically and their debtors (people who owed them money) decreased, along with their stress levels. They no longer felt sick in the stomach about where they were going to get the money to pay the wages – all from simply identifying and honing in on the target market they wanted to service.

Chapter 4
Blue Ocean Thinking

☐ **What is unique about your business?**

What differentiates your business from others? Why would your prospects buy from you over your competitors?

....

....

....

....

....

....

☐ **Who's your ideal client?**

How would you describe your ideal client as an avatar?

....

....

....

....

....

....

☐ **How can you market to your customers?**

Where are your customers hanging out and what challenges can you solve for them?

....

....

....

....

....

....

....

....

"Be genuine,
be remarkable,
be worth
connecting
with."

Seth Godin

CHAPTER FIVE

Know the Game You're Playing

True to his word, my dad gave us our first year rent free at his office which was an amazing benefit. Having very few fixed expenses was a great advantage and afforded us the ability to make a profit each month. As a result, we finished our first year of business with a small net profit which was an awesome achievement. With no other source of income, we had no choice but to make it work. We didn't have an overdraft to fall back on and being a start-up business with no prior track record of financial success, we had no evidence to give to the bank for an overdraft, even if we had wanted one.

We simply worked our butts off to make sure we were making sales and turning a profit. There was also the added incentive of trying to keep our mortgage payments up on our home that we had managed to save and renovate after the fire, thanks to some funds from the insurance company. We were determined not to default on our mortgage and run the risk of losing our precious home.

When the time came for us to leave my dad's office and create our own business space, I researched many businesses. I discovered that most of them leased their premises for around five years. With this information, naturally David and I were about to do the same. However, Dad explained to us all the hidden traps that leasing can incur, and encouraged us to do some more homework before we jumped into leasing. After looking at all the pros and cons, David and I were dumbfounded that there were so many factors for us to consider. We had never thought of buying our own business premises, it sounded way too daunting. Nevertheless, we decided to do a comparison to see if we'd be better off buying a business premises, and if that was even a possibility for us.

To our surprise, after working out the numbers, we found it was actually cheaper per month to buy, rather than lease. The added bonus was that every single month we were going to be ahead because we would be buying an asset, compared to if we had just done the same as everyone else and leased an office. After much research, we shortlisted three properties that were within our size, budget and location criteria.

Finally, we settled on a beautiful little building, approximately 16 months after we started our business venture. It was an early 1900's railway cottage on the outskirts of the city with loads of character – a perfect place for us to run our business. We aptly named our new premises, our *Business House*. It was another milestone and step forward for us and our business. We felt as if we were slowly rebuilding our lives and beginning to chart the course for our future once more. It was a wonderful feeling after all we'd been through together.

Not long after we moved into our Business House, my grandmother (who we all affectionately called Nanna) fell gravely ill. I remember receiving the distressing news that she was in hospital. I was extremely upset as we were very close, and I loved her dearly. Poor Nanna was so sick that when her sister passed away during this time she was not well enough to leave hospital to go to her funeral. To help keep her company and lift her spirits, I went to visit her on the day of her sister's funeral.

As we sat together, she said to me through tearful eyes, "There's no point in living anymore. I may as well die and join my sister."

Devastated at the thought of my Nanna dying, I replied, "You can't leave yet Nanna! You don't have a great granddaughter yet."

At this, she managed a little smile and asked, "How long do I have to wait for that?"

Wanting to give her a glimmer of hope, I quickly responded, "Well, why don't I go home and make a daughter and you go home and get better? And if you stay alive long enough to meet her, I'll name her Eve after you. Is that a deal?"

Nanna was delighted with my idea and said with disbelief in her voice, "You would actually do that for me?"

From my heart I answered honestly, "Yes!"

Well, Nanna was so keen on the idea of having her first great granddaughter named after her that she recovered quickly. She was home within a week and fit as a fiddle for months afterwards.

Meanwhile, I kept my side of the bargain and was pregnant within a few weeks. Of course, I was eager to have another child anyway, so my ingenious plan suited us both.

Over the months of my pregnancy, I continued to work in our business and enjoyed spending time with my little family, Hamish and David. I loved being pregnant and was so grateful to have another smooth-sailing pregnancy.

By this time, Hamish was three years old and an absolute delight. He loved chatting with everyone in great depth; his confidence and verbal skills were exceptional. David was also a beautiful father. He loved spending time in the park with Hamish walking at a snail's pace so Hamish could look at every single ant or pretty leaf they walked past. Times like these with Hamish brought David into the present moment and distracted him from the constant pain of his burns. Hamish would also delight in coming back to the Business House to do 'business with Dad' after day care. Hamish would help pack up the days' sales orders with David, which made him feel very important. Sticky tape, sticky labels and markers were strewn all over the storeroom, but they had fun together. I enjoyed seeing that trail of packing materials as a reminder of the precious memories David was building with our son.

Of course, we continued to visit Nanna regularly throughout my pregnancy and she was keen to hold her hand on my belly to feel any movement of the growing life inside me. We all wondered if our new baby would be a boy or a girl.

On June 21, 1993, on the eve of Midsummer Night in Scotland, I delivered a beautiful little baby girl. True to my word, we named her Eve. I fell in love again instantly and felt so lucky to have had such a different birth experience from Hamish's. I was able to give birth naturally with no pain relief; little Eve was delivered straight into my arms.

Sadly, Nanna had a cold when Eve was born so she couldn't visit us at the hospital straight away. Finally, when Eve was around six weeks old, we were able to visit Nanna at her house. She was so overwhelmed with joy to meet her little namesake, she kept saying she couldn't believe that anyone would actually name their child after her. Nanna cuddled Eve in her arms and it was magical watching the two *Eves*, three-generations apart, connecting in love. Little newborn Eve delicately smiled and relaxed as she contentedly cuddled up in her great grandmother's arms. It was a special moment.

The very next day my beautiful Nanna went out shopping with her best friend, had her hair done and bought some new shoes. All the while telling everyone she met about little Eve, and saying that meeting her was the happiest day of her life.

When she arrived home that afternoon, she sat down in her armchair, nodded off to sleep and peacefully passed away. It was as if she had stayed around long enough to meet her great granddaughter, but after achieving this goal, it was time for her to go.

I had never experienced the loss of a loved one who was so close to me before, so I was heartbroken at Nanna's passing. While I knew she was elderly and her time to go wasn't far away, the sense of loss I experienced was deep. It was as if my heart received a big bruise; I still feel pain from her loss, even to the day.

At the same time, with Eve's birth, it was wonderful to be parents again; David and I were both delighted. However, the truth was that David was still battling the physical and mental pain of his burns and, with a new business and two young children to care for, I had to think more seriously about our future plans together.

Very mindful of the mental and physical battle I witnessed taking over David's life, I tried to support him, but was increasingly concerned with his downward spiral. I couldn't ignore the fact that his state was a potential threat to our children, the business and our family's future. David knew he had a problem, and he knew it bothered me, but the black dog of depression was ever present in his life. It was as if it slumbered in his mind, only to wake up and peep through the gaps in David's days with daunting regularity. He tried to come up with strategies to stop the drinking and escape the dark side taking over, but the curse was ready to pounce at the slightest opportunity.

Unfortunately, too often than not, it seemed the only time David was relaxed, happy and out of pain was when he was feeding his addictions with alcohol, cigarettes, food or work. David continued to drown his sorrows and was caught in a vicious cycle of being drunk or hung over. He often spent a full day a week being so hung over that he couldn't get out of bed. It was also pretty standard that on a Friday night he would drink so much that he'd eventually pass out at three or four o'clock the next morning.

Added to this, his self-image was terrible. His hands, in particular, were sore to move and the skin often split open with the slightest knock, leaking drops of blood on everything he touched. His calves, which he had to have surgically rebuilt, throbbed when he stood up for too long and these still had weeping wounds. We had come to learn that burns took an incredibly long time to heal, with the inner invisible scars seeming to take just as long. David still didn't recognise himself in the mirror when he saw his reflection each morning; seeing himself every day was a harsh reality and reminder of what he had become. David had also not been able to exercise consistently since the accident, so his weight ballooned each year, but he just didn't care. Despite being drunk or hungover, he poured all his time and energy into the business. He worked long hours, which was also to the detriment of his health.

As a mother with a new baby, David's habits and mental state deeply concerned me. I prayed and hoped every day that David would win the battle with the demons he was fighting inside his heart and mind.

We often spoke openly about his drinking challenges and he understood how damaging it was to his health and to our relationship. Despite the ongoing battles, I knew the depth of love we had for each other was unwavering and that he never intentionally did anything to damage it. Yet, I knew he still held a great deal of sorrow and sadness within. He hated what he had put me through over the years since the accident, for which he took full responsibility. I could also see in his eyes how sorry he felt for the anguish he'd create during his drinking episodes.

Generally, he didn't remember any of the hurtful things said or done while he was drunk, yet he knew he had a dark side which could emerge when he was under the influence of alcohol. The day after such episodes he would always be deeply apologetic and hopeful he hadn't pushed me past the edge of no return, to the point where I would walk out the door and leave him. It was a difficult tightrope we walked together during this time.

Yet, never a day went by without a kiss or a hug from him telling me how much he loved me. Just about every single morning when I woke up, the first thing I would see was David's face on the pillow beside me. He'd be wide awake staring at me in adoration and at times he'd have been watching me sleep for up to an hour, when he couldn't sleep himself. He would say how beautiful I looked and often whispered how he could not believe he was lucky enough to have me as his wife. At the office, our desks were across from each other and just a glimpse of him looking over to me made me feel the love that was ever present between us.

In our first three and a half years of business, David and I learned so much from our experiences. Not only were we building our business, we were also growing our family, whilst contending with the many issues associated with David's accident. We faced mental and physical burdens, the arrival of two babies and the loss of loved ones. Throughout it all, we were still able to move from success to success in our business due to the invaluable lessons we learned along the way.

My recommendation, when dealing with someone in pain or grief, is to be there for them, be present, listen, love with your whole heart, be patient and help your loved one to get some professional help. Everyone has a story, everyone has battles, and there are so many factors that have a way of impacting our relationships, family and business, without us even knowing it.

Your Business Premises

When you're at a stage where you are deciding whether to lease or buy your business premises, there are a few important steps to consider. When my dad had warned us of all the unseen threats around leasing, he brought a few important ones to our attention:

- If you lease a premises, you will most likely be part of a strata group and will have to conform to the rules of the group building.

- If there is any reason that may cause concern for other tenants in the building, these complaints aren't always easily resolved. For example, your regular truck deliveries may interfere with other tenants, or you might end up squabbling over car spaces, noise, bins, common grounds, and even air-conditioning.

- Landlords can increase the monthly rent and even sell the building out from under a tenant's nose.

- If the owner of a building goes bankrupt and the bank forecloses on them, the building is sold, regardless of whether there are leases in place or not.

- Any investment you may have spent on the fit-outs required for your business would go down the drain if you are forced to move on before you had planned.

"This is only the tip of the iceberg," my dad warned.

So, when we undertook our assignment of comparing leasing to buying a property, we carefully compared figures for each option, side by side. Firstly, we identified the annual cost per year of the average lease in the location, price, and size range we were seeking. Then, we calculated our potential future costs if the lease amount increased by the minimum Consumer Price Index (CPI) each year. We tallied up what the total amount paid would be by the time the lease term ended and compared these figures against a comparable premises, if we bought rather than leased (over the same timeframe).

You will have far more control if you own a premises rather than lease it. If you buy, you are also buying an asset that can be held outside the business. When we settled on our business premises, we purchased it in our own names, as we had a small amount of equity in our home. The benefit of this was that our business could rent the office from us and we would receive a total tax deduction in return. Our accountant explained that if we purchased the property in the company's name, it wouldn't have been as tax effective. Here's where having a great accountant comes into play! Plus, real estate traditionally increases in value (not in all cases, so you need to do your research) which provides the potential to benefit on multiple fronts. If you lease, you'll be draining money from your business and after many years, you won't have anything to show for it other than a major overhead expense. It's wise to consider these options to discover what is better for your budget, security and sanity.

Additionally, where your business is located can have a dramatic impact on your business's performance, depending on how many competitors and potential clients are in your area. This will also depend on whether your business is based upon face to face interaction with clients or would benefit from prospective walk-by customers. If your business is all conducted online, however, your location may not have as much bearing on your ultimate success. With David's many years of experience in our industry, we knew who our competitors were and where they were located. We took this into consideration when buying, so we didn't have too many of them in our area.

Research Your Industry

As already mentioned, research in business is vital to your success and this applies to understanding your industry. By undertaking a full and detailed industry analysis, you can find out how large your market is, your industry's annual turnover, learn how many people it employs and pinpoint how many outlets there are for your specific sector. You can also determine where your market is trending and if it is on an upward or downward trajectory. You can source this sort of information through the Bureau of Statistics, local market research companies or online through sites such as IBIS World, where you can purchase full industry reports.[16] Companies that specialise in market research can also provide you with invaluable information about your marketplace.

The questions to answer, when you're considering your marketplace, include:

- Do you know how big it is?
- Do you know who your competitors are?
- What are they offering and more importantly, what are they offering that you're not?
- What are their prices compared to yours? Are they higher or lower?
- What do they do better than you? What do you do better than them?
- Where do you sit in your marketplace and how do you compare to your competitors?
- How secure do you feel that your business has the means, method and ability to surpass your competitors?

If you can't answer these questions, you have no way of protecting yourself from your competition and can't focus on proactive strategies required to take your business to the next level.

Analyse Your Strengths

A *SWOT* analysis is a powerful process used to identify your business's Strengths, Weaknesses, Opportunities and Threats. If you act upon the information you gain from the process, you can improve your position in your market.

To identify your *strengths*, ask yourself what does your business do particularly well or what sets you apart in your industry? For example, your strengths may be that you have a huge amount of industry experience, you might have qualified and highly trained team members, be located centrally, have an exclusive line of products, or you might offer a totally unique service. Perhaps you provide 24/7 live customer support, don't charge a call-out fee or have an experienced team of bookkeepers and accountants behind you? Knowing your strengths is powerful; you can communicate this with your team and your customers, i.e. on your website, in proposals or tenders. If you have over ten years of technical experience in the industry or a national accreditation, tell your clients!

Just as knowing your strengths is important, knowing the *weaknesses* of your business is equally so. By being aware of your weaknesses you can focus on the actions you can take to mitigate them. For example, perhaps you are new to the industry, don't have a national company backing you, have limited financial capital or are a one-man-band? If you know that you or your team lack skills or knowledge in certain areas, compared to your competitors, it's a great idea to focus energy on professional development or training to mitigate this shortcoming.

Sometimes you may even find that a weakness is also a strength. An instance of this is where being a one-man start up business compared to a large competitor can be a weakness (due to fewer resources or less experience), but it can also be a strength because you may be able to offer a more personalised service. Another potential weakness of a small mechanical repair business might be that you do not have a workshop. However, you can turn this into a strength by saying that you can pass the savings onto your customers by charging less and coming out to their premises instead.

Identifying *opportunities* in your business helps you to look into the future. By doing this, you can recognise what hidden potential exists in your business or industry and what you can proactively do to capitalise on those opportunities. The more ideas and information you have to place you at the forefront of opportunities, the better placed your business will be. Often government grants are available to support certain industries or sectors, which can be a huge opportunity for future research, development or capital injection. Technology also offers a huge possibility for new opportunities. There may be advancements in technology in your industry that you can bring to your organisation to optimise the way your services and products are delivered (such as phone apps, payment gateways, scheduling and tracking programs, to name a few). Opportunities are everywhere, so keep your eye out for them.

Lastly, if you can foresee potential *threats* that your business might encounter, you can work to lessen or avoid the blows before they become a bigger concern. Some threats may be outside your control, but there are generally ways to soften the impact of a business threat. For example, if the US Dollar rises, your cost of stock prices may rise which could force you to increase your selling prices. To mitigate this from your end, you might buy your stock in bulk when the US dollar is low, or look at joining forces with another local business to buy in bulk. You could even buy some US dollars when the dollar is low. If you have threats to face in your business, what are you doing to counteract them?

Imagine the possible benefits available to you if you conducted a SWOT analysis on your business with your team each year, and if everyone was involved with reviewing the company's SWOT? By identifying the strategies for improvement, this could make a significant difference to your bottom line. Whether you are a one-man band or have a large company, it is a valuable exercise to do each year. Additionally, by having access to the different points of view from your team, the quality of the intellectual property coming from these sessions will be far greater than if you did the SWOT analysis by yourself. The more informed and proactive you are about what is going on in your business, your industry and the other companies in the same marketplace, the better prepared you will be for any risks that may arise.

Know Your Competitors

Competitors can be classed as *direct* or *indirect*. A direct competitor supplies the *same* or *similar* product or service as you in the same marketplace, whereas an indirect competitor is a company that sells a product that competes with the product you sell in a more general way. For example, an indirect competitor of a swimming pool company might be a travel agent or home renovation company. This probably makes no sense on first appearance, so let me explain. Families often have a certain budget to spend on big ticket luxury items. These categories might include installing a pool, renovating a kitchen or going on a family holiday. They likely can't do all three, which makes these three very different industries indirect competitors. This is why it's worth knowing what other items your customers might be interested in buying alongside yours, as these may be your indirect competitors.

A good example of this can be seen when you're targeted by social media or online advertising. You may be looking for a pool and then an ad comes up for a destination holiday or a kitchen renovation deal. Why? It's called targeted marketing and it's based on data collected from search engines such as Google. When a large portion of customers searching for a pool may also be seen looking at holiday destinations or kitchen renovation websites, Google begins to identify the pattern and will start producing ads in these categories on your web searches. These ads all start to vie for your attention.

Registering or Trademarking

One way to protect yourself from your competitors is to ensure you trademark or register any product, service or process unique to your business so that others can't steal or copy them. If you have created a unique product, do you have a product patent in place or other legal protection to protect your intellectual property? A patent expires after a certain period of time, so putting trademarks in place for a product, service or company name will also give you added protection from your competitors. Many business owners think that just because they have their company name registered and have purchased their website URL that they are protected and that the corresponding name, product or service is theirs. I'm afraid this is not necessarily the case.

For example, Karen, who had a very successful children's dance school, experienced this first-hand when her biggest competitor purchased her website domain – out from under her! Unfortunately, her domain had recently expired and before Karen had the chance to re-register her domain name, it was effectively available to 'buy off the shelf.' Her competitor must have been aware of this and immediately purchased Karen's domain. With all of Karen's classes sold online, this was very detrimental to the success of her business. A distraught Karen came to me asking if I could help her, wondering how she could get back the domain for her business name. Sadly, after lengthy negotiations, Karen eventually had to buy the domain back from her competitor for $20,000. It was an extremely expensive lesson to learn, when this could have been avoided, had she been more proactive.

It is a sad fact, but there are people who specifically look for domain names of large, profitable organisations that are close to expiring, buy them and then demand money to sell the domain back to the original owner. Whilst it's not an illegal practise, it's certainly deplorable and it happens. Therefore, if your domain is important to you, be careful and organised; make sure you are aware of its renewal date.

While on the topic of domains, be sure to have a copy of your website content in case the company which built your site goes out of business. On many occasions, I have witnessed businesses wanting to re-work or modify their website, only to discover the company which built it is no longer operating and their online content has disappeared. Alas, they need to start from scratch all over again which is not only frustrating, but also costly and time consuming.

Benchmarking

Benchmarking is another useful resource that is reasonably easy to access before you decide to open your business. Based on the tax returns that similar businesses have submitted over the years, there are reports produced on standard benchmark KPIs of each industry profession. You can usually obtain these reports from an accountant. The benchmark gross profit for your intended business lets you know how much profit is made, on average, after stock costs or other cost of goods have been paid for. Net profit is an even better indicator for you to assess your potential position. If the benchmark is 10% net profit, that means for every $100.00 of sales you invoice there will only be $10.00 left for you. Revenue to wages ratio is worth looking at too, as this explains how much you are likely to pay in wages for every dollar of sales revenue you receive. All these measures give you great insight, so that you are fully informed before you hit the 'go' button.

By having this information *before* you open your business, you can decide if you are happy with the benchmarks for your industry and whether the numbers are enough to keep you excited about your new venture. If you are an established business, this information offers a great way to measure and compare your performance. The aim of the research is to protect you financially, physically and emotionally.

Appearances May Be Deceiving

Another way to compare yourself to your competition is by studying their websites; it's an excellent resource for all types of useful information. Often, a company will have its history, size of their team, product range, price offerings and projects outlined on their site. By taking this one step further, you can also find out where their physical outlet is and actually walk in and see what it looks like. This is often an enlightening experience, as you will find that some companies appear huge or high calibre on their website, but you might find out they are running out of their garage or a scruffy office that does not truly reflect what their website portrays. I have seen this exercise provide people with a huge sense of confidence when they realise that a competitor, whom they once thought of as their biggest competition, was not as successful as they once assumed.

When you are looking through competitors' websites or physical premises, it's also good to note what works and what doesn't. It might even be possible to have a casual, friendly chat with the business owner about how business is going for them. You can also buy a product or service from them (or ask friends to do this for you) to see how they handle the sale. How does the product arrive or how is the service delivered? Are they a friendly, organised company to deal with? Can you purchase online? Is the standard consistent every time you buy from them?

I have had tradespeople from the same company come to my house; one of whom arrived on time, was friendly, polite and cleaned up after themselves; and another who turned up late, grumpy, smelled of body odour and left the place a mess after finishing off the repairs. It's a great lesson to learn, so you can set your sales and delivery standards to be consistent every time, by everyone in the team. Your reputation depends on it.

Partnerships

Another competitor you may never have even thought of as being in competition with you, is your business partner. If you go into business with someone else, even if it is a family member or a best friend, having a Partnership Agreement in place to protect your business is critical. This form of agreement is about protecting you, your partner and your business for every possible scenario that may occur in the future. A Partnership Agreement is designed to protect parties in case one of you gets sick, has an accident, dies, where one of your life partners becomes incapacitated and your business partner has to look after them, where you have a disagreement, decide to separate, dissolve the business or any number of other scenarios. You might be thinking you're not willing to pay a lawyer to create a Partnership Agreement when your business isn't worth anything yet, or you might be convinced that these types of issues would never happen to you. However, I can assure you that you are not exempt and these things happen more often than you realise.

If you are in partnership now or if you are thinking of going into partnership with someone, I can't stress highly enough how important it is for you to protect each other by having an agreement drawn up. Have an honest discussion around what will happen to the business in the event one of you wants to (or has to) leave the business. If you don't have a Partnership Agreement in place, do it now! Call a lawyer as soon as possible and have one drawn up. Hire someone who has experience in these types of agreements; it's too risky to do yourself or have someone inexperienced do the job. It may just save you a great deal of pain, stress and money down the track – and I promise you, you'll thank me for it.

The same applies to owning shares in a company with a business partner.[17] In this case, it is also imperative to have a Shareholder's Agreement prepared by a lawyer. If you can't afford to pay a lawyer to have these documents drawn up properly, I would suggest you don't start the business until you can. You will save yourself money and time in the future. Among other things, these documents will determine what happens to your shares or ownership interest in a business if you were in a position where you could no longer act, due to death or incapacity. Additionally, it is also worth thinking about Buy/Sell insurance.[18]

I'll never forget Mark and Stephen who owned an I.T. business together; they'd also been friends for many years. Sadly, not long after we met, Stephen suffered a heart attack and couldn't work, but still needed to take a wage from the business to support his family. He had a mortgage to pay and couldn't risk losing his family home. But with Stephen unable to work, he was not doing any billable hours and the business could not afford to pay his wages indefinitely. To add to the pressure, their business was relatively new and only had four people in the team. Mark and Stephen were the only senior I.T. experts, so their business success relied heavily on the joint work they did.

Unfortunately, they had no insurances in place in case of this kind of circumstance and were therefore left in a dilemma. When the business could not afford to pay Stephen any longer, he asked to sell his share of the business back to Mark. However, Mark couldn't afford to purchase Stephen's interest in the business. Sadly, the worse-case scenario eventuated. Mark had to wind-down the business and find another job. Stephen was forced into taking a government funded sickness pension, and Mark and Stephen's friendship was damaged forever, which was difficult to witness.

Last Will and Testament and Death Planning

A plan to cover the death of a business owner or partner is also essential. Please don't be naïve, and think that, "Oh, that will never happen to me." I see this attitude time and time again amongst business owners, and most do not have a Last Will and Testament (Will). It is vitally important you have a Will, and have it properly drawn up by a professional. If you don't have one, you will have no say on the distribution of your assets after you are gone, which can be a massive headache for your loved ones. Furthermore, it is far more expensive to distribute the assets of your estate if you die without a Will in place.[19] It is such a small thing to arrange and the benefits far outweigh the cost.

Having an Enduring Power of Attorney and Enduring Power of Guardianship drafted at the same time means that if something happens to you and you are incapacitated, either temporarily or permanently, your financial and medical decision-making powers will be delegated to someone you trust.[20]

A Power of Attorney is a legal document in which one person nominates and gives legal authority to another to act on and manage their affairs on their behalf. An Enduring Power of Guardianship is a legal document that authorises a person of your choice, to make important personal, lifestyle and treatment decisions on your behalf, should you ever become incapable of making such decisions yourself. The person nominated is known as an Enduring Guardian.

If there was a medical or financial decision that had to be made and you were unable to do so, who would you want to handle these decisions on your behalf?

Insure Yourself

There are many types of insurances to consider that will protect your business assets and your family. If you are the sole breadwinner through your business, what would happen if you became ill and weren't able to run the business? Who would look after your family if you had no Life, Income Protection, Total and Permanent Disability (TPD), Trauma or other relevant key person insurance in place? Ask yourself:

- If you, as the business owner, or another key person in your business dies or is seriously injured or disabled, do you currently have plans in place to meet your ongoing financial commitments?
- Do you have a succession plan outlined to ensure an appropriate transition of ownership?
- If you were unable to work in your business for a year, could you continue to pay the ongoing expenses with funds held within your business?

If the answer to any of these questions is 'no', or you're not sure, I encourage you to speak with a reputable, qualified Personal Insurance Broker about your insurance requirements. They will assist you to identify the type of insurances available to you, to protect you in the event of worst-case scenarios.

It's crucially important to protect your equity and to make sure the future control of your business stays with the most important people, without jeopardising the business and its financial future. As a business owner, you may also be personally liable for any loans or expenses incurred by the business. Importantly, in these situations, insurance cover can be set up to protect your personal assets from being at risk.

Diagram 5.1 shows a basic table of personal insurances available to consider.[21]

Personal / Key Person Insurance Table

Category	Brief Description
Life Cover (Also known as Term Life or Death Cover)	Insuring your life for a set amount of money, which will be paid to your nominated beneficiary/ies when you die to help eliminate debts and support the loved ones you leave behind.
Income Protection	Replaces up to 80% of your pre-tax salary if you can't work due to sickness or injury, so you have income to support your living expenses plus debts such as your mortgage.
TPD Cover (Total & Permanent Disability)	Covering yourself if you suffer an illness or injury that results in you becoming totally and permanently disabled. A lump sum benefit is awarded to you in such an event, often used to pay for medical expenses or fund permanent lifestyle changes required.
Trauma Insurance (also known as Critical Illness Insurance)	Trauma cover insures you for an agreed amount to cover you in the event of many trauma related events, such as cancer or a heart attack or intensive care. The funds provide money to cover immediate medical expenses and other financial needs when a critical illness or injury occurs.

Diagram 5.1

Insure Your Business

Insurance for your business is also essential to consider, when consulting with your specialised insurance broker (such as a dedicated General or Business Insurance Broker). Along with loss of income, there are various other insurance covers available for business owners.

Diagram 5.2 shows some of the main risks to which businesses can be exposed.[22]

Business Insurance Table

Category	Brief Description
Property Damage	Loss or damage to buildings, glass, etc.
Business Interruption	Loss of income following loss or damage to fixed assets
Crime	Theft of property following illegal entry to premises
Equipment Breakdown	Cost to repair machinery following mechanical or electrical breakdown of plant and equipment
Motor	Comprehensive and / or third party liability for motor vehicles
Public Liability	Bodily injury arising from business activities and / or property owner's liability
Product Liability	Property damage arising from business activities, products manufactured, sold, exported, imported or serviced
Professional Indemnity	Damages arising from the professional advice and / or errors & omissions/civil liabilities of an organisation
Management Liability	Directors & Officers Liabilities, Employment Practices Liabilities, Crime, Statutory Liability, Internet Liability
Employer Liability	Liability for employment related issues such as wrongful dismissal, sexual harassment, and discrimination
Worker's Compensation	Employers' liability for injury to employees, Act benefits and at Common Law
Cyber Risks	First and third-party loss cover for cyber theft or breaches of customer information, extortion and damage to systems
Corporate Travel	Covering Business and associated travel expense losses including medical, evacuation, cancellation, baggage and business equipment etc.

Diagram 5.2

Know Your Team

Sometimes, our biggest threats comes from right under our noses and we are blissfully unaware that anything untoward is occurring. A horror story (to get this point across) comes from Luke, who had an engineering business. He came to me saying his bookkeeping was not making sense, so we needed to get to the bottom of the issue. The office admin person who was doing his accounts was not a qualified bookkeeper, so I asked a trusted professional bookkeeper, Joan, to have a look over Luke's accounts.

Surprisingly, after Joan had looked through the accounts, she rang me over the weekend in tears. I was quite taken aback by the call and the distress I heard in Joan's voice. Joan had discovered that the accounts person had been stealing from Luke's business and had apparently been recording the business's tax as being paid, but instead was paying these funds into her own account. She had stolen over two hundred thousand dollars from the business. Worse still, the office admin lady was Luke's daughter-in-law, the mother of his only grandchild. To complicate the situation, she, Luke's son and grandchild all lived together with Luke. Luke was helping the young family by giving his son and daughter-in-law a job and a roof over their head to support them with a good start in life.

I felt sick to the pit of my stomach. How do you tell someone that the person they love and are living with has been stealing from them for quite some time? As you can imagine, this situation ripped Luke's whole family and business apart.

In over a decade of business coaching, I have gone on to see at least three more businesses where team members have stolen large amounts of money. Two were family businesses where the person they trusted was in fact not trustworthy at all.

So, I hope you have received the message that when it comes to employing family members, do so with extreme caution. They should be screened the same way, using the same methods you would use to employ another employee. I'm certainly not saying it can't work; I have successfully worked with my husband for over 20 years and my daughter now works with me too. It's just important to do it prudently and correctly.

Think Long Term

How many times in your life have you seen or heard of an unexpected event happening in someone's life? They happen all the time and can dramatically affect the future of loved ones. It saddens me when I see those effects on the immediate family of the owners and other people involved.

Without doing due diligence, you might not stand up against your local competitors. If your business cannot make enough profit, you may be forced into closing your doors and declaring bankruptcy. I've seen this happen before, and it crushes lifetime dreams, leaves a massive mental burden and creates long-term financial repercussions. In some countries, bankruptcy lasts for five years, which usually means you can't have a credit card, leave the country without permission or even start another business.

In many cases, challenging situations can be avoided if business owners simply carry out a thorough market analysis, draw up legal documentation and insure themselves and their assets. In a nutshell, considering the long-term impact of every business decision you make can have a massive difference to your success, both now and in the future.

Seth and Emily

When a friend, Seth, passed away unexpectedly, he didn't have a Last Will and Testament drawn up and all his family's bank accounts were in his name. Seth had always dealt with the money and business 'stuff', so it made sense for him to keep it all in his name.

After Seth's death, even his wife, Emily, couldn't gain access to any of their bank accounts, leaving her with no way of supporting their three children in the immediate term. It was gut-wrenching to see and is certainly not what Seth would have wanted for his grieving wife and family. Imagine how difficult this was for Emily dealing with her husband passing away, raising their children and not having access to any funds?

Because Seth died without a Will, his assets (the house and a little cash) were split equally between the three children and Emily. In the short term this was OK, but as the children grew older, they wanted access to their inheritance. The children's share of the inheritance equated to three-quarters of the house value between them, so Emily was regrettably forced to sell their family home to divide the assets between the children. This was definitely not what Seth would have wanted either, but it's the way it panned out because of the simple mistake he made of having no Will drawn up while he was still alive. Seth's beloved wife, Emily, after years of wealth creation and making a living with her husband, had no other option but to rent a house and was not in a position to buy her own home.

This is not an isolated incident. Unfortunately, it happens over and over again to many families, more often than you'd imagine, as people always think they have time to sort these things out. I implore you please, please consider what assets you have to protect and what insurances you can put in place to take care of yourself and your loved ones.

Chapter 5
Blue Ocean Thinking

☐ **How well do you know your industry?**

Review where your industry is heading and who the big players are. How do you measure up?

☐ **Who are your competitors?**

Who are your direct and indirect competitors? Conduct a SWOT analysis against them.

☐ **Protect yourself and your assets**

Book an appointment with a trusted insurance broker and consider the relevant personal and business insurances available to you.

"Profit is not something to add on at the end, it's something to plan for at the beginning."

Unknown

CHAPTER SIX

Making Money

After Eve arrived, my weekly routine had to be rearranged to accommodate all the moving parts in our lives. A typical week for us became David working the normal nine-to-five Monday to Friday and, only a week or so after her birth, I took Eve with me to the office to work three days a week. This gave me the chance to keep in touch with the business and focus my brain on something outside of home and childcare. Hamish went to day-care two days a week, which he absolutely loved. Tuesdays were his favourite days, spent with my mum; he called them 'Nanna days.'

We were slowly building a little team at work. We had one admin lady who had been with us from the start, as well as a full-time technician to repair and install the equipment we sold. On my first day back at work with Eve in my arms, I interviewed an intelligent young 16-year-old girl, named Jenny, straight out of high school for a trainee administration support position. She was a quick learner who also loved children, and we connected instantly. Jenny was perfect, and felt like an angel sent from heaven to a young mum who was running a business with a toddler and breastfeeding newborn. The added bonus was that by employing Jenny straight out of school, we trained her in the culture, philosophies and systems that were important to our business. In Australia the government even incentivised small businesses to hire trainees, so it was a win-win all round.

By this stage, the business was providing us with consistent and healthy profits and we always had money in the bank. In September of 1993, we went on our first big family holiday since starting the business. We enjoyed two glorious weeks in Port Douglas relaxing in a seaside resort which we all absolutely loved. We were lucky to have built our little team to a level of trust, whereby the three of them could competently run the business without us for the two weeks we were away. It was a wonderful time for our family and showed us that we could indeed leave our business from time to time to enjoy our life outside of the business.

In early 1995, David and his mate (who both knew they had problems with alcohol) had a bet on who could go three months without drinking. To my great joy, David achieved this goal – despite his mate giving up well before the three-month period was over. David said he couldn't believe how clear, simple and clean his life seemed without alcohol. He commented that it was like a fog had been lifted, or that someone had cleaned the windows of his mind for the first time in years. Life seemed to be so much easier and it was the most amazing three months for me. Yes, David found it challenging, but it was a huge step forward in his awareness of how different life could be without the constant presence of alcohol.

In the middle of the same year, we received the news that David's mum had passed away after many years of illness. It was a very sad day, especially for David, as it meant the final chapter of his life with his mother had closed. Fortunately, he had managed to fly home the month before her death to say goodbye, but he still wondered if he had said everything he wanted to say. He questioned so many things about his life. However, we both knew she would have been happy to have had the chance to see her son one last time, and to hear the words, "I love you, Mum."

At the time, I was happy in the knowledge that, even though I was only working part time, our business was running well enough to allow David to be by his mother's side in Scotland before she passed. It was a position that we had worked hard to achieve.

Only two months on, still grieving the loss of David's mum, I received a phone call from my own mother.

"Come home, love. Your dad has just died," she said.

As I put down the phone and told David, I was somehow not shocked. Despite looking like a big, strong, healthy man, Mum and I both knew Dad's heart was weak. We rang our other family members, and Dad's sister brought his mum, my grandmother, over to see him, which was heartbreaking. She broke down and wept, saying, "As a parent, your children aren't meant to die before you."

Mum and I organised Dad's funeral and hundreds of people turned up to pay their respects; so many people loved my dad. To many of the business community he was the tall, strong, confident, funny and astute businessman. To me, he was simply my 55-year-old dad, a family man, and the person who had first helped David and me begin our own little business. I had a heavy heart; my dad had always been there right beside me if I ever needed help or advice.

As if this period hadn't been challenging enough, exactly 14 months after the death of David's mum (and less than a year after my own dad's passing), we received the harrowing news that David's dad, Robin, had tragically died. David and I were fast asleep at home in bed when the phone rang at 3.00am. I immediately felt sick at the thought of what might be so important for someone to call us at that time.

On the other end of the phone was David's sister, Deb, who told us that their dad and new wife Sheila were killed in a plane crash on a routine flight that Robin was piloting.

We were rocked with disbelief as we had only recently received a letter from his dad in the mail, telling us the exciting news that he'd met a new lady and fallen madly in love; they were getting married and would be flying over to see us at Christmas! Sadly, we hadn't been able to make the wedding, but enjoyed a toast over the phone with them to celebrate the happiness of their nuptials.

Eight days after they wed, they were both killed. After I hung up the phone, David and I were both totally numb; we had no idea what to do or say.

I convinced David to fly back to Edinburgh and had him on a plane by lunchtime. Meanwhile, I was at home looking after the kids and the business. I wished I could have gone to support David and pay my respects, but I knew it was best for David to have the time to grieve without a six and three-year-old in the midst.

I was in total shock; I couldn't believe Robin and his new wife were dead. I had looked at him as my second father for a long time and since David's mum had passed away, we had become very close. He would write letters to me every month. I loved him and was very much looking forward to meeting Sheila as well. We were all excited about the prospect of having the first family Christmas together in 12 years. Plus, the kids couldn't wait to play with their adventurous grandpa who flew a plane, and their new grandma whom they hadn't yet met.

After I put David on the plane, I was a total mess. My brain was numb, my head was throbbing, and the tears were endless. My stomach was tied in knots. I kept running to the toilet every ten minutes and shook uncontrollably with heart palpitations. I was experiencing the physical impact of the emotional shock.

Beautiful Jenny from the office, forever poised and ready to do whatever needed to be done, just took over all the face to face client interactions and did everything she could to help me keep it together. While I was emotionally absent and David was away, our wonderful team managed to keep the business functioning well and looked after all our clients and suppliers. My symptoms slowly went away as my body got used to the shock, but the one thing that didn't go away was the throbbing headache from trying not to cry. I had never considered myself a teary person, but this was different; I just couldn't stop.

As far as the kids went, Hamish was a total angel; so helpful, caring and sensitive. His emotional intelligence for a six-year-old was incredible. He knew exactly the right things to say at the right time, and where to put his dear little hand to show me how much he cared. Eve, at three-years-old, was too young to understand but must have picked up on all the sad vibes as she was really uncooperative and super cranky the whole time. Thank goodness I had my wonderful mum and some beautiful friends, especially Fran who always came to my rescue to help me in whatever way she could. I don't think I could've kept it together if it wasn't for them and my amazing team at the office.

Losing three parents in such a short space of time was like walking around with a gaping wound in my heart. I wondered if the pain would ever heal and if I would get over the fear of bursting into tears at the subject of death. It was impossible to be truly happy. I couldn't remove myself from the fact that three people, whom we loved unconditionally, were gone forever. At the same time, the world just kept spinning and other people kept getting on with their lives. As we picked up the pieces in the aftermath, we accumulated new scars and hid away the painful ones so we could carry on. We now refer to that time as *the death year*, with so many of our loved ones passing away in such quick succession.

Most of us will experience the death of loved ones, but nothing ever prepares us for the pain that their passing creates. It is a time of growth we will all undoubtedly go through in our lives. I learned so much about how much grief affected me physically, how it affected my brain function and who my true friends were. I had no idea how much control I would lose, and how I would need to rely so heavily on the support and understanding of those around me.

I have come to learn that the more we talk about death, rather than hide from it, the quicker the pain lessens. If somebody close to you loses a loved one, I recommend that you do not ignore it, and instead reach out and acknowledge their loss. I really appreciated the people who openly asked how I was, what they could do to help or just gave gestures of kindness to make my life easier. A simple phone call to say, "Hey I'm coming past your house; I'll pick the kids up on the way to school." Or, "I've just made a double batch of pasta; I'll drop some off to you." These little gestures made such a difference and it helped to know how much people cared.

The losses we experienced made me realise that as a small business owner, nothing was more important than our own health and happiness and that our business wasn't the be-all-and-end-all. I also realised that everyone went through challenges in their life, so I was less quick to judge. If I was dealing with someone who wasn't giving the service I expected, I'd give them another chance. Perhaps they, too, had just lost someone they loved but had no choice but to turn up and continue running their business? Whatever their reason may have been, I stopped being so quick to judge others.

There have been many instances for David and me when we have had to rely on our business profits to carry us through challenging times. During this time of grief, I was incredibly grateful that our business was able to run without us, as I couldn't have dealt with my heartache, and still pay the bills and make sure the mortgage was paid. Our business and our team were a great asset for us, and I felt proud that putting in the learning and hard yards in our business over the years had allowed us the time to deal with our personal circumstances without completely floundering in our business.

Understanding Money

If you've ever found yourself lying in bed at night worrying about how you were going to pay the bills and the wages, you can turn this around. Lack of cash is one of the biggest stressors for business owners; many people fear looking at their own financial reports. Do your eyes glaze over when your bookkeeper or accountant starts talking about your financial reports, hoping you could crawl into a little hole to escape having to think about them? At the end of the day, money is both a fact of business and a part of life.

If you are willing to invest time into learning the key elements of finances, you will gain more than a valuable skill. You'll get composure when you know what to expect financially. You'll have the peace of mind of knowing where you stand, and you will start to learn the quickest and easiest ways to bridge any cashflow gaps. You will no longer lie awake at night with the fear of the unknown. You will be clear on every line of your profit and loss and how you can do more than just break-even (or worse, go backwards).

As the business owner, understanding your key financial reports will allow you to feel confident that there will always be enough cash in the bank to support your business, your team and your family (with a buffer).

Many business owners have a basic understanding of where they sit, but don't have an in-depth understanding of financial literacy or sufficient knowledge of their own business numbers. Thus, they don't keep up with the bills and their long-term aspirations slip further and further out of reach.

Understanding the key numbers in your business, or what is required before you start, will give you an advantage over many other business owners who don't put in the time to learn them. You'll have the ability to make sound business decisions based upon what your key financial reports tell you is the best decision, not based on a hunch or if there is money in the bank. Remember, money in the bank doesn't necessarily mean you're making a profit, or heading in the right direction.

Two great questions to ask yourself:

- Where can you pro-actively change things in your profit and loss so you're making long-term headway?
- In going through each area, can you identify ways to bridge the gap in the numbers?

I'll provide various examples of how to do this in the next chapter.

Your Financial Dashboard

Being aware of what your optimal financial dashboard looks like for your business will enable you to get a quick visual snapshot of where you are, financially, at any given time.

Which financial reports could you review on a weekly, monthly or annual basis? What financial areas can be assessed to determine your success? What ought to be tracked in order to meet your financial outcomes? In looking at the revenue of your business, are you clear on what you need to achieve in sales for you to achieve your financial outcomes? Are you clear about the different product groups that you have and how much you pay for those products? Are some products more popular than others? Do you pay for stock or labour in every product group, or just some? Which product groups have the most amount of profit, which ones are most popular and who is the target market for these product groups?

I am always amazed to hear how many business owners don't know how many sales, or the revenue, they need to achieve in order to reach their financial outcomes. Some questions to answer are:

- What is your break-even point?
- What is the minimum number of sales you need to make to reach the revenue to carry you through another month?
- Based on your current conversion rate, how many people (and who) do you need to talk to in order to reach those targets?
- Which products could you focus more on selling?

If you don't have sales targets or goals, you won't ever know if you are operating successfully or which actions are required to be carried out to achieve good results. How, where and when are you going to measure your financial success? How regularly and what metrics need to be measured? Schedule time to assess your prospects on a regular basis and look at what's in your sales pipeline.

The clearer you can be on what success is for your business and what has to happen for success to be reached, the easier it will be for you to achieve your desired outcomes. Falling in love with numbers can be a wonderful thing.

Profit and Loss

A common question I hear is, "How can we be so busy in our business, have an endless supply of customers, but still have no money in the bank?" Sound familiar? If you have ever asked this question, you're not alone. You are the same as thousands of others who fear that their business will fail, and feel incompetent or downright stupid for not understanding the ins and outs of their own business.

What business owners ideally want is to understand how to make proactive business decisions based on their financials, and to be able to plan sustainable growth in their business whilst maintaining a profit. It *is* achievable if you put your mind to it! It all starts with a plan for success that is based on your goals, then getting clear on the numbers you wish to achieve. This is why knowing how to read your numbers in the profit and loss statement is vital to business success.

I'd like you to consider that looking at a profit and loss statement is like looking at a scene from a movie. Your profit and loss shows data from one date to another date (which may be over one week, a month, quarter or year), where all the sales and all the expenses in that period are shown. The profit and loss statement will be measured in either cash or accrual (you might have heard your bookkeeper talk about this), which is simply the way of reporting your numbers (money in/out of the bank, or money invoiced).

If you're talking about a profit and loss in cash, you'll be looking at the actual cash in your bank, exactly what has gone in and what came out in that period. Basing your financials on an accrual system, this means that if you invoice a sale but haven't received the money yet, it would still be included as a sale for tax purposes in any given period. Similarly, if you are billed for business expenses, even if unpaid, when entered as an expense, they would be included as well. An accrual basis is the standard way to report a profit and loss for larger corporations and as your business grows and gets bigger, often the tax department might ask you to report on an accrual system rather than cash.

Starting at the top of your profit and loss statement, you'll be able to see five important sums that result in a positive or negative net profit in a particular period:

1. Sales, Income or Revenue (all names for the same thing) – this is how much money came into the business in sales generated.
2. Cost of Sales or Cost of Goods Sold (COGS) – these are the expenses that directly relate to the sales generated in the same period, which may include stock or contractor fees.
3. Gross Profit – calculated by deducting the COGS from the Revenue.

4. Fixed Expenses, Operating Expenses or Overheads – these are the business expenses that are non-specific to the sale generated and may include items like accounting and bookkeeping fees, insurance, rent, telephone, wages, etc. They would be paid regardless of sales being made or not.

5. Net Profit – the final calculation shown at the bottom of the Profit and Loss statement, which is calculated by deducting the Operating Expenses from the Gross Profit.

Diagram 6.1 shows a simple example of a Profit and Loss Statement where you can see the sums mentioned above.

Profit & Loss - Made Simple

XYZ Widget Pty Ltd
Profit & Loss Statement

Sales / Income	Red Widgets	$ 50,000.00
	Blue Widgets	$ 44,000.00
	Green Widgets	$ 21,000.00
	Yellow Widgets	$ 7,000.00
Total Sales		$ 122,000.00
Cost of Sales	Red Widgets	$ 25,000.00
	Blue Widgets	$ 15,000.00
	Green Widgets	$ 17,000.00
	Yellow Widgets	$ 6,000.00
Total Cost of Sales		$ 63,000.00
Gross Profit		$ 59,000.00
Fixed Expenses	Bank Charges	$ 2,500.00
	Bookkeeping	$ 4,100.00
	Interest	$ 2,200.00
	Misc. Expenses	$ 1,500.00
	Office Supplies	$ 3,000.00
	Postage	$ 1,200.00
	Printing & Stationery	$ 2,000.00
	Rent	$ 5,000.00
	Sales & Marketing	$ 4,000.00
	Staff Amenities	$ 800.00
	Telephone	$ 3,500.00
	Wages & Salaries	$ 12,000.00
Total Fixed Expenses		$ 41,800.00
Net Profit		$ 17,200.00

TOTAL SALES / INCOME

COST OF SALES =

GROSS PROFIT

FIXED EXPENSES =

NET PROFIT / LOSS

Diagram 6.1

Balance Sheet

Once you're clear on your profit and loss statement, you can move on to the balance sheet and how that relates to your profit and loss. A balance sheet will show you all your assets (everything you own) and all your liabilities (everything you owe) broken down into short-term and long-term amounts. The difference between your assets and liabilities is referred to as the equity of your business (assets minus liabilities equals equity).

Diagram 6.2 shows a simple example of a Balance Sheet where you can see the items mentioned above.

Balance Sheet

The difference between everything you own and everything you owe

BALANCE SHEET
As of December 21, 2019

Assets		Liabilities	
Cash at Bank	$89,315	Acct Payable (Creditors)	$135,399
Acct Receiveable (Debtors)	$253,938	Overdraft Debt	$98,849
Inventory (Stock)	$5,095	Taxes Payable	$19,508
Other Current Assets	$7,148	Accrued Expenses	$0
Total Current Assets	$ 129,294	Total Current Liabilities	$253,756
Gross Value of Property,		Long-term Debt	$90,609
Plant & Equipment.	$1,400	Total Liabilities	$344,365
Accumulated Depreciation.	$(500)		
Net Property, Plant &		**Owner's Equity**	
Equipment.	$900	Retained Earnings from P&L	$1,323
		Total Shareholders Equity	$ 140,002
Total Assets	$485,690	Total Liabilities and Equity	$485,690

What the Company Owns (left side arrows for Assets)

What the Company Owes (right side arrows for Liabilities)

Shareholders Equity (right side arrow for Owner's Equity)

Diagram 6.2

Each amount in the line items of the balance sheet (both the assets and liabilities) are amounts that have been carried forward from the very start of the business on day one. The aim of the balance sheet is to increase the equity as your business grows, while reducing your liabilities. It reflects the health of your business at any given date, and is like a still picture of the age and history of your business. It's important to review both your profit and loss *and* your balance sheet because some items which come out of your balance sheet do not show up in the profit and loss.

Mark-Up vs Margin

Sometimes, the terms used around money and business financials are confusing and misconceptions can leave your mind spinning. An example of terms that people often find difficult to distinguish between is *margin* and *mark-up* – they are not the same. An easy way to remember the difference is:

- a *margin* comes down from the total price that you're selling an item for; and
- a *mark-up* is marked up from the cost price of the item

For example, if you sell something for $100 and you bought it for $80, the margin is $20 (or 20%). The margin is based on the sale price and is a percentage of the sale price, so it's how much you get to keep out of each dollar sold. Mark-up, on the other hand, addresses the cost price of the product and the percentage of the cost price that you can increase the cost price by. In the same example, the mark-up is 25%.

Diagram 6.3 shows the mark-up and margin % on an item that sells for $100.

Diagram 6.3

Tweaking margins in products is a powerful way to increase your profits. There will be more cashflow for you to pay for your business operating expenses and more net profit, too.

Numbers as They Relate to Your Team

When you're looking to delegate tasks within your business, it's a good idea to break down the team into how they correlate with your profit and loss. For example, who is responsible for closing the sales (revenue) and who deals with suppliers and pays the bills (COGS and expenses)? Who pays the wages? By breaking down your profit and loss into departments or people who do those tasks, you can start to clearly delegate actions into relevant areas, and everyone will know their responsibilities. Each team member's actions can be based on the outcomes that you want them to achieve, both for the short and long term. If each team member knows what they are responsible for achieving, the pieces of the puzzle can come together.

It may also be helpful to work backwards on your profit and loss to determine what actions are required. For example, perhaps your regular weekly expenses equate to $10,000 and your cost of goods are $5,000. This means that generating $15,000 in revenue would leave you with no profit. To achieve a net profit greater than nil (leaving you cash in the bank), you'll need to work out how to increase your revenue above $15,000. Perhaps this means making one more product sale, and the action might be to train your sales team to up-sell at the check-out. Maybe the accounts team can negotiate a lower price with a supplier so that expenses are reduced, and the net profit increases again? Maybe your marketing team can focus on advertising the product with the biggest margin, so you can work on selling more of that product and less of the ones that don't have as much bang for their buck. These are just a few quick ways to increase your net profit.

Budget

In assessing your overall financial position, budgeting is key. Producing a budget ahead of time (for the year, quarter or month) will let you know what income you expect to receive, what the cost of goods for that portion of revenue will be, and your expected expenses in that period. In tracking to your budget and assessing your budget to the actual results of that period, you will be able to identify quickly if there are any variances to the budget and if so, evaluate why they're more or less than expected (to make a judgment on what you need to change going forward).

Diagram 6.4 is an example of a Budget that is based on Profit and Loss figures.

Profit & Loss Budget Projection

	January	February	March	April
Sales / Income	$66,950	$60,450	$69,550	$74,750
Cost of Goods	$26,780	$24,180	$27,820	$29,900
Gross Profit	$40,170	$36,270	$41,730	$44,850
Accounting	$1,650	$1,650	$1,650	$1,650
Bank Fees	$10	$10	$10	$10
Marketing	$6,350	$6,350	$6,350	$6,350
Rent	$4,000	$4,000	$4,000	$4,000
Staff Expenses	$385	$385	$385	$385
Telephone	$1,600	$1,600	$1,600	$1,600
Wages	$16,500	$16,500	$16,500	$16,500
Total Expenses	$30,495	$30,495	$30,495	$30,495
Net Profit	$9,675	$5,775	$11,235	$14,355

Diagram 6.4

Cashflow

The next level of achieving financial independence is having a cashflow projection to monitor future income and expenses, alongside a solid budget model for success. Regardless of how small or large your business is, if you have these in place, you can take into consideration business growth and future expenses when making important decisions in your business.

Diagram 6.5 shows a simple cashflow projection that takes into consideration liabilities from your Balance Sheet that wouldn't show up in your Profit and Loss.

Cashflow Projection

	Week 1	Week 2	Week 3	Week 4
Opening Bank Balance	$8,000	$8,830	$10,205	$12,180
Cash In				
Sales	$15,450	$13,950	$16,050	$17,250
Total	$15,450	$13,950	$16,050	$17,250
Cash Out				
Materials	$1,500	$500	$850	$2,450
Accounting	$1,650	$0	$0	$0
Bank Fees	$10	$0	$0	$0
Car Repayments	$575	$575	$575	$575
Directors Loans	$3,500	$3,500	$3,500	$3,500
Marketing	$850	$1,500	$2,500	$1,500
Rent	$1,000	$1,000	$1,000	$1,000
Staff Expenses	$35	$0	$150	$200
Taxes Payable	$1,100	$1,100	$1,100	$1,100
Telephone	$400	$400	$400	$400
Wages	$4,000	$4,000	$4,000	$4,500
Total	$14,620	$12,575	$14,075	$15,225
Cash Flow	$830	$1,375	$1,975	$2,025
Closing Bank Balance	$8,830	$10.205	$12.180	$14.205

Diagram 6.5

Financial Strategies

Starting with the end in mind, what does a successful month look like in your business and what actions are required to achieve this?

- What is your target revenue?

- Where is that going to come from in sales (how many products or services need to be sold to reach that revenue) and who is accountable for achieving those sales?

- What is the margin in those sales, and how can you increase the margin?

- What are the budgeted expenses for the month, and how can they be reduced?

- Who is accountable for sticking to the budget?

- Who is responsible for all the marketing activities?

- What wages are being paid? Who is responsible for putting out the rosters?

- What is the wages to revenue ratio? (How much are you paying in wages compared to the revenue you generate?)

- Are your financial ratios consistent? (i.e. Have you increased wages without increasing sales revenue, thus reducing your profits?)

Numbers are not just numbers. They tell a story and if you learn to read numbers as a story then you will become better at forward projecting what actions are required within your business. Numbers are a result of previous actions, so if you want them to be different, change your actions.

For example, Leroy had a small I.T. consulting business; just himself with one other technician assisting him. The work was often unpredictable, break-fix work and his cashflow was as random as his clients trying to predict when their computers were going to have a meltdown. He decided to add a new service product, which he would strategically sell when he was fixing up any I.T. crisis. He offered regular proactive monthly maintenance programs for his clients, much like a car service, giving the client a far greater chance of avoiding future computer disasters before they happened.

Leroy focused on this strategy for a year, and slowly built up this managed I.T. side of his business. The next year, he started offering backup services and cyber security services as well. Slowly, his cashflow not only became consistent but dramatically increased as well. The add-on services became a win-win scenario for him and his clients, as he was giving them more proactive services (better than reactive break-fix service) and Leroy's company had more predictable cashflow. With more stable and more predictable services, Leroy's business started booming. Six years on, the company grew and developed interstate. Now, all his fixed expenses are covered by just the regular monthly services provided to his clients. All the extra work is a bonus.

Just Over Broke (JOB)

Financial freedom ultimately comes from building up cash reserves by regularly making a profit.

Is your business actually doing what it's supposed to do? Is it creating wealth to provide you with the freedom of choice both now and in your future? If you're spending all the money you make, or your business isn't making enough profit to build your wealth, your business is not properly providing for you. If your business doesn't work for you, you're working for the business. You effectively have managed to be 'just over broke' and have a JOB. Is this why you decided to own a business?

If your financial situation is the same every year, you're probably one of the many business owners I know who either don't understand their financials, don't track them regularly or don't know how to read between the lines to improve their situation. If your budget is only ever set at break-even, how are you ever going to pay off the overdraft and other liabilities to create extra income for investing into your wealth creation?

Creating Wealth

If you haven't been making headway for many years, it is not healthy to continue down that same path. Living with stress and financial uncertainty is horrible. Looking at the grid below, there is a great exercise to do. Mark off all the numbers up to your current age, then all the numbers beyond the age you'd like to retire. How many years do you think you have left in business?

Based on average global life expectancy statistics, we have marked off all ages beyond 71 (the average age of death) as well as the numbers from 1-18 (before most people start work). Once you've marked more off, you'll see there are only limited years left to create your wealth. If you're already closer to retirement age, this is a great visual to see how much impact you need to make and how much time you have left to do it.

Diagram 6.6 shows a grid that you can use to predict how many working years you have left to create your wealth.

How Many Years Do You Have To Create Your Wealth?

~~1~~	~~2~~	~~3~~	~~4~~	~~5~~	~~6~~	~~7~~	~~8~~	~~9~~	~~10~~
~~11~~	~~12~~	~~13~~	~~14~~	~~15~~	~~16~~	~~17~~	~~18~~	19	20
21	22	23	24	25	26	27	28	29	30
31	32	33	34	35	36	37	38	39	40
41	42	43	44	45	46	47	48	49	50
51	52	53	54	55	56	57	58	59	60
61	62	63	64	65	66	67	68	69	70
~~71~~	~~72~~	~~73~~	~~74~~	~~75~~	~~76~~	~~77~~	~~78~~	~~79~~	~~80~~
~~81~~	~~82~~	~~83~~	~~84~~	~~85~~	~~86~~	~~87~~	~~88~~	~~89~~	~~90~~
~~91~~	~~92~~	~~93~~	~~94~~	~~95~~	~~96~~	~~97~~	~~98~~	~~99~~	~~100~~

How old are you now?
How many more years do you want to work?
How much money do you need to retire?
How much do you have invested in superannuation?
What other passive income or investments do you have?
What is the gap?

Diagram 6.6

Exit Date

The previous section leads onto some pretty serious questions you can ask yourself. These include:

- Have you thought about when you want to retire or when you want to exit your business?

- What do you want to do with your life once you stop working?
- Have you considered the amount of money you should be putting aside to live your life beyond your business?

A popular book that may help with your personal finances is *"The Barefoot Investor"* by Scott Pape, which simply explains how to 'fill up your buckets' for future wealth creation.[23] I found it brilliant; I wish I had read it in my early 20s instead of 30 years later in my 50s. Scott recommends to split your income into three main buckets. You can find out more about the breakdown of percentages in his book.

Once you have invested the time into improving your financial literacy, it's something you'll have for the rest of your life, like riding a bike. Learn the skill once, and you'll have it forever. If you want to be an entrepreneur and be successful in business and wealth creation, you'll use the knowledge of financials over and over again.

A Plan for Your Life After Business

Wealth creation for one person will be very different for another. You may be comfortable with building your superannuation and low-risk investments. For others, it might be investing in property, business or shares. I strongly suggest you speak with an experienced financial advisor about your wealth creation plan, so that you can work on creating passive income for many years to come. If you originally went into business to create wealth, to provide you with long-term future security, don't let your business take all that away. Have a plan and strategy in place, so you can track your progress and be rewarded in the long term.

If your income doesn't support your life goals or isn't reliable enough, how can you change things to create wealth for your future to give you more choices? Do you have enough in superannuation and investments to live comfortably? If not, what long-term wealth creation strategies can you incorporate to create residual income into your retirement?

Matthew

Matthew had never closely looked at his financials before. He was a one-man-band, running his business blindly and didn't know the first thing about his numbers and what they meant, other than knowing whether or not he had money in the bank.

In one of Matthew's first coaching sessions with me, I educated him on his profit and loss, and we worked step-by-step from the top of his profit and loss statement to the bottom. That was the first time Matthew really understood what his Gross Profit and Net Profit were. He also grasped his Cost of Sales, Fixed and Variable Expenses, not only the figures but their percentage to revenue earned. It was an enlightening process and opened up many doors in his business.

When we looked at Matthew's cashflow, we could see how inconsistent it was, so we looked at how we could build that up. With his budget projections in front of us, we addressed where costs could be saved, as well as looked at the details of where his revenue was coming from (including product margins) so we could fine-tune how the business could run more efficiently. Matthew was excited that so many action items could come from just looking at his financial statement. Without seeking help, he may never have asked himself the questions that transformed his business.

After some time, Matthew became so confident in his ability to look at and understand his financial reports, that he delegated the reporting to someone else and merely oversaw the numbers to see what actions were required. Matthew went around the learning quadrant from not knowing what he didn't know, to knowing what he didn't know, to knowing what he knew and being confident enough to delegate. In the end, Matthew became rather quick at being able to review the numbers each month and to see if anything was out of place, such as big jumps in expenses or drops in sales, and instantly acted on what needed to be done to address the concerns.

Chapter 6
Blue Ocean Thinking

☐ **Know where your money is going**

Create an up-to-date Budget and Cashflow forecast based on your previous 12-month financial reports.

☐ **Book a regular date in your diary to review your financials**

Review and track your financial results on a monthly basis, and act on anything required.

☐ **When do you want to exit your business?**

Set a date, and plan towards it. Book a meeting with your trusted financial advisor to consider your options for wealth investment and determine how much passive income you'll need for your retirement.

"Stop being afraid of what could go wrong and start being positive about what could go right."

Zig Ziglar

CHAPTER SEVEN

Do What Matters

By the eighth year of running our business, things were still going smoothly. We knew what our margins were, down to each order, and we had a great local team with whom we worked well. David looked after the purchasing and I looked after the financial reporting. We had a successful little business, a great lifestyle and were achieving regular profits. We had worked so hard that we even managed to pay off our home which was an amazing feeling. This only left the mortgage on the business premises, which was being covered and paid off by the business renting it off us anyway. Business-wise, we were in a good position.

David poured himself 100% into everything he did at work, but it was affecting his health in a negative way. He had put on a great deal of weight and was still addicted to alcohol, despite knowing how bad it was for him and our family. He was a damaged man, still hurting internally. He had never seen anyone professionally about facing all the post-traumatic stress that he had as a result of the burns accident. I also knew having both parents gone weighed heavily on his heart. It was an underlying unhappiness that he tried hard to hide, but he would often talk about the emptiness he felt within. Many times, we'd go to ring his parents or want to send them a photo of the children, only to be quickly reminded that they were no longer with us. The pain we felt was hard to articulate.

A huge turning point for me came when I met an amazing couple, Vicki and Gary, who introduced me to the sport of triathlon. One of my long-term goals at the time was to get into a sport or hobby that would increase my fitness and get me involved with people who were not all about drinking and partying. I had never even heard of triathlon – but swimming, cycling and running sounded like fun. Vicki introduced me to a group of women in their mid-30s, like me, and I decided to start training with them. I left home at 5.00am each morning, returning by 7.00am in time to see the kids wake up.

Often, I would be leaving to go to training in the morning and David still hadn't gone to bed; he was still drinking or drunk from the night before. He'd yell out from our balcony, "Go, Suzzie! Go get 'em, Suzzie!" or some other supportive cheer which always ended with, "Love ya, Suzzie!"

He was battling his demons, but was genuinely supportive and proud of me for my newfound love of the sport. I'd just hope that the kids didn't wake up until I got back from training. These dawn sessions gave me a couple of hours of freedom each morning to start the day and I loved the endorphins it gave me. It was a relief to be accountable only for myself, and no one else. It was a liberating feeling to be someone other than a mum, wife and business owner. I was just me. I loved training, and I loved competing.

One Australia Day, January 26, 1998, I competed in a Triathlon event at the beautiful Matilda Bay along the Swan River. It was a race I will never forget. David was so proud of me; he got up early that day to come and cheer me on. The sun was searing, it must have been at least 38 degrees and the water was glistening a perfect turquoise. I was on the third leg of the triathlon, running along the melting tarmac track beside the water, and all the competitors were excited to be approaching the home straight. Nothing could stop me now.

I remember passing one friend who shouted, "Yeah, go girl," in encouragement, as we passed each other and gave each other a high five. There was a small crowd of people at the water station cheering me on, too. They called, "You're doing great; keep going!"

It was a euphoric feeling; until all of a sudden, my bliss came to an abrupt halt. I felt a sharp pain deep in my abdomen, as if a knife had stabbed me. It was so excruciating I couldn't breathe.

I started walking to lessen the pain and began taking tiny shallow breaths to focus on something else other than the pain.

"Don't stop, keep running," said a man as he passed me, so I made an attempt to run again to acknowledge his support.

But instantly I was pulled back by the horrendous pain. *"What if I need an ambulance?"* I thought. I started to panic. *"What if my appendix has burst? What if I'm having a heart attack? What if there is really something wrong?"* My mind raced; my heart pumped even faster.

I wondered if I should pull out of the race, but I'd never done that before, so it was definitely the last resort. After a few minutes, the walking slightly dulled the sharpness of the pain again, but I still had an inkling that the pain wasn't normal.

The scorching heat of the mid-summer sun zapped every bit of energy from me. *"Is a triathlon really worth dying for?"* I asked myself. Not really, considering my worst fear was dying as a young mother and leaving two children motherless. I didn't know what to do, but I knew I was close to finishing, so I just kept going as fast as I could.

I finally saw the finishing line and David was relieved to see me. I had taken far longer than expected to finish the race, so he had started to worry. As I sat and recovered, I felt reassured as the pain seemed to disappear again. *"Thank God,"* I thought, and figured the pain must have been exhaustion from the heat or just a bad cramp.

The following morning, however, I awoke to more intense pains and immediately knew something wasn't right. I went straight to my doctor to find out if there was a reason for the excruciating pain.

"The first thing we need to do is book you in for an ultrasound to find out what's going on," said the Doctor calmly. "No need to worry until we know what it is."

Within hours I was at the radiologist having the ultrasound test, and as the cold wand slid over my abdomen, a large growth on one ovary was quickly revealed. *"Oh, it's just a cyst; nothing to worry about,"* I thought. Cysts are harmless. In a few short minutes, the scan was over, and I was on my way home.

Over the next few days as I waited for the results, I started overthinking and questioning my initial self-diagnosis. My mind was filled with conflicting thoughts, *"What if it is something worse than a cyst? What if something is seriously wrong with me? What if it is ovarian cancer? Isn't ovarian cancer the worst? Isn't ovarian cancer the one that women do not survive from? No way, not me."*

Back with my doctor, she had the horrible task of telling me that my worst fears may actually be coming true.

She explained, "The shape, texture and size of the growth are all characteristic of ovarian cancer, a fast growing cancer. You must see a specialist as soon as possible."

Gasping for air, I couldn't believe this was happening to me. Not after everything I'd already endured with David. My doctor rang an oncologist, while I was still sitting with her in the room to arrange the first available appointment. My head was spinning with shock and fear.

Within two days, I was seated in front of yet another doctor for more pathology tests. I felt like a zombie. No emotions yet, just quiet disbelief. My worst fear in the whole world could be coming true. I didn't want to go through chemotherapy. I didn't want my kids to lose their mum.

On February 24, 1998, my 33rd birthday, I sat alone in the deadly quiet, sparkling white, clinically cold, specialist's room with one of the best oncologist gynaecologists in Perth. I'd had enough of tests; I was fed up with waiting. I just wanted to know what the test results had revealed. It was just another day at the office for the oncologist, as he delivered the news I had rehearsed in my head over a hundred times.

"I'm sorry to say that it does look like ovarian cancer. We'll need to operate as soon as possible to take the growth off your ovaries. You will probably lose your ovary."

Yet again, I was numb. I trembled uncontrollably, trying to keep myself together.

"I will get you admitted into the oncology ward here at the women's hospital as soon as possible. After we take the tumour off, we'll run some more tests, so we know what the next step is," he said, in a very matter-of-fact manner.

It all felt so rushed, my mind couldn't comprehend what he was saying. I had another brutal physical and internal examination, and was scheduled for surgery the next day.

I was totally devastated. I had been competing in a triathlon only a few weeks earlier. I was a fit young woman; my nickname was *Wonder Woman,* for goodness sake. How could this be part of my story? I felt horribly sick and upset; I could hardly walk through the hospital corridors back to the car park. The weight of what had happened, feeling mentally shaken up and physically violated from the internal examination, made each step seem heavier and more impossible.

I finally reached the car and sobbed uncontrollably, letting go of all the tears I'd been holding back. I forced myself to get it together enough to drive; my hands still shook uncontrollably, and tears streamed down my face between sobs.

Within twenty four hours, I was admitted into hospital. The surgery went smoothly but unfortunately, I lost the ovary that the growth was on, as predicted. After a week of lying in hospital, I still didn't know the pathology results. *"Did I have ovarian cancer or not,"* I wondered? The waiting game was torture, yet all I could do was hope and pray for the following two weeks until I received the confirmed results.

David knew how worried I felt and was a total darling. He was gentle, caring and supportive, which was just what I needed. Repeatedly he kept telling me, "Everything will be fine. It'll be OK, Suzzie."

After the wait of over two weeks, it was finally time to see the doctor and find out my fate. David joined me; the car journey was silent; we both felt sick.

Within seconds of walking into the doctor's office, he coldly remarked, "The good news is that it is not cancer, but it may as well be. It is a cell like disease that grows just as aggressively as cancer and it can destroy everything in its path. It's called endometriosis."

I was instantly taken aback by this man's cold and impersonal approach; I wanted to launch across the desk and shake him. What ever happened to a doctor's bedside manner? No polite explanation, no asking if I was OK, nothing gentle about sharing this news at all. But, it was about to get even worse.

He continued to explain, "As far as we can see, your whole abdomen is riddled with the disease; there's not much we can do. With the extent of damage you have already sustained, you probably only have around five more years to live before the endometriosis consumes so much of your body that your organs will fail."

His words descended upon me without warning, like a hard punch in the gut. He showed no care, no emotion or compassion. We couldn't believe what he had said. How could a disease I knew nothing about be killing me? I felt a deep lump in my throat as I looked across at David, and tears welled in my eyes.

In the doctor's cold, clinical, smug manner, he explained that my bowel and uterus were also consumed by the disease. He then casually went on to say that my bowel wall had partly collapsed during my last surgery so I needed another surgery immediately or would risk getting toxaemia and dying.

"What the hell was going on?"

I struggled to digest all the news. It felt like a bomb had just hit my heart and blown it into pieces. David was ordered to take me straight to hospital, where they were expecting me. I was not even allowed to go home to collect my personal things, or see Hamish and Eve. My whole world had been broken apart.

Twenty four hours later, the emergency operation went longer and was much more complicated than expected. The extent of the damage was far worse than they had initially thought. There was an excessive amount of internal bleeding, so they performed a total hysterectomy and also had to remove my appendix and lower bowel at the same time. My fears and my reality collided.

Any hope of having more babies was crushed with that news and my body now had five body parts fewer than I had earlier that day. I was also fitted with a plastic bag (ileostomy bag), where liquid faeces dribbled out of my tummy instead of passing through my bowel. My once-tanned, flat and scar-free tummy now had a huge bright silver line of shiny staples starting from my belly button going all the way down to my pubic bone. I felt obliterated and in a world of pain that I can't even begin to describe. Both physically and emotionally, I had a long road of recovery in front of me.

I was forced to get the hang of living with an ileostomy bag; there was no choice around that. Days turned into weeks. I was grateful to be alive but angry and depressed at the thought of living with a poo bag for the rest of my life. How was I going to swim with it? What about tight fitting clothes, sexy underwear, or even sex for that matter? How would it all work? It was a bitter pill to swallow; there was nothing fair about this situation. The doctors told me that there was still a chance they would be able to sew up the stoma (the hole in my stomach that attached the poo bag) and redirect my faeces, if my bowel recovered well enough. But I didn't hold much hope for anything at that point.

Not only was I scared and worried about my prognosis, but I was also concerned about David. He was stressed out trying to keep it all together, run the business, look after the children, drive back and forth to the hospital twice a day and attempt to keep a positive face, whilst he handled the real possibility of losing me in a few years. He didn't cope well with stress, so it made it worse for me seeing him like that when I was stuck lying in hospital unable to do anything.

Worse still, when I smelled alcohol on his breath when he visited, it made my blood boil. He knew that drinking made things worse, but he did it anyway due to his addiction. My body shuddered with a cold, sick chill running through me -which only a mother would know- at the thought of her kids being at risk. I wanted to scream and slap David across the face to wake him up every time I smelled booze.

To calm myself, I would remember our wedding vows, "For better, for worse, for richer, for poorer, in sickness and in health." We had been through so much together; we had a deep bond that connected us. I was determined to stick by David's side, as he did mine. The love and vulnerability we shared united us. I knew he was a gentle and beautiful man deep inside. He loved us all incredibly, and would never intentionally do anything to harm us. This was just another challenge we had to rise above.

Still in hospital three weeks after my surgery, I slowly began to feel a little better each day. I counted down the tubes as they were removed one by one from my body. I missed feeling fit and healthy. I missed my old life which I knew wouldn't be the same for a long time. I missed our little family. I missed seeing the children running down the hallway of our home. I missed our morning cuddles, hearing their laughter and holding them tight.

Strategic Planning

One thing I am forever grateful for is that through this horrendous ordeal, I was not worried about our business as I knew we had worked hard to get it to where it was. We had strategies in place to cover my absence and ensure our business still ran efficiently, which was a true gift in the midst of yet another difficult time.

Strategies are about setting up the foundations of your business and making sure those foundations are strong, so things don't fall over when the going gets tough. There's no point working like a bull at a gate to get more business in the door, if your foundations are not strong. If things are in a mess now, then you will just get into a bigger mess if you grow your business without first putting strong strategies in place. When I discuss strategies with clients and which ones to initially focus upon, we always look at their business as it stands in that moment. From this point, we then decide which areas will help improve the business the most in the immediate future.

Where to Start?

A common mistake I see, when people are looking for more money, is they go straight to trying to increase their number of leads. By default, and lack of business education, lead generation is where most business owners consider they can make the biggest difference in their business profit. They think that if they have more customers, surely they will make more money, right? Not necessarily. This is normally the last place I recommend focusing on because it generally costs money to generate more leads (Google ads, SEO, paid or sponsored marketing, referral arrangements, etc.) and it doesn't guarantee a higher profit in the business. There are often many other potential areas overlooked that can bring more cash to the bottom line first, before you look at increasing your number of leads.

I recommend focusing on strategies that are going to give you a fabulous result the first time – I call these strategies 'low hanging fruit.' In each strategy outlined below think about how much impact they would have on your business, and which ones would be the most leveraged to use. Once you've identified the top strategies to adopt, then the goal is to implement, test and measure the success of each strategy. If it proves to be successful, then make sure it's a strategy that continues within your business and becomes part of a team member's job description.

My advice is also to not take on too many strategies at once, or you'll become overwhelmed and it will make it difficult to measure which strategies are working and those which aren't.

My suggestion is to look at perhaps two to three strategies per quarter, depending on how big your business is. For a large established organisation, there could be a proactive strategic plan working in the background behind everyone's role and functional area. This way, each person has a strategy that they are working on to improve the effectiveness and efficiency of their role and ultimately contributing to the big picture of the business.

Strategies that can be implemented once, such as a pricing increase or changing the templates of your quoting system, are great strategies to begin with because after the initial change they will continue to give you results over and over again. The key is to make sure that you're working on the right strategies and ensuring that the most effective ones (proven through testing and measuring) become a part of the way things are done in your business in the future.

Ask Your Team

The people in your team working in the core areas of the business will often have better first-hand knowledge and ideas of what would give them better efficiency and results than someone observing your business from a distance. Some organisations only include strategies recommended by the top management. However, strategies from the front line people (the ones actually doing the job) are generally the most relevant and successful. From my experience, I have seen that often top management haven't been down to the front line of the business for a long time and can become removed from the actual processes.

My recommendation is to have a place where all the wonderful ideas from different people within your organisation can be collected, instead of them being thought of and forgotten along the way. However, there's no point getting loads of feedback and having a huge list of strategies from your team if they're never discussed, brainstormed or implemented. To manage this, monthly or quarterly strategy meetings are a good way to get the whole team involved to brainstorm ideas and decide which ones to implement.

Once all the low hanging fruit has been implemented, learn from other people's success to decide 'Where to next?' There are many amazing books, podcasts and YouTube videos available, with strategies that have worked for other people. So, there's never any shortage of ideas and no excuse not to learn from others. With seeds and ideas planted from others, and your own business expertise, you'll be able to develop on those strategies or think of new ones to give you the edge on your competitors.

To give you some ideas to get started, here are some of the top proactive strategies I have seen implemented within the businesses I have worked with. These are categorised in order of the quickest results achieved. I have seen these strategies implemented in start-up businesses as well as multi-billion dollar businesses. The size is irrelevant, if the strategy is implemented well.

Cashflow Strategies

Starting with cashflow strategies, my top strategies are:

1. Implement a debt collection system
2. Reduce your stock levels
3. Review your fixed expenses
4. Look at your wages to revenue ratio

Debt Collection

Creating and implementing an effective debtors' system can impact your cashflow in a huge way, although this may not be applicable if you have a straight forward cash-on-delivery or online shopping cart structure. However, if you have a large amount of money owed to you, this will be dramatically impacting your business. If you have an overdraft which you're paying interest on, then you're effectively funding your debtors. If you had that money in your bank instead of theirs, you could use it to avoid paying interest on your overdraft, as well as invest in your business in a variety of ways that could work wonders for your business.

I'd consider this strategy a top priority so you can get the money you're owed into your bank account as soon as possible. You've done the job and provided the products or given your service. Now, make sure you get paid for it. Have somebody accountable for doing the debt collection on a regular basis with a target of reducing the number of debtors outstanding;

effectively, reducing the amount of money out in the world that is owed to you. To get started, set and agree upon targets, such as when the debt collection process begins. For example, is it when an invoice becomes more than seven days outstanding? Then decide how many companies to follow up a week, in priority from the highest amount owing to the lowest. This will depend upon what is relevant for your business and what is realistically possible.

Documenting the process (including time-lines, scripts and templates for each step of the way) will enable you to improve the system on an ongoing basis and keep accurate records of what's promised by clients, and when. The important thing to remember is to have it completed on a consistent basis, then your clients will know you're serious and will be more likely to pay you. The other reason to clearly document what is said and done is that if the person accountable leaves, goes on holiday or is sick, then someone else can take over the role where they left off.

Reducing Stock

Reducing stock (if it's applicable in your business), particularly slow-moving stock, can have a positive impact on your cashflow. There is no point in having a large amount of dead stock on the shelves for months and months, reducing in value every day it sits on the shelf. In fact, it is worth getting rid of all stock that doesn't sell very well as it is effectively cash sitting idle which could be better utilised. I have seen some businesses who keep stock for over a decade; it's not a good look and doesn't amount to positive returns. If you have stock that has been on the shelf for years, it's better to get a small amount of cash for it now than have it sit there indefinitely.

Another option with stock is to consider having some on consignment, so it's not pre-paid for, or it may be appropriate to ask your supplier if you can just pay a deposit upfront for stock, with the balance payable on delivery instead. These little changes can make a big impact on your cashflow, especially when dealing with large amounts of stock.

Fixed Expenses

When clients review all their fixed expenses, so many are surprised by how many costs they can cut back. Looking through all the money that is going out of your bank account every month, can you pin-point if some of these expenses are no longer necessary? My clients often notice subscriptions and small recurring fees coming out every month that are not used by the business any more. Even though they may be small amounts, they all add up. Alternatively, if you can't find any expenses to cut, can you look at moving direct debit dates to the same cycle as your billing cycle? If you notice that certain debits are coming out at your quietest time of the month, maybe you can move them to earlier or later in the cycle when you're due to be paid from your clients. Most businesses don't mind what day of the month they get paid, as long as you pay them.

When you're reviewing your contracted expenses, such as insurances, telephone and internet costs, car repayments, memberships, bank fees, etc., it can be a powerful exercise to do an annual price review of these, as you can usually reduce your fixed expenses. You may not even need to change suppliers either, but if you see that their competitor is offering a better price and you're a loyal customer, you can ask your supplier for a reduction in your costs or a 'price match.' If they don't want to lose your business, they will probably choose to reduce their fees or premiums in order to keep your business for the long term, even at a lower price.

Expense reviews are important for the bigger items too – the ones that come around for renewal less frequently. If your premises lease is up for review, don't just renew it without giving it a second thought. Do your homework and make sure the rent you're being charged is comparative to current market prices.

I recall encouraging Sally to do a rent review comparison with the rates of other vacant units in the block of shops she was renting, and she ended up negotiating a $20,000 reduction on her annual lease. How do you think that helped her cashflow? The building owner was happy to keep her as a tenant on a lower rent rate than lose her altogether. Otherwise, the landlord would have had another vacant shop to lease which would have also cost them more time and money to co-ordinate.

If a team member has it written into their job description to review all expenses and the budget on a monthly and annual basis, you'll see that your cashflow can be maintained more consistently and accurately.

Diagram 7.1 shows the impact that reducing your fixed expenses can have on your Net Profit.

Increasing Net Profit By Reducing Fixed Expenses

Reduce Fixed Expenses by 10%

Sales	$100,000	Sales	$100,000	
Less COGS	$30,000	Less COGS	$30,000	
Gross Profit	$70,000	Gross Profit	$70,000	
Less Operating Expenses	$50,000	Less Operating Expenses	$45,000	
Net Profit	$20,000	Net Profit	$25,000	↑ $5,000
Net Profit %	20%	Net Profit %	25%	

*$5,000 Increase In Net Profit

Diagram 7.1

Wages to Revenue Ratio

The last strategy to look at to improve your cashflow is focusing on decreasing your wages to revenue ratio. If you have contractors or casuals, keep a check of the wages to revenue ratio when you're doing the rosters so that as your sales go up, the wages bill isn't going up at a proportionately higher percentage ratio. Sometimes these little details aren't calculated accurately, and you end up overpaying contractors or casual team members, without increasing the sales by the same value. In this case, you end up going backwards. A little extra attention to detail here can make a big difference. Another way to reduce wages is by reducing overtime costs. If you deliver a service that is labour-based, look at reducing overtime by re-jigging and regularly checking your rosters.

Lance used this strategy to reduce his wages bill considerably, by reducing overtime and changing the roster around a little to find a win-win for his budget and his team. Some of his key people opted for less overtime in exchange for a shorter four-day-week. The outcome for the business was reduced overtime wages by $15,000 per month and a happier team who had more time to spend with their family.

Gross Profit Strategies

The second group of strategies I recommend you look at, directly relate to increasing your gross profit. My top gross profit strategies are:

1. Review your products
2. Increase your prices
3. Negotiate better prices for stock
4. Stop discounting

Review Your Products

When you're looking at your products or services, do you know which ones have a higher gross profit margin? If you start to put more emphasis on selling the products with the higher margins, your gross profit will increase with little effort.

A great example of this was when Bob (who owned a bed manufacturing business) excitedly discovered that some beds he was selling had a much greater margin than others. When I asked him what he found most valuable about identifying this information he said, "Imagine if we put more of those beds on the floor than the ones with less margin, how much more money we'd make in our business?"

"Fabulous," I thought. "He's got it!"

It was such a simple discovery, but so many business owners don't check their products for the best profit margins. Remember, the margin of your products may change with time and other variables, so don't assume that your most profitable product or service from five years ago is still the most profitable one today.

Diagram 7.2 demonstrates the power of knowing the gross profit percentage margin in each of your products.

Power Of Selling Products With Higher Gross Profit %

What product has the best margin?

Product Sales	A	B	C
Sales of $100,000 – COGS	$ 100k 50%	$ 100k 80%	$ 100k 20%
Gross Profit	$ 50k	$ 20k	$ 80k

How would your sales look if you focused more on product 'C' ?

Diagram 7.2

Increase Your Prices

Increasing your prices is a strategy that many business owners are too scared to adopt, but if you think about it, don't most of your suppliers increase their prices? Just about every product you buy and every service you use will increase in price over time. Every year, you expect to receive the letter from your insurer saying that your premiums are going up. The same goes for your electricity and other household bills, as well as your grocery shopping. Do you pay more to get your lawn cut now than you did ten years ago? You'd be hard pressed to find a product or service that hasn't increased in price over time.

Most customers are loyal (or they will be if you take care of them and deliver exceptional service), so increasing your prices to reflect the value you provide and in line with your own increasing expenses is generally well accepted. Again, this is a strategy that can be implemented just once, and it will impact your bottom line straight away. If you're still not convinced and worried your clients or customers will complain, or go elsewhere, increase your prices by a small portion. Most clients will not even notice.

If you are invoicing $500,000 per annum and you implemented this one strategy, with only a 5% increase in your prices, you would have an extra $25,000 on your bottom line. In contrast, if you discounted by 5%, your gross profit margin reduces by $25,000.

Diagram 7.3 shows the impact that increasing your prices would have on your gross profit %, compared to discounting.

Increasing vs Discounting Prices

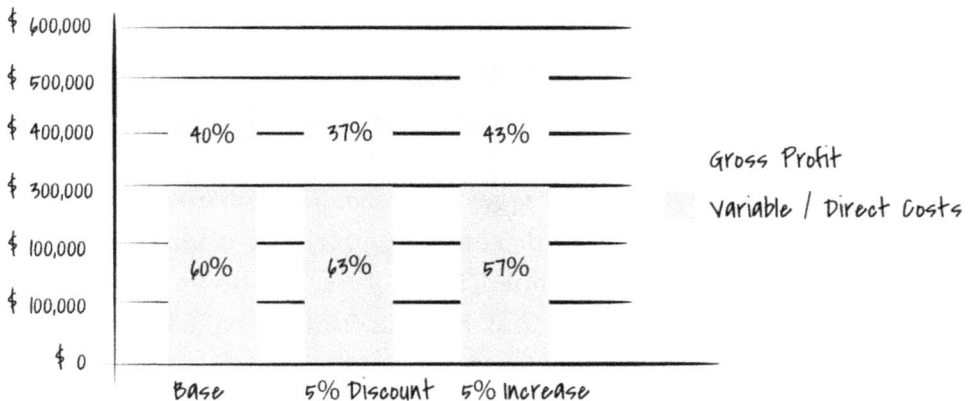

Diagram 7.3

Negotiate with Suppliers

When was the last time you rang up your supplier to negotiate better prices on your stock? Imagine if you could get your stock for 2% lower in cost, what impact would that have on your margins and your bottom line? Ordering a larger quantity of stock, joining orders with another one of your distributors, to increase buying power, or even ordering overseas direct from the manufacturer are a few ideas to reduce your stock prices. This, coupled with increasing your retail sell prices very slightly, will impact your gross profit dramatically without getting any more leads or more sales. If your business is service based and doesn't have stock, this may not be applicable, however you may still be able to negotiate costs with suppliers which you buy from regularly.

Cut Out Discounting

My final gross profit strategy is to stop discounting! Funnily enough, I have found it is usually the business owner who offers the most discounts. My client John is a perfect example of this. He said his company, "never discounted," and even laughed that, "If we discounted, we wouldn't make any money." Keen to confirm this, we logged into his accounting system and looked at his chart of accounts. When we got to the discounts line, we saw there was almost $50,000 discounted every year from the total sales. Fifty thousand dollars just thrown out the window! Shocked, John couldn't understand how this could be.

We looked deeper into the accounts to see who was actually allocating those discounts, as each team member had a code to enter into their sales system so the company could track individual sales. To John's surprise, it turned out that the majority of discounts were applied by him! He was the biggest *softy* in the business and even though he thought he wasn't discounting much, or often, each little discount he gave to clients ended up costing the business $50,000 every year. John had no idea that his discounting added up to such a huge amount. With this realisation, he decided to stop offering discounts altogether. He delegated the job of taking orders to another team member, to make sure that he didn't waver on this decision. In that one strategy, he added $50,000 of cash onto the bottom line of his business in just 12 months.

Average Dollar Sale Strategies

The third category of strategies you could look at are strategies to increase your average dollar sale. These strategies include:

1. Upselling
2. Educating your team and customers
3. Analysing your competitors

Learn to Upsell

Upselling is about offering something else to customers when they purchase from you. McDonald's well known phrase, *"Would you like fries with that?"* is a famous strategy that would have increased their average dollar sale, increasing their total sales by millions and millions of dollars all over the world. Most businesses have *fries* of some kind – a little extra 'add on' their customers can buy with their purchase that will enhance the product they're already buying.

If you can upsell to the clients who already buy from you (and trust you), it's far easier than getting brand new customers. For every sale you make that is higher in value, your average dollar sale will increase and your revenue will grow.

It is common that clients don't know all the products or services you supply, so when they ring and order, it's definitely worth having a conversation with them to let them know what other products you provide. If you provide an online purchase facility, that's another great opportunity to upsell. When you're purchasing something online, you've most likely seen a pop up appears at the check-out, saying something along the lines of: *"People who have purchased your product also bought this,"* or *"Before you check out, would you like us to add this to your order for just $5.00?"* It's effective. Even if only one in five say 'yes', it's going to increase your average dollar sale and directly impact the cash on your bottom line.

This strategy can be adopted in the service industry too. Ask your customers, *"While we're out doing your service, we could also check your – insert service item – as well, to save you an extra call out fee. Would you like us to book this in for you?"*

Train Your Team

By educating and training your team to understand more about the products you are selling, and which products complement others, you can help to increase your average dollar value. Selling in bundles instead of just one product at a time can have a huge impact on increasing your average dollar sale. It also gives your clients more value when they better understand your products. This particular strategy worked really well with a retail store I was working with, who trained their team to better communicate with their customers about the benefits of the products they were selling. Good old-fashioned customer service can go a long way.

When you're looking for something in a shop and not sure exactly what to get (whether it's a book, groceries or a gift), sometimes it's really helpful to get guidance from the people who work there. As long as the communication is friendly and informative, it can help you make a decision and you may end up buying more from them. When a client implemented this one strategy at her retail store, their average dollar sale more than doubled – almost immediately.

Check Out Your Competition

Conducting a current competitor analysis is about seeing where you can expose opportunities to increase your average dollar sale. If your competitors are offering the same service or product for a higher fee, you have leeway to increase your prices as well. This will depend on your margins. However, to give yourself a competitive edge, you could still keep your fee lower than theirs. Often your competitors can provide great clues about the market and save you time on starting your research from scratch.

Conversion Rate Strategies

The final area of strategies to look at are conversion rate strategies. Successful ways to increase your conversion rate are by:

1. Being Consistent
2. Tweaking your sales process
3. Training your sales team
4. Improving your sales scripts

Being Consistent

You've heard it before; *consistency is key.* If you consistently market your products and services with a consistent message, if you consistently follow your sales process and deliver the same great customer service, you will build a rapport and improve your reputation. A better reputation = higher conversion rate. No big feat in life will ever be achieved without consistently working on it. A famous author of new thought metaphysics, Robert Collier, once said, "Success is the sum of small efforts, repeated day in and day out."[24]

Tweaking Your Sales Process

Sales processes can always be improved and expanded, no matter how confident you are with your current process. I've seen conversion rates go from as low as 15% to as high as 80% by tweaking, improving and standardising the sales process. This will occur more so where the whole team knows it and sticks to it. If you are delivering a product or service that your customers need on a regular basis, it's your responsibility to give them great customer service and then follow up and remind them when they're due to come back. Wouldn't it be great if your mechanic took the hassle out of remembering to service your car by keeping a log of when your car is due for a service and sending you a reminder? Having a follow up system is an easy way to get your clients to come back, rather than relying on them. It puts the power in your hands. Much of this can be set up automatically in a simple customer relationship management (CRM) program, so you can systemise the tracking and contacting of all your clients.

Training Your Sales Team

Training your sales team can have a massive impact on conversion rate, as when a salesperson is genuine and they relay accurate information to customers in a professional and friendly manner, they're likely to have a higher conversion rate than a salesperson who has insufficient training or doesn't relate well to the customer. Some powerful training ideas for salespeople might include:

1. Increasing product knowledge, to increase confidence with explaining your products.
2. Developing body language knowledge, including looking at customers in the eye to increase trust.
3. Learning to understand personality profiles, to talk to your prospects in the language and style in which they best take in information.
4. Creating sales scripts for phone or face to face salespeople.
5. Understanding how to dress for the customer, to look presentable and professional at all times.

Implementing Your Strategies

Each of the strategies I've spoken about in this chapter will feed another. When carried out in the correct order, you can grow your business in a leveraged manner. As I mentioned earlier, lead generation is the last strategy that I would work on because if there is hidden potential in the other four areas, it is more logical to work on them first to capitalise on what you already have in place.

Sometimes it's good to draw up a basic chart of pros and cons for each strategy, including time, effort and cost, versus the impact each strategy will have, to determine the priority order of which ones to work on first. The main thing to understand is how a very small change can have a compounding impact. Implementing continual proactive strategies in your business will be crucial to your long-term success and will help you get through the times of mayhem and madness.

The same goes for anything in life, if you have strategies in place, you'll cope better when you're hit with an unexpected curve ball, as happened many times with David and me.

Greg & Alicia

Greg and Alicia came to me one day with a barely profitable car detailing business. They were eager to learn how they could increase their profits, so they could put money aside to invest in their future wealth. We got very clear on what their model of success looked like and went about prioritising what proactive growth strategies would impact their business in a positive way.

One of the first quick and easy wins was reducing the amount of stock sitting on their shelves. We negotiated the return of some stock for a credit and even developed a plan with the supplier whereby they started providing samples to give clients, to encourage clients to buy their products. It was a win-win for both the supplier and my clients.

Next, we reviewed all their operating expenses, and managed to trim about 10% off their total costs. Some of their regular expenses simply weren't necessary anymore. They were just being direct debited each month and had been forgotten about, adding up over time.

Greg and Alicia's business then increased its average dollar sale by offering other services to their clients that they weren't already providing. They implemented a regular booking schedule for busy clients, and worked on grouping products together, as well as having package offerings available for appropriate clients.

Through a few simple and effective strategies, Greg and Alicia stopped 'spinning their wheels' and were actually able to put money away each week. They ended up increasing the value of their business by so much that they sold it for twelve times the price they purchased it for only six years earlier. They were then able to invest in their wealth and create some monthly revenue from investments in property and shares, creating a very good living for themselves.

Chapter 7
Blue Ocean Thinking

☐ **Decide which strategies will be most powerful in your business**

What will be the quickest strategies to achieve, and have the biggest short-term impact?

☐ **Diarise when you will work on each strategy**

Put time aside for whoever is accountable to work on your chosen strategies.

☐ **Test and measure each strategy**

Decide how you're going to track each strategy, so you know if and when you achieve your desired result.

"People don't care how much you know until they know how much you care."

Theodore Roosevelt

CHAPTER EIGHT

Your Work Family

When I was first released from hospital, I was in a wheelchair; I couldn't even walk. My life was altered considerably due to the extra fashion accessory of an ileostomy bag attached to my stomach. The post-surgery pain was excruciating. A friend had been through a similar experience and kindly offered to make me some sexy underwear that covered everything. It even had an innovative little pouch inside to hold the stoma bag, so I didn't feel so gross and unattractive. It was a beautiful, thoughtful gesture and I realised that for all my challenges, there were ways I could overcome them by carefully developing strategies to make the most of my situation.

I must say that having people to support, inspire and believe in me through the tough times made all the difference. My mum helped with housework, drove me to and from appointments and helped with Hamish and Eve. A couple of close girlfriends checked in on me regularly and David was also always by my side. He even cut his drinking right back and was extra vigilant with trying to keep the house in order. I saw a truly beautiful side of David when I was at my worst. He took care of the kids, looked after our clients at work, made me feel loved and beautiful; and treated me like a queen every single day.

David and I even came up with creative strategies to have meaningful intimacy with a poo bag between us; luckily our relationship was made of stronger stuff and we worked together despite our challenges. He really did a wonderful job of juggling all the balls and leaving me with as much energy as possible to focus on my recovery. The simple job of having a shower could often take a couple of hours and leave me so drained and wiped out that I would need a couple of hours sleep straight afterwards.

Along with the help I had in front of me, I was also inspired by reading many non-fiction stories of ordinary people facing extraordinary challenges, and overcoming them through their tenacity and willingness to push through. If others could get up each day and push themselves further with battles greater than mine, then I would be able to as well. *"If I can dream it, I can do it,"* I just kept telling myself. It was the first time I started to believe in my wildest dreams again. I knew that they were possible, if I just kept getting up, day in and day out.

My first goal was to walk to the bathroom and back from my bed, without assistance. This turned into a bigger goal of getting down the stairs. Then a week later, going across the road to the park and eventually walking a lap of the oval. I could have easily felt sorry for myself or fallen short of having any desire to set new goals, but with my mentors cheering me on, I pushed through my fears and pain. I became determined to figure out the strategies which would enable me to achieve my goals in the easiest way possible.

As the months went by, I found it harder and harder to live with the poo bag. My life often felt like a living hell, with non-stop faeces coming out of my stoma, dribbling into a bag stuck to my stomach. The problem was, every time I ripped off the patch that attached the bag to my stomach, some of my skin came off with it, which left my skin sensitive, wet and raw. As a result, my bag often leaked during the day, which meant replacing it, leading to more skin being pulled off and having to shower three to four times a day to keep myself clean. It was a living nightmare and was setting back any progress I was making.

However, motivated to get my life back to normal, I persevered. As the days went on, I slowly increased the distance I was able to walk and gradually regained my strength. Then came the first positive news in quite some time. Four months after the surgery, I was beyond relieved when the doctors told me they could reverse the ileostomy and I would soon be 'bag free' once more. It was such a milestone and I was excited for some normality returning to my life.

Nine months after being given the shocking diagnosis that I had a maximum of five years to live, David and I decided that we should spend some extended time together as a family. We decided to take a break from the business and travel the world with Hamish and Eve.

With my life expectancy cut so short, still battling with the disease that was eating me up from the inside, we decided that quality time with our family was far more important than running our business. That could wait; my health couldn't.

David sold his beloved motorbike which paid for the around-the-world ticket for four. With Eve and Hamish only five and nine years old, we both knew that traveling the world could only benefit their education. However, to ensure they kept up with the regular school curriculum, we enrolled them both in the School of Isolated and Distance Education (SIDE) which provided the curriculum for us to follow in fortnightly packages. I became Hamish's grade four teacher and David, Eve's grade one teacher. Our friends lived at our home while we were away, giving them a chance to do their house renovations without having to pay for a house to rent. This also meant our home was cared for, so we were all happy with the arrangement.

Thankfully, we still had Jenny, our wonderfully capable manager, who treated the business as her own. We trusted Jenny implicitly and loved her like a member of our family. We knew she would look after our business in our absence and, in line with her additional managerial responsibilities, we took a cut in our wages and gave Jenny a wage increase. Jenny was the first to step-up and was pleased to be able to help us so we could take a trip of a lifetime.

As we were preparing to embark on our world trip, in late January 1999, I couldn't believe we were about to face yet another setback. I was at home with Hamish and Eve packing up boxes and cleaning out cupboards, and David had set off for a session at the gym. Perhaps only 30 minutes after he had left home, I received a frantic call from David.

"Suzzie, I've smashed my finger. It's really bad and I'm waiting for the ambulance."

David had somehow managed to drop a dumbbell directly on top of another set of dumbbells and smashed his index finger in between them.

I hurriedly raced to the gym and could see that David was not in a good way. As he stepped into the ambulance gingerly cradling his hand, I could see his finger was really messed up and dangling off his hand. After an excruciating five hour wait in the hospital emergency room, finally a doctor examined David's finger; and scheduled surgery the next morning. I couldn't believe it had taken so long for him to receive medical attention.

The specialist surgeon inserted a small steel plate into David's finger and hoped that it would be enough to help it heal back together. However, he said that the chances for a full recovery were only 50-50 and if it didn't heal properly, he'd have to amputate the finger. My heart sank for David; I couldn't believe how seemingly unlucky he was. The pain of his injury was intense, because his nerves were crushed, but we were due to fly out for our trip in less than two weeks and nothing was going to stop us. After all, we'd faced bumps in the road before, so this was just another obstacle we had to get through.

As I reflect on the challenges we have faced, in hindsight I can appreciate that I learned many coping strategies and tactics which I've called on again and again to get myself through tough times. I gained much inspiration and hope from those who travelled a similar path before me, acquired knowledge from others and developed insights from various mentors who had battled similar challenges. My heart was ignited by people who opened their hearts to me, keeping me going when I had little strength.

The biggest lesson I learned was that there is always a way to overcome each and every challenge and that it's important to never give up. Don't be afraid to accept help and allow yourself to be vulnerable and trust those you love. The biggest help came when I learned to say, "Yes," to the people around me who offered help. This applies to both your personal and professional life.

Everyone has to start somewhere, as I did from my bed after excruciating surgery and as David did after the horrific house fire. It is just a matter of taking one step at a time and identifying one strategy after another, that are in line with where you want to get to. If you have a rough time in life or in business, it's not the time to be too proud to ask for, or accept, help when people offer it.

Possibility Thinking

What could be possible for your life if you took the time to really think about and plan it? Could you say, "I'm taking a year off from my business because my priorities have changed?" If not, how could you set up your business so that you are not totally indispensable, so that if you wanted to take a year off and still take a wage, you could? What would need to change to make this possible? Who else in your team knows what you do? If everything is all in your head and no-one else knows what to do, it might be time to start sharing, training and documenting your intellectual property.

A local business owner, Paul, exclaimed to me, "I couldn't possibly take two days away from my business without things falling in a heap." He then proudly stated, "I haven't had a holiday in 12 years," as if it was something to be pleased about. I asked him how his wife and kids felt about that, which got him thinking. Was his business really serving him or was he serving the business?

If you can't take one or two days away from your business, let alone longer, it's time to do something about it now so you're not always tied to your business.

Building a fully engaged, trustworthy team who are able to follow procedures and get the job done correctly (the first time) is the biggest asset you can create for your company. It will allow you the freedom of being able to step away from your business, when needed, trusting that it will still run efficiently without you there.

Being a Great Leader

A colleague once told me, "You get the people you deserve." Ultimately, you are responsible for the team you have. In order to create a team who care as much about your business as you do, you have to work for it. Great team members may seem like they are rare to find, but if you take the time and attention it requires to find the right people, you can find a pot of gold at the end of the rainbow.

The first place to start is to really look at yourself and what kind of leader you are. Are you the kind of person people like to work with? Are you the kind of person people trust? Are you a leader who inspires your people or are you a manager that pushes your people around? Being a leader and being a *boss* are two very different things. If you are a great leader, you will create an engaged workplace where everyone in your team is rowing together in the same direction.

Diagram 8.1 compares some examples of behaviours displayed by a leader versus a boss.

A Leader vs A Boss

Inspires	Pushes people around
Develops people	Uses people
Gives credit, reward and recognition	Takes the credit for themselves
Coaches their team	Points the finger
Says "We"	Says "You"
Bases their decisions on goodwill	Bases their decisions on authority
Generates enthusiasm	Generates fear
Fixes breakdowns	Places blame on you
Shows people how things are done	Tells people how it's done
Asks their team questions	Gives their team commands
Says "Let's Go"	Directs you to "Go"

Diagram 8.1

Are you a leader or a boss? There are many differences between being a great leader or just a boss. One of the first places to create a good team is to look at yourself and ask how you can change your actions to be a better leader, and inspire positivity and growth in your team.

Your Dream Team

Creating an awesome team is based on finding the right people for your business and choosing the right people for the role they will fill (and that includes you!). Look at the people currently in your team and identify if they're the right fit for your business. Coaching your team to *step up* or *step out* is a great way to go about improving your team – if they're not prepared to do what is required of them to be successful in their role and contribute to the success of the business, perhaps they're not in the right job.

If you haven't chosen the right people, or you haven't nurtured them to be the team members you need them to be, you will likely have a disconnected, disengaged team who are dragging your company backwards. No one wants a team which doesn't care about their jobs or the business, and no one wants to waste money and time training new team members for them to soon leave. Worse still, you also don't want unmotivated team members to stay around and actively *sink the ship.*

Disengaged employees are more likely to be making recurring errors, too, and mistakes equate to inefficiency and reflect poorly on your business. Not only that, but around 34% of a disengaged employee's salary is wasted, so you're pouring money down the drain with team members who aren't engaged with what you do.[25] These alarming global disengagement statistics are a great cause for concern as in 2018, it was determined that only 27% of the workforce was Highly Engaged, 38% were Engaged, 21% Disengaged, with 14% Actively Disengaged.[26]

Around two out of ten people in your business are actively *rowing the boat* and pulling your company in a forward direction. There will be about six out of ten people doing only *as expected*, or *less than expected*, and alarmingly one or two people out of ten in your business who will be actively *sinking your ship,* meaning they are dragging your company backwards and preventing your company from reaching its potential.

Diagram 8.2 shows a visual of global engagement statistics.

Global Engagement Statistics

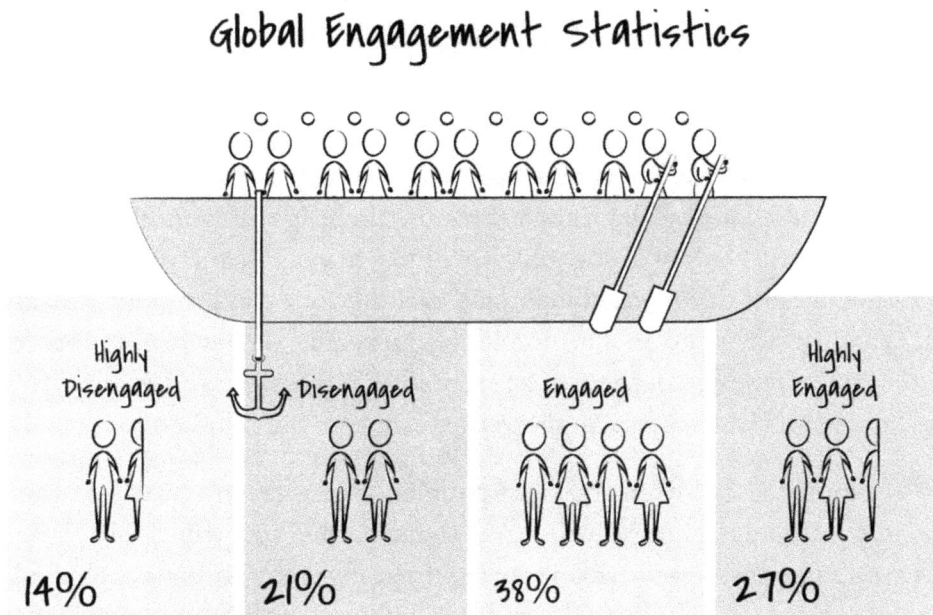

| Highly Disengaged | Disengaged | Engaged | Highly Engaged |
| 14% | 21% | 38% | 27% |

Diagram 8.2

Find the Right People

Finding the right people starts with a vision of what you want your team to be, then in following some simple recruitment steps to find the right people for the positions required in your team. Ultimately, each new team member you hire should add value to your organisation. Recruitment is not just a lottery, where you hope for the best. Let's break it down into some steps that I have successfully used myself, and with my clients, to build a great team:

1. Draw a future organisational chart outlining what you want your company to look like.
2. Write a clear job description in line with your organisation chart.
3. Create an awesome advertisement that will appeal to the person you're seeking to find.
4. Shortlist the top applicants.

5. Conduct phone screening with those shortlisted applicants.

6. Offer a face to face interview with a small number of those who impress you during the phone call.

7. Follow up references, before offering a trial period to the most promising applicant.

8. Perform a trial / skills test.

9. If the applicant proves themselves capable, offer them a position in your team.

10. Provide a solid induction and training period.

11. Nurture your team on an ongoing basis.

Where Do Your People Fit?

An organisation chart (or org chart, for short) is like a family tree, showing a hierarchy of positions and departments, with the people who work in each area.

Diagram 8.3 shows a basic org chart example of an average company.

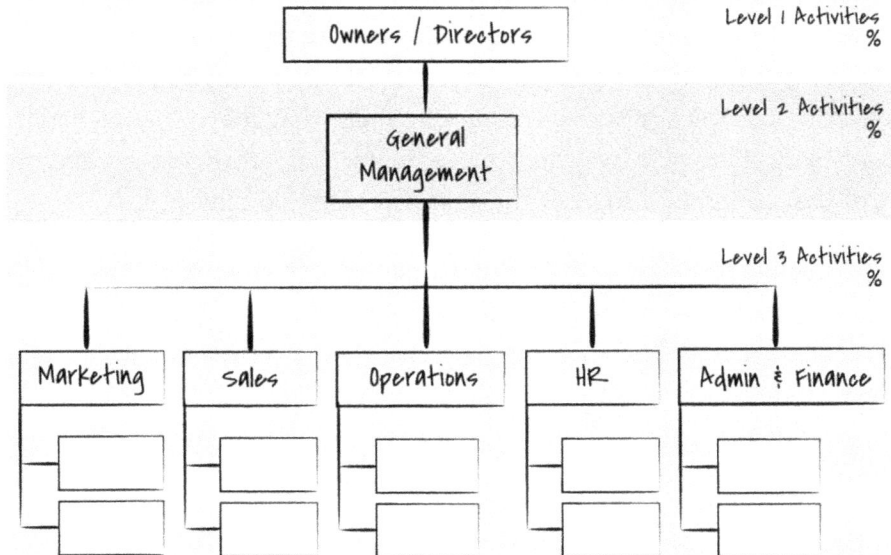

Diagram 8.3

There are the Owners and Directors at the top (who perform what we call Level 1 Activities), then General Management or Upper Level Management underneath (conducting Level 2 Activities) and finally all the Level 3 Activities including Operations, Marketing, Sales, Human Resources, Admin and Finance, etc.

Looking at the people in each area of activities, how much percentage of your (or their) time is spent in Level 1 activities versus Level 2 and Level 3 activities? As you progress from working *in* your business, to working *on* your business, you will do less of the Level 3 activities and more activities in Level 2 and Level 1. Most business owners take an average of 12-18 months to get out of Level 3 activities and *only* manage the business or even, in some cases, become a silent partner or owner. If you are spending too much time doing activities you dislike or that you would be better off delegating, having those areas outlined in an org chart will help you when you're looking at future team member placements.

An interesting exercise I did with Brian was to draw up an org chart for where he wanted the business to be in five years' time. He then displayed it in the office for all the team to see, so they could identify where their career paths were headed and what positions may be coming up in the future. If anyone was looking for a career promotion or area to develop, they could see what was possible in the future in line with the company's goals. I bumped into Brian not long ago and was pleased to hear that they far exceeded their five-year org chart plan, way before the time was up. It was so exciting to be part of that company's success and see their plans be achieved.

A fun creative exercise is to draw an org chart of your business as it is now, then do another one of what you would like it to look like in three, or five, years' time. You will learn who is coming on this journey with you, and who else you need to recruit on the way. It is much easier to forward plan for budgets, production and geographical expansion if you have a picture of your growth plans.

What Roles Are Played?

Creating a clear picture of who best fits the roles you're filling will help you to identify the dream person who would be *just perfect* for the job.

Being clear on the ideal candidate for each role that you recruit for will dramatically increase your chances of success. Remember, skills can be trained but ethics, morals and values cannot be.

Some questions to ask yourself:

- What will their tasks be?
- What skills are required?
- What qualities should the person possess?
- What are the key performance indicators that will determine their success in the role?
- What personality traits would be ideal for the role?
- What qualifications are required? And are they preferred, or essential?
- How much experience in the industry would the ideal person have?

Once you have these questions answered, you can write up the position description, which will make it so much easier when you are advertising the role and interviewing. When it comes to advertising the position, so often people advertise a job for a person they think they need, but don't include the important details of the role.

I was once told by a business owner that the person he recently hired was, "An idiot who couldn't do the role properly."

I asked him what the job description contained, only to be told there wasn't one.

"Well then, who is the idiot in this situation?" I replied.

If you hire someone primarily because you got on well with them in the interview, chances are they may not be the perfect person for the role.

It must be confusing for someone to take on a role without really knowing what is required of them, and then to actually do the role without knowing if they are doing it correctly or not. I'd strongly recommend going through an outline of the job position description with every employee in your business, both current and new employees, so you are all on the same page.

Advertise the Right Way

When advertising, the goal is to attract the ideal candidate by asking leading questions relating to the essence of the role, such as, "Do you love technology?" or "Does developing new systems excite you?"

If the right candidate is reading the job, they'll be sitting there in excitement answering, "Yes, yes, that's me!"

At this stage they won't know anything about you or your company, so the initial aim is to make sure they feel like this job is made for them. They won't care about your company, until they have found a job that is great for them.

After you have attracted the candidate in the first couple of paragraphs, then you can explain more about the role and your company. If the candidate is passionate about what your organisation is about, it will fuel the vision of the business and inevitably help you to achieve your goals. If your company has a particular passion – such as conservation, organic food or fitness – hire people with the same passion.

Asking applicants to respond to questions in a cover letter when applying for the position will ensure that they are providing more than just their resume. This will push them to think about the role and formulate a response to match the desired criteria. When considering a large number of applicants, this will help you to short-list the right people; those who don't provide a cover letter, or those who don't formulate an appropriate response, could be eliminated right away because it shows that they can't follow procedures or don't meet the criteria you have set.

Narrow Down Your Top Candidates

When you're short-listing applicants, make a list of the top five qualities or expertise you're looking for, that are relevant and essential to the role.

From there, I'd recommend phone screening your top applicants before wasting precious time with a large number of face-to-face interviews. You can condense your list by seeing if you connect on the phone and if their telephone manner is up to scratch.

If you have the time and capacity, I suggest calling five to ten applicants, asking questions relative to the role and their application, as this will test their ability to answer honestly and accurately on the spot. If you call them out of the blue, you're more likely to get the *real person*, not the *prepared version* who has a rehearsed answer. I like to start with asking questions such as, why they're leaving their current role, what they're looking for in their new role and ascertaining their desire to stick around for the long term.

Following this, I ask specific questions related to the role, such as their willingness to travel (if required), what their passions and strengths are, examples of how they have used their strengths in their previous roles, areas of weakness (and how they are working to overcome them), what their goals are, what their salary expectations are and what other roles they have been seeking. If they seem vague or unclear on the role they are looking for, perhaps they're just after any old job rather than a long-term career with your organisation. The aim of your conversation is to ensure they are confident in what they're looking for and that they meet the requirements.

Another question I like to ask is, "What would your previous three employers rate you on a scale of 1 to 10, with 10 being an exemplary team member?" This way you're reinforcing their strengths and the way people perceive them, and preparing for reference checks later on if they make it that far. Make sure you use this phone interview opportunity to be clever with your screening. Look for patterns and listen to what is really being said. When you ask questions, dig deep and ask a lot of "how" and "why" questions. You want to have the chance to get to know them better, without just asking vague surface questions. Ask things such as, "What's an example of that?" or "What happened next?" or "How did you deal with that?"

Getting your candidate to open up and be clear and honest with their answers will provide you with the insights you require to decide whether to offer them a formal interview. If you are confident you have a promising candidate, invite them for an interview. If you're unsure at the end of the call, don't offer an interview on the spot as you can always call back later. If you know they're not right, it's best to be upfront and say that unfortunately they don't appear to be the right fit for the job.

Meet Your Prospective Employee

By this point, hopefully you will be able to identify your top three candidates to either bring in for a group interview, (generally suited if you have a large amount of people you want to screen) or individual interview, depending on your preference and available time.

Before the interview, I obtain a personality profile of each candidate to make sure their natural personality, values and motivators suit the role requirements. This way, if the role requires someone to have very high attention to detail and their natural personality profile shows they're not good with follow through or don't have a high tendency towards compliance, they're not going to be right for the role (but may, in fact, be more suited to another role in your company, if you're looking to fill multiple roles).

There are various online reports available; I use *DISC and Motivator Profile Assessments* created by Dr Tony Alessandra.[27] DISC traits can be very helpful in ascertaining whether someone is suited to the role for which they are applying. In simple terms, DISC is an acronym that refers to the styles of Dominance, Influence, Steadiness and Compliance. You may sometimes see small variations on those acronyms, but they all relate back to the same sort of style (for example, 'I' might stand for inspiring, or 'C' may stand for conscientiousness). Each style is associated with behavioural tendencies that are observed between people of the same DISC style; noting that it's possible – and quite common – to possess multiple styles and traits.

Diagram 8.4 shows examples of DISC characteristics exhibited by people in each style.

Slower-Paced
Task-Oriented

C

Faster-Paced
Task-Oriented

D

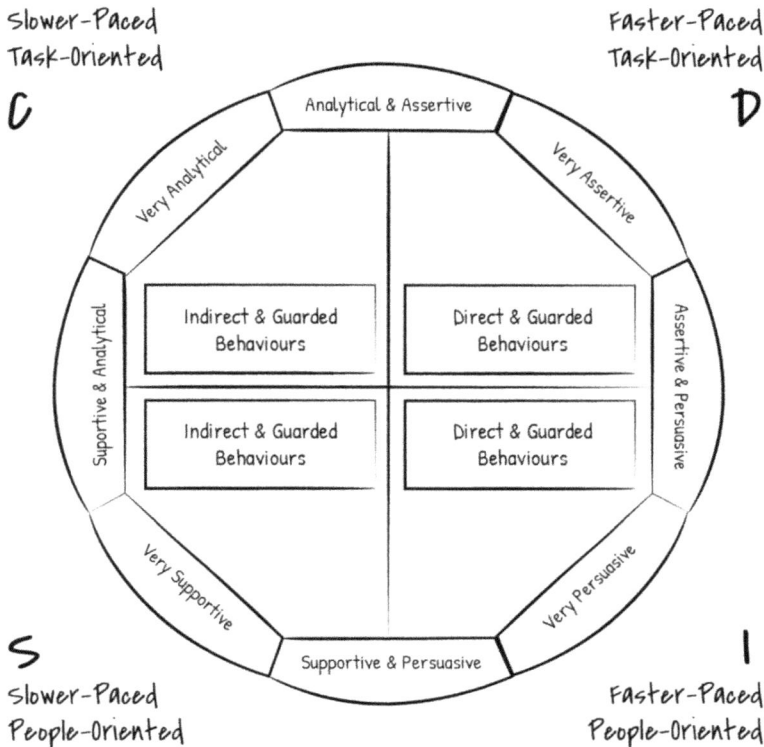

Diagram 8.4

Slower-Paced
People-Oriented

S

Faster-Paced
People-Oriented

I

If you have not conducted an interview before, here's a small checklist of things to go through with each applicant. Remember to take notes so you can remember each person clearly.

- Tell them about your company and its history, and the products and services you sell. Remember, you have already attracted the right person for the role based on the advertisement and pre-screening, so it's OK to talk about your company now.

- Talk about the future vision of the company, your mission, and how you deliver your products.

- Ask them what attracted them to the role.

- Ask them about their passions, their hobbies and interests.

- Show them who's currently in the team, what their roles are, and how they fit into the big picture (org chart).

- Show them where their prospective role sits and talk briefly about potential career opportunities in the future.

- Explain your company values and behaviours.

- Ask them about their employment history and what they did and didn't like about each role.

The purpose of your interview is to elaborate on what it is you're offering, and align each applicant's suitability to the role. When talking about their specific position, make sure they know the purpose of the role, the tasks expected to be completed, the corresponding KPIs and the documented job description. Go through their resume, ask questions along the way and do a little test with them. An example of this is asking them what they know about your company, as this will show you if they are really keen about the job and have done some research. The more talking they do, the better.

I also ask what they think their greatest assets are that they could bring to the company and what are the areas they could improve on? What are their long-term goals and aspirations in life? What does their family do and what was their upbringing like? These questions will offer clues about the type of person they are, who their mentors and teachers were growing up and what direction they are heading in life.

Check Out Their References

When you have finished the interviews, don't just take their word for it; follow up and verify with job reference checks and any other validation required, such as a skills test. Some roles require a range of skills and seeing as *we don't know what we don't know* (and everyone's perception of their skill level is different depending on their experience), it's a good idea to get applicants to do a skills test in the interview as it helps to confirm qualifications and experience.

I usually get two or three references to verify all my notes from the interview. I speak with previous employers who are able to give more insight into the candidate's abilities and strengths, verify what they wrote in their resume about the role, confirm the applicant's answers to the questions around what they liked about their role, what they were good at and not so good at. Lastly, I authenticate why they left the role.

I don't always just ring the people who have been listed as the references. I also try to find someone to call with whom they have worked, or to whom they reported. Make sure you also verify all documentation that is relevant to the role you are filling, be it a driver's license, police clearance, certain level of university education or qualification.

Your New Team Member

I recommend giving a potential new team member a minimum of one-day or even a one-week trial, to see how they go and how they gel with your team, before offering them a firm position. If they pass this final hurdle, you can provide them with an employment contract that outlines their job description, start date, working days and hours, remuneration conditions, entitlements etc. Once you have reached this point, you are now ready to induct the successful candidate into their role.

It's great for each team member to have their action plan, outlining what they can work on to achieve their goals and can see whether they have completed what they set out to do. Do you have long and short-term goals written up for each team member? This is very helpful in motivating people, as having goals is a great way of maintaining focus and staying on track.

Communication is key in developing and maintaining successful relationships in the workplace; make sure you are both on the same page with what is expected. A fun exercise is for you to write down the top ten things you consider are important in their role and ask them to do the same. If they don't match up, have a discussion about how to rectify the differences. Often, the business owner and the employee have different expectations of what is required of them, so it's critical for there to be an open dialogue for best results.

Create an Engaged Workplace

If you've achieved all this so far, congratulations! Now you have a great team of amazing, passionate people who are going to help your company to achieve its goals. You can now focus on creating an excellent work culture.

One way of making sure your team remains in sync and inspired to achieve great things, is by having regular team meetings. This way, everyone can share their progress and you can determine if everyone is on track to achieving their goals. Full transparency holds the team together, so everyone knows whether to celebrate as a team, or buckle down and roll up their sleeves. I often have people discuss their culture statement or rules of the game, but then don't follow through in their actions. Culture should be reflected in everyone's behaviours and agreed upon as a team. Having the right culture comes from the top – the business owner.

Reward and recognition is always ranked high on people's motivators, and far outweighs the motivator of money. Part of having a great team culture is making sure your team knows when they've done a good job and are rewarded and recognised accordingly. If they don't know what the goals are, they won't know whether they have achieved them. If the goal posts change, make sure your team knows if their KPIs need adjusting. No one can read minds; honest and upfront communication, together with understanding and respecting your team, will go a long way towards the success of your business. A great acronym to remember is T.E.A.M. – *Together Everyone Achieves More*. Your team are members of your work family and by supporting and treating them accordingly, you'll all reap the rewards.

Having a framework in place where you and your team can provide honest feedback and communication, is a great way for everyone to work towards constant progress in all areas of the business. Both the business owner and team members should be able to communicate what is working well and what isn't, so the team can collectively work towards improvement.

Maintaining integrity in your team environment is vital, and studies show that companies who listen to their team and value their feedback, perform far better. Through the work I do with *Engage and Grow Global*, it has been fascinating to see research about what truly motivates and engages human beings. A classic picture that we share with business owners who are looking to increase the engagement of their team, is the *Science of Motivation*. It shows people are *more motivated* by measures such as having a greater life purpose, love, relationships, human connection and making a significant contribution; over money, promotions and other similar rewards and benefits.

Diagram 8.5 shows the science behind our neurological motivators, how we learn the quickest and our core human needs.

Science Of Motivation

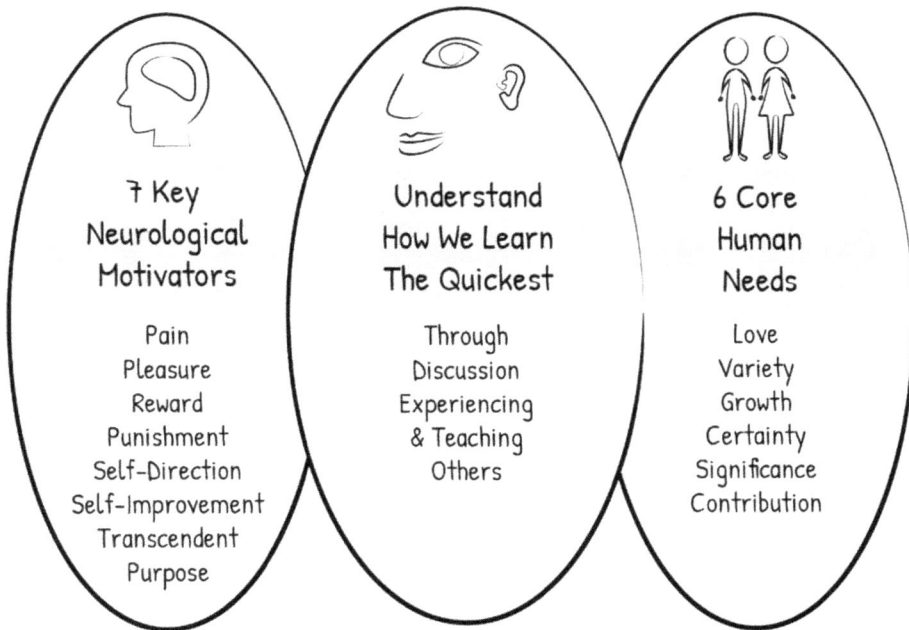

7 Key Neurological Motivators	Understand How We Learn The Quickest	6 Core Human Needs
Pain Pleasure Reward Punishment Self-Direction Self-Improvement Transcendent Purpose	Through Discussion Experiencing & Teaching Others	Love Variety Growth Certainty Significance Contribution

Diagram 8.5

Once people know about who you are and what you're about, there becomes an underlying trust which is beneficial to your organisation as well as your interpersonal and professional relationships. If you respect your team and provide interesting work that challenges them and is in line with their values and purpose, your team will be powerful; they are your vehicle to being even more awesome in your business.

Laura

When Laura first took over a business from a relative, there were people working for the business who ultimately weren't the right fit. Because of this, the business didn't have the capacity to grow and Laura wasn't confident that her team could handle any extra workload. She knew that her existing team had to *step up* or *step out* and she needed to find the right bums for the right seats.

We discussed the recruitment process extensively, from advertising the position to appealing to the right people, to short-listing the top candidates, screening and profiling them, right through to offering them a trial, and eventually a role in the organisation. By asking Laura the right questions, she was able to make sure any potential candidates had the same values and ethics as her organisation, making sure they'd be a viable fit for the future of the business.

We also explored *offshoring* and how Laura could create a successful business model with team members who weren't located in the same country. There was a lot of extensive planning, which led to a trip to Vietnam, followed by more brainstorming; but eventually Laura employed a mix of in-house and external employees which created an awesome balance for her company and budget.

With the right people in the right positions in her business, Laura now has a solid and supportive team that has transformed the way her business operates and ultimately, her business success.

Chapter 8
Blue Ocean Thinking

☐ **Create a current and future org chart**

Who currently fills each functional area of your business and who's missing from your team?

☐ **Write job descriptions for each current and future team member**

Get clear on specific duties each team member should carry out to meet their KPIs.

☐ **Decide how to best nurture your team**

What's one thing you can do to improve the relationships with your team members? If you don't have a team, how can you improve relationships with your suppliers or customers?

"The secret of getting ahead is getting started."

Mark Twain

CHAPTER NINE

Putting It All Together

In the first week of February 1999, we embarked on our family world trip. We packed only three backpacks for the four of us which included the kids' school books, one toy each, some basic clothes and a second-hand laptop so we could communicate with our team.

We flew across Australia, from Perth to Sydney, to spend a week with some friends before flying onto our first international destination, New Zealand (NZ). We had originally planned for David to do some farm work whilst we were travelling, but that was before he had smashed his index finger, so this was no longer an option. He was in so much pain that he was unable to handle any sort of manual labour, so instead, we moved to plan B and hired a motor home to live in whilst we travelled. It ticked all our boxes – we had transport, somewhere to sleep, and a clean, quiet table to do schoolwork with Eve and Hamish. Most weekdays, we spent the mornings doing the core school activities, which freed us up for full afternoons of play and adventure.

We spent a month travelling around the North Island, and another in the South Island. We were totally blown away by the beauty of New Zealand, with its spectacular glaziers and breath-taking mountains, alongside its rugged coastline. Nothing could have prepared us for its awe-inspiring scenery. We lived every day as if it was our last, waking up, reading our map and deciding which majestic spot we'd visit that day. We enjoyed quality time chatting with the kids as we travelled through the magical countryside. Each evening after the kids were asleep, David and I stayed up chatting, just the two of us, by the campfire under the moonlight. It was so nice to spend quality time with David and re-connect. Having no television or internet created the opportunity to have some deep soul-searching conversations; it truly was a treasured time for us all.

For the whole of our NZ adventure, we *free camped* at the most isolated, picturesque locations we could find each night. Our bed (which doubled as a table by day) was situated at the back of the van, which meant it had a massive window behind it. Each evening as we positioned the van, we made sure we woke up to a scene straight out of National Geographic Magazine[28] – a perfect start to our day. I frequently found myself caught in moments of wonder and even gasped at the sheer beauty of this country.

As a business owner, I will never forget the feeling of being free; it was exciting, fun and exhilarating. We were able to go anywhere and do anything we wanted, every single day. Our only deadline was getting to Auckland on the day our return flights were booked (and we could have changed that too, if we had wanted to). I'm sure our sense of freedom worked wonders on our nervous systems after the high degree of stress we had endured over the previous decade. The feeling of putting my feet up on the dashboard of the van with a map on my knees and the window down, was truly amazing. Eve and Hamish were a total delight, and made everything more enjoyable with their thirst for knowledge and eye for wonder.

At the same time, even though David was totally loving our adventure, with his throbbing finger and the constant reminder that I may die in only a few short years, he couldn't escape his addiction and still succumbed to the lure of alcohol. I had come to realise that no matter where we were or what we were doing, David's only escape from pain was to drink. It was hard to watch as he made one small step forward, followed by two steps back. I was also battling my own health challenges, so between us it wasn't all rainbows and sunshine. But we were determined to push past our issues and enjoy our time together, so we relished the beauty around us more than we dwelt upon the negatives.

Some of the highlights of New Zealand included experiencing luminescent glow worms twinkling in pitch-black caves, seeing living dinosaurs (Tuatara, which have been on Earth for 225 million years), and waking up to discover that one night we had camped right in the middle of a seal colony! We also loved getting to know the first nation Maori people and their incredible culture. We enjoyed their Hangi Feasts where they cooked food buried underground over hot coals, and the kids joined in their traditional dancing on stage.

Our next stop was the idyllic South Pacific islands of Fiji. For a treat, we stayed for a few days in a hotel which gave us a break from washing in rivers and digging holes to go to the toilet. It was absolute bliss. The people of Fiji were gentle, smiling, relaxed souls which made it a stark contrast to our next stop in Los Angeles (LA), where the people seemed to live at a frantic pace. Going to LA was the kids' one and only wish-list item of the trip; all they wanted was to see Disneyland. In just three days, we spent our whole monthly budget, but it was well worth it. We all had a ball. After LA, we flew straight up to Vancouver, Canada.

We had enjoyed our motor home so much in NZ that we decided to do something similar across Canada. David found a brown 1977, V8 Ford Chevy Van which the children named *The Bear*. It had four big swivel captain chairs, which not only spun around a table but reclined, too, and a couch at the back that converted into a double bed. Even though it was a total rust bucket, we all fell in love with it instantly. Every part of the interior was covered in either crushed velvet or shag-pile carpet. It had a least a dozen stereo speakers throughout, but no stereo system; it was the perfect hippy van.

On our first day on the road in Canada we saw snow, as well as a wild mother bear with her two cubs. It was love at first sight with the Canadian countryside. We spent the next few months driving leisurely across the country from west to east, spending time in libraries doing school work along the way. It was such a delight to experience The Rocky Mountains and glaciers, and the amazing variety of wildlife that the children had never seen before. We regularly saw bears, moose, elks, squirrels and many other unfamiliar creatures.

However, Canada was not so supportive of free camping, so we had to be a bit more creative in finding places to camp for the night. We didn't have a bathroom, toilet or stove, so we washed in rivers, toileted in the forests and collected firewood to make a little campfire each night to cook our dinner. I became an expert at making pancakes on the fire; flipping them up as high as I could always entertained the kids. David become the master at making what we called *Dad's Mush*, which the kids just loved. It could never be replicated, as it was basically everything he could find in the food box in the van, mixed together in a pot on the campfire.

As the van had only one double bed, which converted into a bench during the day, the kids slept there. David and I bought a second hand two-man tent that we pitched next to the back of the van, so we were not only close to the kids, but we also had some privacy. Wherever we were camped, I would try to get some exercise time alone, often going for an early morning walk or jog. Too often the pain in my abdomen reminded me that endometriosis was slowly taking over my insides. David's finger was also a constant source of pain, but we tried not to let these problems dampen our spirits.

One of my favourite encounters took place in Thunder Bay, where a local librarian fell in love with David and Eve. David had been teaching Eve to read in the children's section of the library, and the librarian was enchanted by Eve's golden blonde locks and five-year-old Aussie chatter with her daddy. Eve happily told the librarian all about our world adventure and, captured by her charm and whimsical nature, she invited our whole family back to her house for a hot meal, shower and to meet her husband.

Eve couldn't wait to tell Hamish and me, but David stubbornly said, "No way! We are not going to a stranger's house." The kids were disappointed as they loved meeting and chatting with new people.

Later that evening as we were leaving town, we experienced our first and only flat tyre in *The Bear*. The kids screamed with excitement shouting, "It's a sign! We should have gone to the librarian's house." We were on the outskirts of town with nowhere to go, so our choices were limited.

With a family vote, three to one, we slowly made our way to the lovely lady's home. When we arrived, we warily knocked on the door, but were welcomed with great excitement as the librarian screamed with glee when she opened the door and declared to her husband, "The Aussies are here."

Our hosts, Carolyn and Tom, were generous, warm people; they loved children but had never had any of their own. They were also small business owners of a bike shop and with Van Morrison playing in the background when we arrived, we instantly knew we had much in common.

The trust and kindness of Carolyn and Tom was overwhelming. We ended up staying with them for three nights. They spoiled us, fed us, and even entrusted us with their house keys and security alarm code! It was absolute heaven to sleep in a real bed and wash in a shower. They even loaned us their three-man tent for the remainder of our travels, which was wider and longer for my six foot body. Their kindness was heart-warming to say the least.

After three months of camping non-stop across Canada, we'd had enough of roughing it, so drove to New York City and booked ourselves into an apartment for a few days.

It was total euphoria! We had a two bedroom apartment all to ourselves. We jumped on the beds and danced in the shower with joy. It was even a novelty to light a flame on the stove with a click of a button and have toilets that flushed. The feeling of gratitude for such small things we normally took for granted was overwhelming. I will never forget the delightful sensation of the clean sheets on my skin after a shower and how happy I felt when I hopped into bed; no sand or mosquitos, no damp or dirty bedding. The crisp, dry feeling was incredible. We loved New York. It was just as it appeared in the movies and lived up to all our expectations. The saddest part of leaving, however, was saying goodbye to our much-loved Brown Chevy Van, *The Bear*.

Our next stop was London, staying with David's favourite auntie and uncle in Kent, where spoiling us was taken to a whole new level. Scotland followed, where we shared some special time with David's family in his hometown of Edinburgh. Then, it was off to Ireland to see some friends and explore more of the striking country.

Finally, we visited Paris, which was *my* must visit destination of the trip. Ever since we were married, David had promised to take me to Paris. Our budget didn't allow for much, but we still managed to stay together in a tiny hotel room overlooking the Eiffel Tower. I loved Paris; it was just as I'd imagined in my dreams, and we even saw the Mona Lisa at the Louvre.

By mid-August, we were all starting to miss home. We had planned to visit a few more countries, but decided it was time to head back to our life in Australia. As soon as we arrived back, David went to see the finger specialist to find out if he could help save his blackened and throbbing finger. He had done all he could in the nine months since the gym accident, trying desperately to keep it. He soaked it in antiseptic liquid multiple times a day, to stave off infection and encourage healing. I'll never forget the strong smell of the antiseptic that filled our motor home each day; it is one of the main sensory memories I have of our trip. Sadly, the surgeon took one look at David's finger and told him he had no other choice but to amputate. It was another tough blow.

Unfortunately, the disease which was killing me, one organ at a time, had also not given up. Despite already consuming my uterus, cervix, appendix, lower bowel and one and a half ovaries, the disease was still not finished with me. It had started making its way through my stomach and lungs. I was coughing up blood daily and often had bleeding from down below as well. My future was not looking too bright. I went on a never ending merry-go-round of alternative doctors and naturopaths in an attempt to conquer the disease. At the same time, my heart was breaking as I felt deep grief and turmoil at the thought of leaving our children without a mother and David without a wife.

Can Your Business Operate Without You?

When asked, "What is my greatest business achievement?" without a doubt I always answer, "When we took time away from our business to backpack around the world with our kids." David and I are forever grateful that our business afforded us the time and money to go on our trip to spend quality time with our children when we needed it most.

If you want a thriving business, it all starts with looking at the vehicle driving your business – *you* – and the systems that keep it all together. Ultimately, creating a business that works without you is about building an organised, systematised, measurable business which won't fall in a heap if you're not around. This level of order doesn't happen by accident; it takes vision, clarity, planning, strategies and action.

Occasionally, I have seen businesses start in the right place, at the right time, with the right product and they succeed with little effort or concern. However, later down the track their biggest challenge is they have no idea how to handle their business growth, or their people, and their business falls down like a house built of cards. The more systematised your business is, the easier it will be for your team to support the company's vision and the more attractive it will be for someone to buy it or take it over, if that's in your future plans.

Systematise

Systems are designed to *save you serious time, energy and money* (S.Y.S.T.E.M). In systemising your business, you are leveraging your knowledge and skills (and those of your team) *to do ever more with ever less*. If everything you do in your business is all in your head (or worse still, in someone else's), it is useless if you or that person are absent for any reason. Find a way to get the business knowledge, processes and procedures in your mind, and the minds of those on your team, out into documented systems which are easily accessible by others. As you work through each part of your business, you'll steadily feel as if a huge weight is being lifted from your shoulders. It will take so much unnecessary pressure off you by creating a solid structure to hold your business framework together instead of you attempting to do a never-ending juggling act where you are an indispensable part of your operation.

If you run your business like this, those juggling balls will invariably be dropped at a cost to you and your business. Remember, you're creating a way of systemising the routine tasks and activities of your business, but humanising the exceptions. Systemising your business as much as possible will result in fewer opportunities for your team to make their own assumptions with how they think things should be done. Instead, you will remove the guess work and ensure that all tasks are performed the same way each and every time.

I understand that the idea of creating systems may seem like a long and daunting project, but it's an investment of time and effort that you won't regret. However, the essential nature of systems becomes especially apparent when mistakes keep occurring in your company, when an employee quits and you need to train someone new, when your business is expanding or under pressure, or when you go on holiday and no one has a clue what they're doing without you. Not only will creating systems give you peace of mind, it will directly contribute to better profits by ensuring operations are being performed efficiently and consistently.

By documenting your knowledge and skills, you can start to trust the processes and in turn, trust your team to deliver the same high quality. If I had a dollar for every time a business owner said, "I just need to clone myself," I'd be a millionaire. Wouldn't it be wonderful for you to go on a holiday and know that everything will run just as well as if you were there? If you could feel confident that even in your absence, your customers would still be happy to deal with your team, and that your team will deliver the same great service as you do, wouldn't that be awesome?

Policies, Processes and Procedures

When you give it some thought, you will probably be able to identify where the gaps are in your systems and training. Which tasks are you repeatedly training your team to perform, that no matter how many times you show them, problems and errors still occur? Where are you losing money or respect from your customers? Also, look at the cost of inefficiencies in your business and which areas are leaking the largest proportions of your profits. These are the areas you could address first. Find out why the discrepancies are occurring; then ensure you create a suitable process to iron out the errors, so they don't continue to happen. The next area of systems to develop could be the items you use most often or those that have the biggest impact on your business.

As the business owner, it's important to take ownership of training your team correctly, with relevant, up-to-date and correct systems in place. You can't expect the same results and standards from different people if your policies, processes and procedures are either non-existent, non-compliant or ineffective.

The three Ps that form a system are:

1. Policies – A set of ideas or plans that is used as a basis for making decisions.[29]
2. Processes – A series of actions or steps taken in order to achieve a particular end.[30]
3. Procedures – A way of doing something, especially the usual or correct way.[31]

There are a number of steps to create a bullet-proof system. Start with a check-list or bullet points of the basic must-know steps, then build in all the finer detail. To ensure the process is the best it can be, it should be regularly tested, and relevant tweaks made to improve it. Here are seven steps to follow to make your systems as complete as possible.

1. Identify the rules – What are the constants and what are the variables? What compliance is needed?
2. Document the method – How will you carry out the tasks, step-by-step?
3. Map out, and write, the process – Who, what, where, when, why? What needs to be done at each point? What are the milestones?
4. Build in the procedures – Details, details, details!
5. Test and measure (assess and re-assess) your processes – Make sure they're helping you and your team to do their job in the best and most efficient way possible.
6. Make your systems scalable – Standardise your routine tasks and keep them simple!
7. Integrate your learning – Continue to work *on* your business and put aside time to build the systems you have; one by one.

Define the Rules

There may be policies and guidelines applicable to your industry or particular rules to which your organisation is obligated to adhere. Regulations need to be crystal clear to the team member following the process, to ensure that compliance is maintained. If you're an electrical company, you might need to fill in a certain electrical certificate after each job. The process ought to identify the industry standards and build in the relevant information to make sure that every electrical certificate is compliant. It may be a checklist that needs to be signed off, timing rules, or specific guidelines that need to be met before lodgement. These aspects will determine how fine-tuned each process is required to be documented. For example, the compliance of a brain surgeon will be different to that of a gardener.

Document the Method

Start by deciding the best way of documenting each process required, including any tools, guides or references that will make the process easy to follow. There are mapping diagrams available in computer programs such as Microsoft Word or Excel, plus other online programs, to help you create an org chart and process map. Think about how your team members following the process will be carrying it out. Will it be best for them to read the process in written format, or would it be easier to follow by watching a video, looking at pictures or listening to an audio? Perhaps it will be a combination of all of these.

Some third-party apps might also become part of a process. For example, if a process involves sending out bulk emails, a tool such as *Mailchimp* would be advantageous so that you're leveraging time by sending out multiple emails at once rather than hundreds of individual ones.

Map Out the Process

Each process shows a set of logically related tasks performed to achieve a defined outcome, setting out how the company or person following the process will translate the rules and policies into actions. When writing each process, there should be a list of sequential steps taking the reader through each task, listing what needs to be done. There are basic principles when mapping out processes, including a starting and ending point, a sequence of steps in between, as well as the consideration that there may be alternative steps needed, dependent on certain variables, decisions or parameters.

A process can be multi-faceted too, or split between more than one person. For example, the process of delivering a product to a customer may involve:

- Taking the order, in person, online, via phone, etc.
- Entering data and other various administrative work, including contracts, emails, invoicing, etc.
- A compliance aspect of the order, such as product check and matching the order against the products being delivered.
- Packing the order, which may involve another party.
- Delivering the product to the customer.

Importantly, for every process, there should be a means of identifying that the outcome has been satisfactorily achieved.

The task of mapping out which processes you need to document could be based around the key functional areas of your business, including the key performance indicators (KPIs) in each of them. It's important to have KPIs for each team member, the manager and the company overall, which relate back to the systems people have in their roles. For each functional area in the org chart, you can map out the list of systems you require, the frequency of each process and the priority order (what needs to be done first, and so on).

Once you identify the processes required, start writing a list of what is required to systemise, i.e. *Open a new order, Create an invoice, Train a new team member, Lodge a form online*, etc. The title for each system should be simple and easy-to-understand, so it's easy for the user to find when needed.

Create the Procedure

The more detail included, the easier a process will be to follow! Details add value. Feel free to use checklists, templates, maps or diagrams. One of the tools we use for creating systems and checklists is *Trello*. It's a free computer and phone app, especially helpful for writing *To Do* lists as well as processes that include procedures and checklists.

Your procedures are formed in the details of each part of the process. For example, one step in the process of '*How to save a document*' might be to, '*Save document in the 'Z' drive*', but there will need to be details accompanying that statement to explain how this is done. That's where the procedure comes in, as it articulates the method of how to carry out each step of a process, as shown below:

1. *Click on File* on the top left-hand side of the screen
2. Click on *Save As*
3. Find the 'Z' drive icon on the left-hand side of the pop-up box
4. Re-name your document with the current date at the start of the document title (YY-MM-DD format)
5. Click on *Save*

Once a process is created, make sure it can be easily accessed by everyone who needs it. It might be appropriate to save in a cloud-based system, internal system or server, or in a client management system. Wherever you decide to store your processes, make sure everyone knows where they are; there's no point in creating systems if your team can't find them!

Assess Regularly

Last but not least, make sure your processes are regularly assessed to ensure there are no faults to correct or improvements required. Aspects of business change over time and you may find that you can make small, ongoing tweaks to improve your systems. It's wise to have someone within each key functional area of your company responsible for assessing their relevant processes on a regular basis, to ensure they are still serving the desired outcome as efficiently as possible.

One particular client, Josh, came to me worried as he and his team were always flat-out with work and good at what they did, but weren't seeing the results on their bottom line.

"If I'm busy all the time, why is my bank balance going down every month? What am I doing wrong?" asked Josh.

Concerned about potential discrepancies in his accounting system, I asked him to pick three random quotes that he had given out for jobs, match them with the time sheets and then, compare the time sheets and quotes to the paid invoice for each. With the task completed, Josh looked like he had seen a ghost! He realised he was making a loss on every single job because he was under-quoting and not telling the team how many hours he had allocated for the job. On top of that, often jobs had variations along the way which weren't being added onto the quote or invoice, so each job was costing them more than they were making.

For any service business, it is essential to align each part of a quote with work completed along the way. It's wonderful now with cloud-based accounting systems and electronic live banking that your sales team can even have an app on their phone to provide a quote on the spot. This quote can then turn into an invoice and be linked to purchase orders for stock, labour and more. It makes it so much easier to track the profitability of each job. Once the job is complete, you can take payment with a credit card or online system, which can be reconciled to the invoice with one click of a button.

Scale Your Systems

Your company should always be striving to deliver high customer service with consistent results, and this is where systems become a valuable asset in your business. If you invest the time in systemising routine tasks for your team to adhere to, it will create substantial returns in the long run. There are so many seamless systems available, many specific to various industries. My recommendation, when choosing yours, is to make sure there are as few processes as possible, to keep it simple.

If each system is scalable, then as your business grows, your systems will still be able to deliver. Your systems then become an asset to your organisation, where knowledge is documented and accessible not only to your current team, but also to any future team members. Don't store the knowledge away in your brain and do nothing about it or before you know it, the great ideas will disappear. Looking at the functional areas of your business, you can break up your systems and procedures depending on the people you have in your team.

Diagram 9.1 shows the internal and external areas of a business as they relate to sales, starting from lead generation through to the sale and the profits made.

Functional Areas Of Business

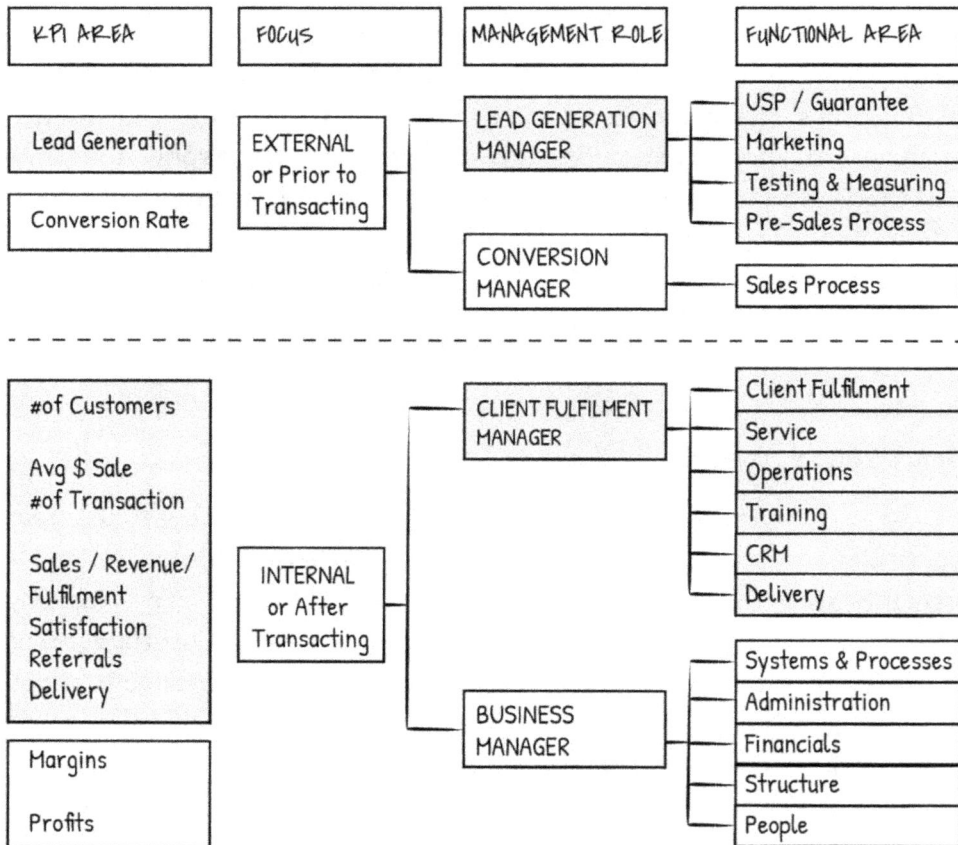

KPI AREA	FOCUS	MANAGEMENT ROLE	FUNCTIONAL AREA

External or Prior to Transacting:

KPI AREA	FOCUS	MANAGEMENT ROLE	FUNCTIONAL AREA
Lead Generation	EXTERNAL or Prior to Transacting	LEAD GENERATION MANAGER	USP / Guarantee
			Marketing
			Testing & Measuring
Conversion Rate			Pre-Sales Process
		CONVERSION MANAGER	Sales Process

Internal or After Transacting:

KPI AREA	FOCUS	MANAGEMENT ROLE	FUNCTIONAL AREA
#of Customers	INTERNAL or After Transacting	CLIENT FULFILMENT MANAGER	Client Fulfilment
			Service
Avg $ Sale #of Transaction			Operations
			Training
Sales / Revenue/ Fulfilment Satisfaction Referrals Delivery			CRM
			Delivery
		BUSINESS MANAGER	Systems & Processes
			Administration
Margins			Financials
			Structure
Profits			People

Diagram 9.1

Relating it Back to Your Business

If you are intending to build a house, how much planning would you put into it before you spent a cent? How many different pictures and versions of the finished product would you review before you started construction? Think about it. Would you build a house without a plan? No. Without a plan, your house wouldn't be safe enough to live in, you wouldn't get a full picture of all the details and you'd have no clue what to expect of the final product. You definitely wouldn't get bank finance. You would never just *wing it* and see how it goes, or you might end up with only half a house. That's insane, isn't it? Imagine not having a budget for how much you could spend or a break-down of all the costs involved. I'm sure you wouldn't be surprised at how quickly it could add up and blow your budget out of the water.

Believe it or not, after speaking with thousands of business owners over the last few decades, I'd say that 95% of them don't have an up-to-date plan or budget, and most have never written a business plan at all. If you're one of these business owners, does this not seem absurd to you? To me, it's as silly as driving a car with your eyes closed. You are just heading for a crash. Maybe that is why so many people fail in their business.

Creating a comprehensive business plan is about pulling out all the critical thinking and knowledge from a business owner's head and delving into the little nooks and crannies to find hidden gems of gold. The process is where the learning comes from, and integrating that learning to see how the success unfolds, is key. It's the *process* of planning that is crucial, not the printed document that's produced at the end. Like anything in life, if you've got a plan, but aren't doing anything with it, you won't see the results.

You might now be thinking, "There is so much to do; where do I start?" The answer is to take things one step at a time. Start with asking yourself all the 'who, what, when, where, why and how' questions. Write things down, brainstorm with as many of your team as possible, and importantly, keep in mind that you must act in order to turn your dreams into reality. Remember, you are the vehicle who is driving your business to success and your team is the engine. So, having time to work with them is essential for trust, communication and transparency. If this time is not mapped out in your calendar, it is unlikely it will get done. Similarly, if it is not in a job description, or it's not clear who is responsible for a duty, it won't get done.

Booking regular time in your calendar each week, month, quarter and year will allow adequate time for you, or whichever team member is accountable for that area, to work pro-actively on the development of your business. Make sure this time is kept sacred, or you'll find more often than not that these sessions are postponed due to urgent or unexpected events that crop up in your business. All of a sudden, you're six months down the track with little or no progress made, and you'll let yourself down or break promises with yourself or your team members.

When we left Jenny in charge of our business when we went on our world trip, the team had full clarity of what was expected – by us and our clients – through each functional area of the business, from taking the order through to delivery, invoicing and taking payment. Little did we know that this would be a huge asset further down the track when we decided to sell the business.

Jarrod

Jarrod said his sales process was systemised and very clear within his team. He was also pretty confident about the procedures he had in place for his business. To put that theory to the test, I asked him if I received a quote from each of his team members, would they be exactly the same. "Of course," Jarrod said. He was confident that his team had a template for quoting, price calculators and agreed timelines to get them out.

"Fabulous," I said. "Let's try it out and see if we can improve it."

We used a strategy that I call *mystery shopping for your own business* which tests aspects in your business without your team knowing. I asked some friends to get quotes from Jarrod's business and asked three different people in his team to quote on the same product and same quantity. The result? I'm sure you can guess. We got back three completely different quotes for the same product, all in totally different formats in varied time frames and for different amounts. One quote came through the same day, one three days later and the other a week later.

Jarrod got a stark reality check, but it was a wonderful insight and opportunity for him to work with his team to improve. All five of us sat down (Jarrod, his three team members and me) and spent an hour going through the quotes and getting super clear on what we all agreed was the best way to go forward. In this way, they would all be producing a quote in the same format and for the same price, within the same time frame.

It's a good idea to review your current systems with your team, to make sure the interpretation of each system is flawless. If there are inconsistencies in your processes, or customer service standards, then you'll need to tweak your systems to improve your efficiency and consistency across the board.

Chapter 9
Blue Ocean Thinking

☐ **Create effective systems**

Carry out a full audit of where your system gaps fall, and decide which ones to work on first.

☐ **What are the functional areas of your business?**

Who is responsible for carrying out each process in your business? How can your processes and procedures be tweaked to achieve better results?

☐ **Diarise and map out your actions**

Set aside regular time to work ON your business, and with your team, instead of just IN it.

"Your health
is your real
wealth."

Mahatma Gandhi

CHAPTER TEN

Honour Your Temple

One night in June 2000, David and I went to a friend's fancy dress birthday party. Everyone was having so much fun, dancing and partying the night away. I remember feeling a veil of sadness descend over me. The next day I was due for surgery to remove the last remaining half of my ovary. Following this, I was to commence a heavy drug program which was the doctor's final hope of ridding my body of the endometriosis that was still taking over inside of me. My heart felt so filled with despair that I drank three-quarters of a bottle of gin in two hours. I had never consumed that much alcohol in one night before in my life, but I was close to rock bottom.

The following day I was admitted to hospital with the hangover from hell. My operation was then delayed twenty four hours, so I had a day and a half to ponder my thoughts in my hospital room, where I felt so very alone. My worst fears arose in my mind, and escalated as I worked myself into a state of panic. It was horrible. I sat alone praying and worrying for hours on end. I was concerned about what else they might find wrong with me when they opened me up. If my track record was anything to go by, maybe I'd wake up with a poo bag attached to me again and have to face the shock of finding out, 'Surprise! The bag lady is back!'

I wondered if taking the remaining part of my ovary would even stop the endometriosis. Perhaps the disease would just continue to destroy the rest of my vital organs, eating my kidneys or liver next? I knew it was already in my lungs because of the blood I was coughing up each day. I was also well aware of the excruciating pain experienced after surgery and wanted to avoid it at all costs. Once again, silent tears rolled down my cheeks as I was wheeled into surgery on the cold, hard, silver trolley to the operating theatre.

The last thing I remember was hearing, "3...2...1," and then – the void! It's such a weird feeling having a general anaesthetic; I hate it.

I woke in pain, and to the beeping of machines. A nurse was seated by my side and I prepared for more bad news. However, to my surprise, I was told that my procedure had actually gone as planned, with no unexpected hiccups. The surgeon had successfully removed the remaining part of my ovary, plus a few cysts. He also repaired some additional internal damage and inserted a Hormone Replacement Therapy (HRT) implant. The HRT would hopefully give me just the right amount of estrogen to keep me *female*, but not enough to feed the endometriosis. Once again, I had a cut from my belly button right down to my pubic bone, held together with a shiny line of stainless steel staples.

Despite the surgery being successful, my fight with the dreadful disease was not completely over. My doctor explained that to give me the best chances of beating the illness, there was one last drug I could try. However, I was told that it was a strong medication with potential side effects such as weight gain and depression, to name just a couple. But that didn't matter; I was already suffering and if this could help me beat the disease, even with the side effects, it would be a better outcome than dying. I was determined to get through this final challenge. After all, I only had four years (of the initial five-year life sentence) left, kindly predicted by my lovely oncologist; and I'd do everything in my power to give me more time.

I decided that in order to conquer the disease, I needed to change every negative that was under my control, into a positive. I decided that I was going to get up early every morning to meditate and exercise. I needed to get back into the best shape possible. I started walking around the oval again in front of our house every day, then worked my way up to slowly jogging. I read only positive, motivating books and listened to things that inspired me.

By the end of 2000, I was ready to slowly return to the triathlon community. These people were a group of positive, encouraging individuals who made me feel loved, accepted and motivated to just *give it a go*. I went back to competing in small events, with the sole goal of just finishing, nothing else. The drugs seemed to be working and the bleeding and pain had stopped. I wasn't depressed and had not put on any weight, as predicted. I was doing everything I could to combat the side effects of the drugs, by exercising each morning with an amazing bunch of people and taking care of my mental health through meditation and positive affirmations. I think my efforts counteracted both side effects; I certainly benefitted from them anyway.

After 12 months of gradually getting my strength back and increasing my fitness, I was ecstatic to win the Novice Triathlon Series for my age group. It was great to be involved again and to feel better within myself only one year after my surgery. Even better, I had also finished the course of drugs and the disease hadn't reared its ugly head again. At last, there was now a small glimmer of hope that wasn't there before. I no longer felt the constant gnawing, throbbing abdominal pain in my body and without wanting to tempt fate, started to believe that I might actually be free of the disease – finally!

I kept visioning a long life of health and wellbeing, with the endometriosis gone forever, and trusting I was doing everything in my power to fight my illness.

By the time I was two years into my five-year life sentence, at the age of 35, I was stronger and healthier than I had ever been in my life.

The same year, David had a revelation. He had caught a glimpse of his reflection in the mirror one day and was not happy with what he saw, declaring, "I don't want to be a fat bastard anymore." This was a conscious decision on his behalf, one which he clearly remembers to this day, and it motivated him to start seeing a personal trainer as well as begin a strict fat fasting diet.

Within a few months, he dropped a sizeable amount of weight, and over time went from a large 118kg to a slim 80kg frame. I was very proud of him.

In June 2002, a fellow triathlon friend launched a *Try a Triathlon* event, as part of a study she was doing at university. However, as the date approached, registration numbers were still very low, and she was worried about covering the event's costs. To help out, our triathlon club got behind her and encouraged as many people as possible to get involved. Being the good club member that I was, I managed to convince David, Eve, Hamish, a couple of his mates, and even Jenny from work, to have a go and enter the event. This was the first full triathlon David or Eve had ever tried.

To his great surprise and satisfaction, David achieved his goal of finishing the event. I don't think he ever imagined that he could do it; this newfound confidence was the beginning of a new chapter for David.

I knew he had officially caught the triathlon bug when he mentioned, "If I could do that, I might even be able to enter the novice races next year." He also thought that having this goal would help keep him off the booze, increase his fitness and give him the chance to spend more time with me. David had never really swum or ran in his life and found it quite an exciting challenge.

Much to my delight, he started to spend more time with me and the triathlon community. These people were different from the friends David was used to hanging out with, which is what he needed to ensure his efforts were not wasted. They weren't all about partying; they were simply focused on being the best versions of themselves they could be, having a laugh and supporting their mates.

David soon became loved and accepted by all in the triathlon community. Once seen as a part-time, overweight, wanna-be fossil novice, he was becoming the true essence of an athlete. He grew stronger, leaner and was an inspiration for many. The first person to put a hand out to help David was a man competing in Ironman races, who only had one arm; he'd lost his other one in a motorcycle accident a few years earlier. He knew all about facing challenges and was not interested in any of David's excuses about being too old, too unfit or burnt. David's new friend mentored him to complete his first full marathon, for which he will always be grateful.

It totally blew me away when David completed this event by running a 42.2 km hilly course at Rottnest Island. I had tears in my eyes as I watched him cross the line. It was a wonderful feeling to see him achieve such an incredible feat. My beautiful husband had come such a long way.

David continued being part of the triathlon community and ended up getting a place in the Novice Series the following year. He loved the way they respected him, exactly the way he was. He was not judged on how fast or slow he was or because he had started this as a new sport in his mid-40s. Instead, he was encouraged, supported and appreciated for giving it a go. He even inspired many others to join in along the way.

Two years after the surgery to remove the last of my endometriosis, followed by the drug regime that turned things around, I was still unexpectedly free of the disease. Doctors were dumbfounded, but now somewhat confident that I had beaten the illness which they predicted would kill me. Of course, there was no certainty it wouldn't return, but my specialists were blown away with my health and fitness after battling an aggressive disease that was quite literally eating up my insides. It was a miracle, in their view, but I knew a lot of it came down to how hard I had worked on keeping my body and mind in peak condition.

However, as both my and David's health blossomed, our business started to struggle. We were under pressure because some of the big chain stores had begun to sell the same products as us at greatly reduced prices. We couldn't compete, our margins were getting smaller, we found ourselves in debt and weren't sure what to do next. We tried many new initiatives, but nothing returned us to our former position. As a result, David began to lose the love and drive for the business he had when we started.

My gut told me it was time to sell before David had a heart attack or a stroke from the pressure he was putting on himself. The loss of passion and stress was definitely not good for his health and with my dad's early death always in the back of my mind, I knew what we had to do. After much thought and deliberation, we put the business on the market and began to think about what on earth we'd do after we sold it.

In June 2003, we sold our business to one of our previous employee's parents. In spite of the challenges we were experiencing, it was still a good, solid business. Additionally, the new owners had the drive, determination and passion that we had lost, so we were excited to hand it over to the right buyers. Luckily, because of my dad's sound advice, we also had the building to sell, as well as a fully systemised business. We found a separate buyer for our premises; fortunately, the property had increased in value.

So, despite us having some business debt, we were able to come out debt free and with money in hand. Jenny was quickly offered a position by one of our clients and the rest of the team stayed with the business.

Once the business and property were no longer ours, it was time to re-invent ourselves. No longer on the brink of death, I now had new opportunities ahead of me, so I was determined to make the most of my *second chance* at life.

David and I were both a little nervous about what lay ahead, but the sense of relief was huge. Even though we had no idea of what we were going to do at that point, we knew we didn't want to start up a small business again or buy an established business or apply for a job. Even though we were still in limbo in a professional sense, we threw ourselves into our sport and focused on those dreams.

However, it would soon be time to set a new vision and create a fresh plan for our future.

Looking After Yourself

When you take a step back from your business and look deeper into your personal being, your core self, the essence of what makes you, *you*, what do you see? Your body and mind play a major part in being fit for business, giving you the energy and focus you need to get up every day feeling inspired and empowered. Being fit for business is crucial to being successful. You will earn more income and respect when your vehicle – your body and mind – is healthy. To assess where you are at with this, ask yourself the following:

- What is your quality of life like?
- How much effort, energy and thought do you put into yourself?
- How much time and energy do you focus on caring for *you*, compared to your business?
- Do you have the energy to work during the day and afterwards perhaps go to the beach, take the dog to the park, play with the kids and make a healthy nutritious dinner?

Too often, business owners tell me they have no quality of life. They complain that their business runs their life and they have much conflict between maintaining a healthy business and personal life. It's heartbreaking to see that their business is taking away from their quality of life, instead of giving them the freedom to enjoy it.

Your business and career can make you happy and support your life. If this is not the case for you, what can you do to change the situation? If you are the vehicle to creating your life-long dreams, what are you doing to keep yourself in peak condition? Your vehicle is made up of your mind, body and soul, and it's critically important to fuel each element with the things it needs to run at peak performance. Finding the true essence of your being may not be an easy task, but the rewards will last a lifetime.

You Have a Choice

Most people can identify what is important to them. They want to run a profitable business, be successful in their chosen career and feel balanced by spending adequate time in their business, as well as quality time at home, relaxing with their family and friends (not to mention, having the time to exercise and eat well). Few people have mastered this balance, often due to a lack of energy needed to sustain them through their days.

If you're not making headway with your business and creating wealth for your future, is the time you spend in your business worth the sacrifice of losing time with your family and time to do other things you love? It's certainly not worth the detriment of *losing yourself* or having a decline in your health. Plus, it doesn't have to be this way.

If your business isn't truly supporting your life, you have the power to change this reality. Remembering, your brain and body drive the vehicle of your life. Your brain is like the mainframe computer of your business, so wouldn't it be a good idea for you to support it by giving it the time it requires to perform optimally? Imagine driving a car for 30 years and never giving it down time, never servicing it and continually filling it with poor fuel. Would you still expect it to perform optimally? It's the same with your mind; making time each day for yourself to unwind and re-focus is going to hugely benefit you long-term.

Meditation

The benefits of meditation on brain function and overall mental and physical wellbeing, have been researched and documented for decades. Meditation is free, available to anyone and can be done anywhere at any time. It is definitely one of the most life changing and beneficial practices I have learnt and it certainly helped to take David's and my relationship to a new level. Think about how you would feel if you were regularly able to sit quietly for just five minutes, and come out of that experience with a renewed sense of calm and clarity. Imagine how that would be amplified if you did that for 20 minutes, every single day? Repeated efforts create compounding results.

You may be thinking, "I don't have time for that." I thought the same, until I tried it. Through meditation, I find I actually create more valuable time in my day because I am clearer and more focused with what I am doing. Therefore, my time is more efficient, and I have increased energy to get me through my day.

When David was burnt, he was at his wit's end and suffering with inconsolable pain. He had done just about everything he could do to help relieve some of the physical and mental discomfort he was experiencing. The pain from the burns and skin donor sites was excruciating, which basically left no part of his body that was not wounded. He had lost all sense of self. In an attempt to relieve some of this pain, David was encouraged to try transcendental meditation (TM). To support him, I decided to learn meditation too and we started practising it as a couple to collectively overcome our pain and fears. The results were astounding, to say the least, and we both came to realise the powerful effects that the mind can have on the physical body. The benefits were endless, and the practice supported our whole wellbeing.

Because of this, we have now both been practising meditation daily for over 30 years. Whenever we can, David and I try to meditate together, as it creates a wonderful closeness to be able to sit next to each other in total silence for 20 minutes. No words need to be said; we can feel the love and energy settling.

Sometimes, if we have a few minutes afterwards, we chat about the meditation. Many times, one of us will say, "It seemed like just a few minutes," where the other might say, "My mind couldn't stop." One thing that remains the same is the close connection we create when we meditate together. It is always different, but it's a practice which provides great benefits over time.

If you have never tried meditating, I would urge you to give it a go. All you need is five or ten minutes per day, working up to twice daily if possible. Meditation will provide you with quiet, clean, clear space to *just be*. There are many resources available online to help you learn the fundamentals of the practice (I personally use the 'Insight Meditation' app). In essence, meditation is about giving yourself the time to calm your racing thoughts, reflect and be still.

I remember back in 2010 experiencing a tour of an amazing company called Zappos, in Las Vegas. Even then, they had a meditation room for their team at their offices because they recognised how much it positively impacted clarity of mind and focus. It was filled with pillows, bean bags, and was sound-proofed. Everyone was encouraged to go in there as many times as they needed throughout the day, to re-focus and shift their mindset. Some people dotted their day with a few five minute meditations after intense periods of productivity, while others were more suited to one or two longer meditations. The system was based on trust and respect, and people understanding the benefits. It was openly agreed and appreciated, by both the business owners and the team, that the meditation sessions assisted with productivity and creativity.

Another powerful story about the positive impact of meditation is told in Michael Singer's book, *"The Surrender Experiment."*[32] He explains how he was asked to teach a regular meditation class to a group of hard-nosed criminals in a prison; the results were astounding. In fact, the reoffending rate of his students was close to non-existent. There was a significant decrease in aggression, so much so that many other prisons have introduced meditation groups too.

Imagine how you could use the power of meditation to work for you.

Creating the Right Recipe for You

Other ways to support your mental health and brain function are through better sleep, regular exercise, good nutrition and learning new skills and information. You may be thinking, "I have heard this all before." However, if this is the case, what are you doing about it? It's important to regularly check in and see where improvements can be made. Don't ever stop making improvements in your life. To learn is to grow, and to grow is to better yourself and your life.

A great place to start is by assessing all areas of your life and determining where you are at *now*. For example, are you getting enough of the things that increase your energy and that are fulfilling in your life? What is it that helps you to be the best version of yourself? Think about:

- What makes you feel amazing and ready to take on the world?
- Did you have a good night's sleep?
- Did you eat well?
- Did you start the day with a swim in the ocean and meditation?
- Did you spend time with inspiring people or read uplifting books?

You probably know from experience what creates energy and positive days, and what doesn't, so how are you using this information?

What Doesn't Serve You

Can you identify which toxins or bad habits in your life, those that undermine your progress, you could eliminate? What causes you to feel unmotivated and low in spirit, with no energy? These may be negative thoughts from poor relationships or social media, or maybe you're feeding yourself actual toxins such as alcohol, tobacco or processed foods? By asking yourself these questions, you can find the right recipe for your life and create the rules that make you feel and perform at your best.

Think about what you do each day and ask yourself if it contributes to your life in a positive way? Does it make you happy or serve a constructive purpose? If not, stop doing it! Creating the perfect recipe and rules of your own life are about supporting a whole-hearted, happy and healthy *you*.

Your Identity

An audit of your identity is a great way to assess how you can achieve better results, especially if you keep trying new things but keep getting the same results. Anthropologist Edward T. Hall developed a model known as the *Iceberg Model of Culture*, which compares the appearance of an iceberg to human culture. Where only 10% of an iceberg is shown *above the water*; this is comparable to culture in that only actions, decisions and behaviours can be observed by others. The remaining 90% of the iceberg is hidden *below the surface* which, in comparison to cultural observations, represents the complex human aspects that we possess inside (our skills, beliefs, values and identity).

Your success – or the results you achieve in your life and your business – are created through your actions, decisions and behaviours. However, what you see above the water, only represents around 10% of your identity. If you look deeper, you can reach the areas under the surface that will impact what you do and how you act.

Diagram 10.1 shows the theory of Hall's cultural iceberg model.

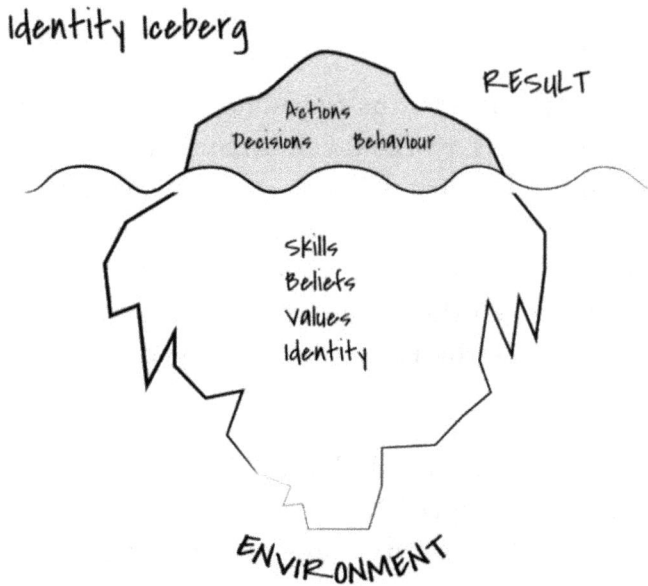

Identity Iceberg

RESULT

Actions
Decisions   Behaviour

Skills
Beliefs
Values
Identity

ENVIRONMENT

Diagram 10.1

Looking below the surface of your identity, what skills do you possess? What are you good at? We naturally do more of what we're good at and resist what we're not good at. So, as you continue to get better at things that you're good at by doing more of them, you avoid improving your skills in the areas which can improve your results. So, in order to alter your results, it's a good idea to increase your knowledge and skills.

Your beliefs impact your skills, which inevitably impact your actions, decisions and behaviours. Your beliefs are things that you hold to be true. However, they may not necessarily *be true*. If you believe you're a good mathematician, you might pursue a degree and career in line with this skill. On the other hand, if you believe that you're no good at maths, you will become resistant to developing that skill and avoid situations where you have to use that skill.

Your values shape your beliefs, so being clear on your values will help with your beliefs, which will impact every decision you make, and every action and behaviour you display. I recall having conflict in my values as a Mum and a business owner – not sure if I should be at work running my business or at my child's assembly. When I got clear that, for me, family always comes first, it made my beliefs stronger and my decisions easier to make.

When you look at your identity, it's about looking at who you are as an individual. Your identity is defined by everything you consider that you are. Brad Sugars, founder of ActionCOACH, sums it up well, "It's what you say to yourself, about yourself, when you're by yourself that matters the most." It's quite a confronting thought. If you are regularly having a conversation with yourself with limiting thoughts such as, "I don't have enough money" or "I'm unsuccessful" or "I'm fat", how do you think that impacts your values, beliefs, skills, actions, decisions and behaviours over time?

A powerful exercise is to write down a list of *I am* statements, finishing off each sentence as you try to define who you are. You may end up with something like:

- I am a mum/dad
- I am a business owner
- I am an accountant
- I am a good cook, etc.

Expanding on those statements, how can you adapt them to empower your values and beliefs? Try writing down some more statements along the lines of:

- I am kind
- I am passionate
- I am not judgemental of others
- I am resilient
- I am intelligent and capable

Speaking to yourself with positive self-love will go a long way towards changing your results.

The water around your identity iceberg ultimately impacts what's on the inside. Your identity is shaped by your environment every day, such as where you live, your culture and how your parents raised you. Later in life, you are influenced by where you work, the people you spend time with, the TV programs you watch, the books you read and the relationships you have in your life. If you choose to live and work in an inspiring environment, where learning, growth and prosperity are encouraged, that will positively impact your identity. Everything in your environment feeds your identity and helps to create the person you become.

If you want better results, look at your environment and the weak points or gaps under the surface first, then decide which ones you need to work on and what needs to happen to change them. It may be changing from negative to positive self-talk, or decluttering your office to make your environment clear or having a think about your top values in life. It's up to you.

The Company You Keep

If the company you keep is negative and drowns your creative self, your hard work will be undone. If you hang out in a negative environment, or with toxic friends, what do you think that does to your identity? Surrounding yourself with happy, positive people goes a long way towards helping you to maintain your sense of belonging and pushing you to continue striving to be your best. It is said that every person is the sum of the five closest people to them, so make sure you choose wisely the people with whom you associate.

The people in your life come in many forms, from your friends, family and neighbours, to your trusted business associates and colleagues, and even those you meet through a sporting club or other social networks. When you have the endearing support of others, it goes a great way to maintaining your positive mental health and your direction in life. Consider whether you have a good tribe of people who support you in your business and in your life? Do your friends and peers hold similar values to you? Do they support you and your pursuits? Whatever you do, keep away from people who bring you down.

Getting Enough Sleep

Another negative habit that many people fall into, is not getting enough sleep. When I researched the recommended hours of sleep a healthy adult should get each night, studies suggested that one in three were not getting enough sleep. Are you getting the recommended seven to eight hours of sleep per night? Do you go to sleep easily, and do you sleep soundly through to the morning? There are any number of techniques to improve the quality and quantity of your sleep. These will, in turn, generate a notable difference in your quality of mind and efficiency throughout the day to support you in your business, relationships and life. I know that I function much better when I've had a great night's sleep, as I'm sure is the case with most people. I am more alert, more energetic, less grumpy, more open-minded and have greater potential to achieve more in my day.

If you are thinking, "I'm just not a good sleeper. I've tried everything; there is nothing more I can do," don't give up. Keep researching and trying new methods until you regularly get an awesome night's sleep, every night. Trust me, I have experienced sleepless nights and used to take a long time to get to sleep. Some of the practices which helped me are:

- Getting up early at the same time every day.
- Exercising early so I'm super tired and ready for sleep by bedtime.
- Limiting screen time at least 30 minutes before bed (or, better still, not using TV, phone or devices for one to two hours before bed).
- Not consuming food, especially anything sweet, for a couple of hours before bed.
- Having a soothing herbal tea before bed, instead of that piece of chocolate.
- Reducing or avoiding alcohol as it can act as a stimulant and keep you awake, and when you do finally sleep, it won't be good quality deep sleep.
- Investing in a great pillow; one of those expensive, weird, contoured ones that chiropractors recommend.

- Having a good, firm mattress to support your back. If your mattress is 20 years old, it might be time to get a new one!

- Using block out curtains, to keep the room nice and dark.

- Removing electronic devices from the bedroom. There have been many studies showing that the electro-magnetic fields (EMF), emitted by mobile phones and the like, stimulate brain activity (some people are more sensitive than others).

- Using an old-fashioned alarm clock instead; Try putting your mobile phone in the next room to see if it makes a difference.

Don't underestimate the power that a great night's sleep provides. Sleeping is an essential fuel; it gives you access to being the most amazing *you* possible. If you are still not convinced to make sleep one of your secret ingredients to being your best self, I have been told that you lose weight when you sleep! Another great reason to nail it!

Never Stop Learning

Learning new skills and fields of study is another way for you to support your brain to perform at a higher level. Our brain is like a muscle – if we don't use it, we lose it. Michael Mosley produced a great documentary on the brain explaining how amazing things can be achieved with our brain when we put our mind to it.[33] It's definitely worth a watch. If you take extra special care of your brain, it's possible to improve your overall function and capacity.

I always encourage everyone to strive to learn new things. It not only helps to develop brain function but ultimately it will increase your chances of success. The more you know, the more you can put into practice. Our brain has millions of neural pathways that help us to learn throughout our lives, so it's important to feed those neurons and always challenge the brain to grow.

There is also evidence supporting the idea that learning to play a musical instrument benefits cognitive development and health. I had always wanted to learn to play the piano, so decided to take up classical piano lessons in my forties. Music doesn't come naturally to me, but I enjoy practising. I find it beneficial, as I have to concentrate on all the various aspects such as tempo, speed and the notes I'm playing. Because I never learnt music as a child, playing piano still remains a challenge for me, but I can feel my brain having a work-out each lesson. In fact, after a one-hour session, I feel amazing (much like a workout at the gym)! I feel happy, clear in the mind, focused and feel a sense of achievement. I just love it.

If we stop working on developing our brain, it will slowly start to deteriorate. What new areas could you learn or read about to support *your* brain function?

I think it is a great idea to base your learning and reading around your goals, then you are motivated for a purpose. However, these don't have to be focused on your business. They can be whatever it is that interests you. In fact, combining creative as well as logical learnings will further develop both sides of your brain. The right side is associated with creativity, emotion and intuition, whilst the left side is associated with logic, such as in science and mathematics.

Consuming Alcohol

In my early years with David, we would often drink alcohol with every evening meal. However, since I have been working on creating the best recipe for me, I now aim to have a minimum of four alcohol free nights per week. In relation to the brain, studies seem to have bad news for even moderate drinkers, indicating that even low-level alcohol consumption is associated with shrinking areas of the brain involved in cognition and learning. From experience, I can feel a huge difference in myself the next day when I have avoided alcohol the night before.

After seeing the effects that alcohol has had on many people in my life over the decades, including David, I would strongly recommend for every entrepreneur or business owner to steer clear of alcohol or limit their intake considerably. Your brain, body and the people with whom you share your life, will love, respect and understand you more for it.

Only recently, I sadly endured the loss of my sister-in-law of thirty years, who 'just had *a few wines* every day.' Her alcoholism wasn't extreme or obvious, and she still managed to function as a school music teacher. To the outside world, it appeared she was functioning fine, but over time, those close to her noticed her inability to go a day without drinking, and it became a concern. Eventually, after years of regular alcohol consumption, her liver started failing, which quickly resulted in total organ failure. Only four weeks after her diagnosis of liver failure, her illness took over and she passed away at age 55, leaving her husband and two young daughters grief-stricken. Alcohol is a powerful drug; its impact on our health is, in my opinion, heavily understated.

Exercise

While we're focusing on ways to improve our brain, it's significant to understand the connection between the brain and body. Exercise directly supports brain development and positive mental health by providing natural endorphins and igniting energy. Dr Wendy Suzuki, who has extensively studied the effects of exercise on the brain, says in her TED talk, "Simply moving your body has immediate, long-lasting and protective benefits for your brain." She goes on to say that exercise is, "critical for things like decision-making, focus, attention and your personality," and that it actually "changes the brain's anatomy, physiology and function."[34]

If you're working on your mind alone, this is just one half of the equation to keeping it healthy. We are all suited to different types of exercise, but if you want to improve your overall quality of life, please consider including whatever exercise you can as part of your daily routine. It is sure to have profound effects, both short and long term.

Maybe you're not a runner and that's fine. Take regular short walks, instead. Perhaps you can't do high impact training (HIT), but might enjoy body balance, pilates or yoga? Maybe lifting weights isn't your thing, but there are many free home workouts you can do without any weights or machines. The focus is just to get your body moving (however able it is), concentrating on the three areas of physical health:

1. Strength – Developing your muscles, to protect bone health and muscle mass.
2. Cardio – Raising your heart rate, for cardiovascular health.
3. Flexibility – Keeping your joints and body agile, for greater mobility.

If you think you don't have time to exercise, I assure you everyone can find time. Getting up a little earlier every morning will at first be hard, but it won't take your body long to adjust and you'll be forever thankful you made the change. Many times, I've heard people say, "But I'm just not a morning person." Trust me, I was the same, until one day I came home from a trip in the Eastern States which resulted in me experiencing a three-hour time zone difference. This meant I was wide awake at 5.00am! So, I decided to get up and go for a gentle walk. I was met with happy, smiling, "Good morning" greetings from other morning people. I couldn't stop thinking, "Ahh, this is what all those exercising, morning people talk about." At the same time, I got to watch the sun rise and breathe in the crisp morning air. It was blissful.

By the time I arrived home, I was no longer grumpy and tired mum; I was happy and awake mum, filled with endorphins from the brisk walk and fresh morning air. It was still so early that I managed to find more quiet time to meditate and get organised before the kids woke up. It was wonderful. From that day forth I stuck to my goal of becoming a morning person once and for all. The differences I felt were amazing; the benefits far out-weighed the cost of getting up a couple of hours earlier.

We Are What We Eat

You can't achieve amazing results from a vehicle that isn't running on the right fuel. Filling your body with good nutrition includes eating healthy wholesome meals, drinking plenty of water and reducing the level of toxins that you consume and put in your body. Do you have routine and healthy rituals around the nutrition you provide your body? Your fuel affects everything – your brain function, sleep, energy levels and performance, and can ultimately lower your risks of developing mental and physical diseases.

Most of us can focus on one area in our diet that we know we can improve upon. Even if it's a small step in the right direction, those little steps will add up to great benefits over time. If you think your diet is adequate, but you are still gaining weight each year, maybe you are eating too much food? Imagine if you kept putting too much fuel in your car, it would ultimately overflow. The same applies when we eat too much food; it keeps stores as fat, overflowing all around our body. Some tips which have helped me avoid weight gain are:

- Eating only when I'm hungry.
- Drinking two litres of filtered water each day.
- Staying away from soft drinks.
- Eating slowly and mindfully, thinking about what I'm eating, and savouring every bite.
- Eating plenty of raw, unprocessed foods.
- Cutting back on sugary and sweet foods.
- Cutting out animal meats.
- Reducing my meal portion sizes.
- Only ever eating to being 80% full when having a meal, as it takes time for your stomach to feel full after eating.

One huge reality check for me was when my personal trainer asked me about my diet. I was certain it was very good, but he suggested I tracked what I ate for a week to see where we could tweak my diet (there are many free tracking apps that can track this for you; I personally use *My Fitness Pal*). Wow, how wrong was I? I was so surprised; my diet was nowhere near as good as I had believed. I was eating way too much, too many carbs, not enough protein and way too much sugar. All the little snacks in between meals were adding up. So, it's definitely worth tracking what you eat for a few days, to accurately assess the nutritional quality and quantity of your daily food intake.

If you are eating OK, but you don't have enough energy, you might not be feeding your body the right balance of nutrients it needs. Alternatively, you may have underdeveloped gut bacteria, hormone imbalances, allergies, thyroid problems or other health ailments that need addressing. I personally found it invaluable seeking professional help from a naturopath, alongside my GP, to diagnose what was holding my body back and to identify the right balance of nutrition for optimal health and vitality.

Practising Gratitude

Being grateful for what you have, writing it down as well as declaring it to yourself and others, is a brilliant way to change your attitude in an instant. If I am feeling the slightest bit down, focusing on all the things I am grateful for is an immediate cure. My drive to the office each day is five minutes, so I take that time to think of the people, places, objects, experiences and aspects of life for which I am grateful. The chemical reaction and physiological changes in me are astounding and have a dramatic impact on how I feel when I arrive each day at work. I might leave the house feeling 6/10, but by the time I arrive at work I feel 9/10 or 10/10, in my peak mental state.

Learn to be grateful for even the smallest of blessings, rather than trying to focus on big, amazing stuff. Again, the energy of being still, calm and focusing on the positives in your life, whatever they may be, will help you to feel more empowered. Turn your negative thoughts into positive ones. Be grateful you had warm, clean water when you showered this morning. Be grateful that you are able bodied and independent. Be grateful that you had food to eat and loved ones to share it with.

Who and *what* do you feel grateful for?

Mastering Your Life

Your business can be a powerful tool. If you work hard on yourself, as well as your business, you can use that power to get a return on your efforts. Brad Sugars once shared the formula for success as being the multiplication of your dreams, vision, goals, plans, learning and actions.

Diagram 10.2 shows my *Formula for Success*, demonstrating how you can create greater results in your life by increasing your score in each area.

Formula for Success

How clear are you on your success?
Step 1. Score yourself out of 10 in each area to see where you're currently at.
Step 2. What is one step in each area that you can improve to increase your score of success?
Step 3. What is your new score?

Step 1. Current Score		Step 2. One Area You Can Improve	Step 3. Your New Score
Dreams	3/10	Create new vision board	9/10
X	X		X
Vision	5/10	Share my vision with friends	9/10
X	X		X
Goals	2/10	Write my goals and put them up in my bedroom	9/10
X	X		X
Plans	3/10	Diarise actions and space them out in my calendar	9/10
X	X		X
Learning	1/10	Read one book each month	8/10
X	X		X
Actions	1/10	Follow actions in diary, in line with my goals	9/10
=	=		=
Success	90/1,000,000		472,392/1,000,000

Diagram 10.2

Often when doing this exercise, it's easy to see where there is potential to improve. By combining the elements of physical and mental health, excellent nutrition, good sleep, wise habits, continual learning and inspiring company, you will give yourself the best chance of mastering your life balance. In turn, this will offer you the opportunity to create a successful and leveraged business that does what it's supposed to do; create wealth and freedom of choice.

Honouring your temple is about taking care of your body and mind and creating positive habits in your life. Good habits can sometimes take time to develop but will have a massive long-term impact on your life. Once you are in a routine of regularly keeping your body and mind in peak performance, the habits will become second nature to you. The positive actions will become automatic and the benefits will compound over time.

"The Slight Edge," by Jeff Olsen, is another great book which highlights the fact that regularly taking small actions can have a massive impact on your life.[35] Olsen says, "Success is usually the result of small choices made every day – things that are very easy to do, but also easy not to do. Failure is caused the same way. Simple disciplines repeated over time will create success, while simple mistakes repeated over time will create failure. It's the slight edge that is the difference."

Take some time to jot down, in point form, your recipe for success. What rules or rituals can you abide by to honour your temple and fulfil your life purpose? We are all a *work in progress* until the day we die. I work on my rituals regularly and am constantly aware of how I can improve. To build greater energy in your life, and laser sharp focus, it's vital to take care of yourself holistically, gently and consistently.

No business is worth the detriment of your health and no life is worth playing second fiddle to your business. If there is something you are doing that is affecting you in a negative way, is it worth it? If it's not serving you or your loved ones, change it. It's your life, *you* have the power, *you* are in control.

I share this with you because I wish it hadn't taken the diagnosis of a life-threatening disease and a doctor telling me I had five years to live, for me to wake up and start looking after myself. Before I was sick, I never got up early to exercise and look after myself first. My reasoning was that I was a busy business owner, juggling the demands of my work and home life. I had two young children to organise each morning before I left for work, and then afterwards it was school runs, sports activities, making dinner, kids' homework, bathing, reading bedtime stories, etc. I was convinced there was no extra time for me to look after myself. Now I understand that my body is the one, sole vehicle that runs my whole life. In this way, my illness made me grateful for life itself and pushed me to look after myself.

Renee

After just one year of working with me, Renee experienced a frightening autoimmune flare up that left her bedridden and in agony. One moment she was *fine* and the next, in hospital with widespread pain and numbness in her back, face, arms and legs. After vigorous scans and tests, a neurologist finally concluded Renee's symptoms were a result of stress responses which impacted her central nervous system. Together with underlying health conditions, including Fibromyalgia and Arthritis, her symptoms were so exacerbated that, despite her best efforts, she was barely able to get out of bed. Renee's nerves were misfiring pain signals, so she felt a mix of extreme pain, burning sensations or complete numbness, together with chronic fatigue. It took a great deal of trial and error with various medications and rehabilitation to eventually combat her ailments.

After facing health challenges myself, I could relate to Renee's challenging situation yet, knew she had the courage to beat her illness. Renee was also determined to continue working when she could. So, propped up with pillows in her bed and a laptop on her knees, she continued to work reduced hours when she had small periods of relief from her pain. The added benefit of this was that using her brain and body for regular short intervals was beneficial to her recovery. On the other hand, it was second nature for me to mentor Renee through her healing journey. The upshot being, that despite her limited capacity, we continued to work together and Renee remained a vital part of my business during this time. Thankfully, Renee recovered after a few months but she knew she had to make changes in her life to prevent a relapse.

Health for one person is different for another, so Renee sought advice from various health professionals to work out the best recipe for *her life*. Some strategies included spreading out her work hours, getting more sleep, dietary changes, nutritional supplements, medication adjustments, increasing meditation and yoga practises. Only two years after Renee's recovery, she shared with me that, "2019 was the first year in over a decade that I wasn't hospitalised." It was a major personal accomplishment that blew me away. Attributing her improved health to a myriad of reasons, Renee said, "Ultimately, it came down to working hard on always bettering myself, placing my physical and mental health above all else, learning from others, trying new things, listening to my body, trusting my mind and following my heart."

Chapter 10
Blue Ocean Thinking

☐ **Create the right recipe for you (review your habits and rituals)**

Choose what you can do more of to create a meaningful life that supports the direction of your vision.

☐ **What doesn't serve you?**

If there are people or things holding you back, what can you do to eliminate them?

☐ **Write a professional and personal development plan**

What areas can you focus on to improve your results?

"Protect
your hope,
refine your assets,
polish your
talents
and
wow the world."

Robin Sharma

CHAPTER ELEVEN

Recreating Yourself

I had always dreamt of representing Australia in a sport, wearing our nation's colours, the famous Aussie green and gold. Four-and-a-half-years after being told I only had five years left to live, that dream came true in December 2003. My illness was seemingly gone once and for all, I'd had no relapses since my last surgery and the completion of my drug regime. I was elated that my life was back on track. After all, my fate could have been very different, if my doctor's original prognosis was correct. However, there I was competing in the event of my life, selected to represent Australia at the International Triathlon Union's (ITU) World Triathlon Championships in New Zealand.

My event was the world Olympic distance triathlon, and the course was located in the world-renowned, Queenstown. Surrounded by its stunning scenery of snowy mountains and glaciers, I had tears streaming down my face as I ran free and strong amidst the incredible beauty of New Zealand.

I firmly believe that through dedication to my overall wellbeing, I defied my odds and rid myself of the disease that had earlier consumed me. I had come a long way in those few short years since my diagnosis and it felt great to be alive. I revelled in the experience of being able to compete and finish the event, and was wholeheartedly grateful to have another chance at life.

David had also maintained his involvement with the triathlon community. He was regularly training with me and had shifted his attention from alcohol to greater things in life. He'd previously tried many strategies to reduce his alcohol dependence, but at the same time struggled to find an overarching focus that was greater than his pain.

That was until life began to offer him other opportunities which would make a difference in the lives of others, and gave him a total change of focus.

In May 2004, we were told that the school Hamish was attending, Saint Dominic's, was seeking a new member to join their Board of Directors. They asked if David would be interested in considering their invitation to take on the role. When I spoke with David about the offer, he was genuinely touched, and accepted the invitation. This was a huge turning point for David and his self-image. He felt respected and part of something bigger, and that he was providing a valued contribution to the school community. I was delighted for him to 'do his bit' to give back to the school.

Additionally, taking on this role meant that he couldn't regularly drink and be hungover on board meeting days, and he also wanted to do a good job for those who had entrusted him with the role. This was another positive shift in David's mindset and health. His reputation, and giving back to the school, was more important than drinking. After years of seeing David struggle with his alcohol problem, by default, his focus switched to using his time constructively to work on things that were actually more important to him.

David went on to obtain his bus driver's licence and enjoyed volunteering at the school to drive the children to excursions. Eve was so proud that her dad was able to come out for the day with them. David even happily volunteered to drive Mum's Brownie Guide group of 20 screaming, laughing girls, aged from six to ten years old, to their annual camp.

I could see David's whole attitude towards life take a complete 360 degree turn. He went from previously focusing on business, making money, drinking and dwelling on his own situation, to focusing on how he could make a positive difference in the world and to the lives of others. He had somehow worked out a better strategy for life; one that was serving him better than his old strategies that had carried him for decades prior. I loved witnessing the change happen before my eyes.

Meanwhile, in our professional lives, David and I were also following a new path and creating a plan to move forward. After the sale of our business, we researched and discussed at length what our next move would be in regards to our wealth creation. We carefully considered the three traditional areas in which people usually invested:

1. Business
2. Property
3. Shares

As we had already spent a considerable number of years in business and had only just sold ours, we were keen to explore the other two areas – property and shares. David decided to learn how to become a successful share trader and property investor, and travelled interstate for courses and training, as well as reading dozens of books in these fields. He joined an investor's support group and hired a specialised coach to give him the best chance of success possible. I had not seen him so determined and passionate about something since we started our business over a decade earlier.

Interestingly, one of the golden rules he learned from his share trading training was to always trade with a clear, alert mind and never when drunk or hungover. He loved this additional discipline and whilst David further adjusted the focus and direction of his life, I think he was also in the process of *finding himself*.

David continued to learn and expand his knowledge in share trading. However, he was not at the stage of earning income yet, so we still had to find another way of making a living. This was where property investing came into play, and David and I embarked on a new endeavour of buying, renovating and selling properties to earn our income.

As we had fully paid off the mortgage on our family home, the bank was happy to lend us money against the equity in our property. Using some of these funds, we focused on solving the problems in the property market. We ran this new venture just like any business, to cater to the needs of the market and make a profit from our efforts.

Initially, we found that there were country towns close to Perth which had a shortage of rental properties. We purchased cheap blocks in these towns, transported unwanted little wooden houses to them, set them up and then renovated the homes. From there, we either rented them out or sold them at a profit. We also did some suburban block subdivisions and converted a few 3-bedroom, 1-bathroom houses into 4-bedroom, 2-bathroom homes. Effectively, we were using these properties as stock, running the numbers over a deal before we committed and turned them over each year as we hit our profit target.

As well as working on property developments by day, David was busy working on the share trading side of our wealth creation plan at night. This entailed him getting up at very odd times in the middle of the night or early morning to trade on the US stock exchange. He was learning and growing with every trade he did and was excited by his new direction in life.

Perhaps, just as importantly, we loved working together and being creatively engaged in our new ventures. We were making good money from the property side of things as the market value was increasing steadily in Western Australia each year. However, whist I was enjoying the property investing, as the time went by, I knew I wanted more.

I felt I had more to offer and was keen to explore what I could do to make more of an impact in this world. I researched career options and stumbled across business coaching, which I was already familiar with as we had hired a business coach in the past. I knew what it entailed and the thought of doing it myself sparked joy inside. It would combine my two great loves, business and coaching, and I was inspired by the idea of everything it offered. I had never been so excited about a career up to this point. After all, I'd been a sports coach for fun since I was in my teens and could see that business coaching was a perfect way to marry my love of coaching with my 30 years of business experience.

I set about doing a two-year correspondence qualification in coaching. I couldn't believe I was starting a brand-new career in my 40s, but it felt right. It was a perfect new chapter with fresh possibilities ahead and I was super excited to help people to achieve greater success in business and life.

It seemed that our lives were filled with new hope and possibilities, and we were both keen to grow into our new careers. David and I were both giving it everything we had, both professionally and personally. We were literally re-creating ourselves. I began taking on the occasional coaching contract for an executive coaching firm, while continuing my professional development.

One of my first coaching adventures with this firm was to work with the team of an Australian mining company, based in Ulaanbaatar, Mongolia. A small group of coaches from Western Australia travelled to Mongolia for three weeks to coach people from all over the world. Our focus was to teach them how they could all work better together through developing a deeper understanding of their cultural differences. It was an incredible experience.

In August 2004, I had another minor health setback; this time in the form of double knee reconstruction. When competing in triathlons, I would often experience a stabbing knife-like pain in the side of my knees as I ran. When I had my knees examined, it was discovered that I had a misalignment of the patella in both knees. This natural design flaw meant that I needed a patellofemoral reconstruction alignment.

After the surgery, my doctor was very keen to explain all the activities I would not be able to do for the next year. He stated, "Having bones sawed, moved, re-bolted and tendons reattached is not much fun for a super active athlete like yourself. So, there can be no running, no cycling, no jumping, no this, no that…" and so on.

He continued to list all the things I couldn't do, when I bluntly interrupted and said, "Wait, stop! Forget about what I can't do; just tell me what I can do!"

A little taken aback, my doctor exclaimed, "Well, you can swim!"

As he said those words, the rest of the conversation became a blur; I was immediately transported to one of my childhood visions. It was a seed which was planted in my brain long before, a dream of mine to swim the 20km distance between the Western Australian coastline and an outcrop of land off the coast named Rottnest Island.

I thought to myself, "Well, if I can swim, I can fulfil my dream of competing in the Rottnest Channel Swim." It sounded like a great idea to me.

From as early as three years of age, each year my mum, brother and I would catch a ferry to Rottnest Island for a summer holiday, which we all looked forward to. A typical Rottnest afternoon for us would involve Mum sitting in the courtyard of the pub, overlooking the beach at Thompson's Bay, whilst reading the paper and slowly sipping her cold *beer shandy*; beer with lemonade. My brother, Andrew, and I would play in the safe shallow waters of the bay where Mum watched us as we frolicked around without a care in the world. The weather was always hot and the water like a mirror; so quiet and peaceful.

As we looked back across the aqua blue strip of ocean to the distant, faint skyline of Perth, I remember declaring, "I could swim that; it doesn't look that far." Little did I know at that time, there actually was a swimming event entailing just that – swimming from Cottesloe Beach, on the mainland coast, to Thompson's Bay, Rottnest Island.

Eighteen months after my double knee reconstruction, I stood on the shore of Cottesloe beach waiting for the Rottnest Channel Swim to begin. It was before sunrise and still pitch black, my stomach was churning in sync with the white caps of the cold, rough seas in front of me.

Yet I smiled to myself with anticipation as my childhood dream was about to come to life. I had dreamt of this moment countless times. I imagined the soft, white sand of Thompson's Bay between my toes at the end of the swim. It was the same place my brother and I had played some 30 years earlier.

Bringing my mind back to Cottesloe Beach, the sky was overcast, the swell rough and many participants were pulling out before the event had even started. I remained focused and braced myself for the endurance swim ahead. I knew it would take all of my resolve to complete the 20km course.

The starter's horn sounded, and the race began. After swimming the first kilometre by myself, I met up with my canoe paddler, Sean, whose job was to paddle beside me for the entire swim. Sean was the conduit between me and my back-up boat, handing me food and water all day.

My darling 13-year-old daughter, Eve, who had never been seasick, was part of the boat crew, too. However, due to the unfavourable ocean conditions, poor Eve vomited non-stop between sobs of nausea for most of the event. Unfortunately, she didn't think to vomit on the opposite side of the boat to where I was swimming, so I swam through all Eve had eaten in the past twenty-four hours.

Following this rough start, the boat's global positioning system (GPS) failed and we discovered that we had drifted way off course. Our crossing was taking far longer than expected. After paddling for over eight hours non-stop by my side, Sean too became extremely seasick. His face green, he retreated to the floor of the boat curled up in the foetal position. In the handover process, the canoe capsized, quickly filled with water, and left my support team distracted for a moment so they lost sight of me. With a shark sighted in the water less than an hour earlier, panic started to set in amongst my support team.

I just kept swimming. I had swum this journey in my dreams so many times that I was not worried. Instead, I sang the imaginary playlist on my iPod to myself, continuing to move my arms to the beat in my mind. I was cold, and I knew that my lips must be blue. When I stopped moving, my teeth chattered, my legs cramped, and my mouth stung with the familiar burn of putting too much salt on my fish and chips. However, most of all I felt happy. At the top of each wave I could see the island in front of me and I knew I would be there soon enough.

After about 30 minutes of swimming alone in the choppy ocean, my crew found me. What a relief, as little Eve was beside herself with distress by that point.

Nine hours and forty-five minutes after I started my swim, I finally took my first wobbly steps onto the fine, white sand in the shallow waters of Thompson Bay, Rottnest Island. I made my way out of the water, right in front of the pub, exactly as I had dreamt I would all those years ago. I fell straight into the arms of my brother, with whom I first shared my dream when I was only around five years old.

People said I must have been a very determined person to have not given up during my swim. They asked me, "Why didn't you quit in such tough conditions and with so many obstacles?"

Believe it or not, even under such horrific conditions, quitting never even entered my mind. I had seen the movie in my mind of me finishing so many times that I believed it would happen; I just knew it would. I kept my focus on the vision, the end goal and just followed the plan. I knew I could swim; my vision was crystal clear and my four-month training plan was simple to follow. With that, I had faith that my success would follow. For the umpteenth time in my life, the power of visioning and planning had yet again pulled me through the challenges I faced.

Planning Ahead

When I decided to swim solo to Rottnest Island, there was a huge amount of planning that went into the project. I created a calendar of events, actions, milestones and goals along the way. I researched, interviewed past participants and sought as much advice from those who had swum the channel before me. In fact, speaking with people who had been on the same journey was a key part of the learning and preparation process. They loved to help by sharing their own experiences. In learning through other people's challenges, I knew it would help me if I came across a similar challenge.

I learnt that sea sickness was a major hurdle faced by ocean swimmers, and discovered that by having anti-nausea medication the night before and every three hours throughout the swim, it would dramatically improve my chances of avoiding sea sickness entirely. I also knew that being stung by sea creatures, such as jelly fish and blue bottles, would make the almost 20km swim turn into a painful nightmare of burning agony. So, wearing a long sleeved, full body swim suit helped me avoid most of the stingers. Food was also a major consideration, with people telling me time and time again that they ran out of food during the swim. I learned that when the body is cold, and enduring a long-distance sporting event, it uses a huge amount of fuel in the form of food. Therefore, I carefully worked out that if I swam the slowest possible time, I could ascertain how much food I would need to maintain my strength. As you can see, planning ahead and learning from others was an invaluable part of preparing for my Rottnest swim.

Another essential addition to my team was having a buddy and coach who provided accountability; this was a huge asset. I was lucky enough to have a wonderful friend, Lauren, who volunteered to do one ocean swim with me every week leading up to the event. As part of our training schedule, we added an extra kilometre each week, right up until the week of the Rottnest swim. Lauren then joined the boat crew in support of me on the day and was so dedicated to my success that she even jumped into the water to swim beside me for a few minutes after a shark had been sighted. My paddler, Sean, was also a vital member of my crew. Choosing someone you trust to help you execute your project is instrumental, and Sean was both a trusted friend and an experienced athlete so I knew I could count on him to paddle beside me the whole journey in support of my pursuit.

It does not matter what you do in life, if you have an accountability coach or a mentor to help you stay on track; it will be invaluable to your success. We can only ever see our life from our own perspective. So, with people around to support and encourage you on your journey, you will get to see things from an outsider's perspective too.

Planning for Business Success

Business is no different; it is just one of life's many adventures that some people choose to launch themselves into. I can't impress on you enough the importance of having clear goals and a comprehensive plan to increase your chances of success. That way, if 'the going gets tough', you will be able to weather the storm and feel strong and focused in the face of adversity. Planning for success is critical. However, many people don't give much thought to the planning process.

Whether you are thinking of starting a business, if you're in business already or you're wanting to take your business to the next level, planning is essential. Months, or even years, of planning is required in the start-up phase, and then regular monthly planning on an ongoing basis is key to maintaining the momentum and longevity of your business. It's good to plan at the start or end of each month, for the month ahead – and make a habit of it. The same goes for the start of each quarter and each year – both calendar and financial years.

Some great questions to ask yourself and your team in these monthly planning sessions are:

- What revenue do you already have promised for the month?
- How much revenue is required in the business to break-even?
- How much is required to make a profit?
- What is the gap between what you have coming in and what you need to achieve?
- What actions and strategies are required to bridge that gap?
- Who is responsible for each action and when do they have time to carry out their responsibilities?

By following these suggestions and regularly making a habit of planning ahead, you'll start to discover the value of planning and the extraordinary difference it can make.

It is funny how many people think they know everything about business because they are good at their profession, even if they have never had a business before. Being good at a profession does not mean you will know how to run a business, let alone be good at it.

I remember meeting an entrepreneur once who said, "I never buy or start a business that I can work in. That way, I will never get trapped into doing the job."

Obviously, this won't be the case for everyone, but it was a genius thought. If identifying that *working on* the business is more important than *working in* it, then your business model and business plan should support that. If you run a business that you work in, how much time do you set aside to work on it? From my experience with most business owners, the answer is probably *not enough*.

It's quite common for business owners to be holding onto the hidden fear of failure and *I'm not good enough* negative thoughts that have been lying inside their minds since childhood. No one wants to succumb to failure and admit that their business could *go under*, particularly if they have invested their livelihood into the business or even put their house up as security. It is gut wrenching for me to see an intelligent man or woman in my office, sobbing tears of utter despair at the onset of having to tell their wife, husband, mother, sister or brother that their house will be repossessed because their business has failed due to bankruptcy. It is especially upsetting because it could have been avoided.

They just *didn't know what they didn't know*!

A Timely Example

Most people would have heard of the company, Polaroid, best known for their cameras, instant film and one of the first manufacturers of digital cameras. They were leaders in their industry and their products were second to none. You could say they were like the *Apple Company* of the 1900s. They reached their peak in 1991, but just a decade later they declared bankruptcy. Whilst there were various reasons that led to their decline, they ultimately failed to keep up with new technologies and new competitors, such as Nikon and Minolta. It's a good lesson to learn that just because you have reached success, it does not mean your success will continue. It is imperative to maintain your learning, engage in ongoing research, know what your competitors are doing, as well as understand the trends in your market.

In contrast, when you think of technology giant, Apple, the founders were visionaries who pushed boundaries and inevitably provided the market with what it wanted. Through constantly bettering their products, using fresh ideas and always expanding their reach, Apple was able to rival other tech giants, such as Microsoft and Samsung. Their success soared as a result. Since their founding, they have gone from strength to strength with hundreds of billions of dollars in assets because they recognised the need to keep up with the changing market and meet their customers' desires.

Therefore, it's clear that regardless of where you are in your business journey, your company can always focus on new, proactive strategies to improve, innovate and increase business performance.

If there is not constant improvement, it means that, in effect, your business is going backwards.

Proactive Business Planning

Business planning is about getting everything out of your head and into a clear plan so that it can be shared with the people who are going to help you achieve your goals. The process of planning is beneficial for getting laser-focused clarity on what strategies you need to implement in your business, and why. It's about forecasting potential opportunities and seeing all the separate areas of your business come together. A business plan is not *just a document*, it's a clearly mapped out roadmap of how you're going to achieve your vision and your goals, with every path and hurdle considered and mitigated before they happen.

If you start out having a clear vision of where you would like to take your business in the long-term future, you can then create a mission of how you are going to achieve it. Identifying your purpose comes next, together with identifying your unique selling point: What is so special about your business and your service? And your brand promises: What you promise to deliver to your clients?

Then, looking at the key outcomes you'd like to achieve in your business plan (and having very specific goals in each of these areas), will help you to define a clear path to follow in line with your goals. By going through your goals and outcomes in greater detail, alongside your team and financials, you will uncover areas that need to be improved which will form part of your strategies. Proactively and consistently working on your business strategies, and tracking against your goals at regular intervals, will ensure that you are actually getting closer to your desired results. Testing and measuring your results is paramount, so you know if you're on track.

Understanding your clients and what problems your product or service is going to solve for them is vital to sustainable success in your business. It's important to be continually researching, innovating and adapting in your industry to ensure you keep up with your market demands. How will you communicate with, and educate, your target market so that they know what problems you can solve for them?

Having a strong and engaged team, who work together with you to achieve those goals, is a great asset. Finding the right people you need in your team, by creating a current and future org chart and visualising the gaps, is a great first step. Your team can help you from the front-line, to build solid systems and processes that will add significant value to your business in terms of consistency and customer service.

Once you have created a comprehensive business plan, you'll have a blueprint for achieving success. I recommend checking in with how you're tracking to your plan, at the very minimum once a quarter, so that your plans are always up to date and you and your team members can adjust strategies as required. Planning and tracking your progress is a continual journey, and is often the key factor that sets apart highly successful entrepreneurs to those business owners who are just 'getting by.'

Diagram 11.1 shows my recipe for proactively planning your business for greater success.

Proactive Business Planning

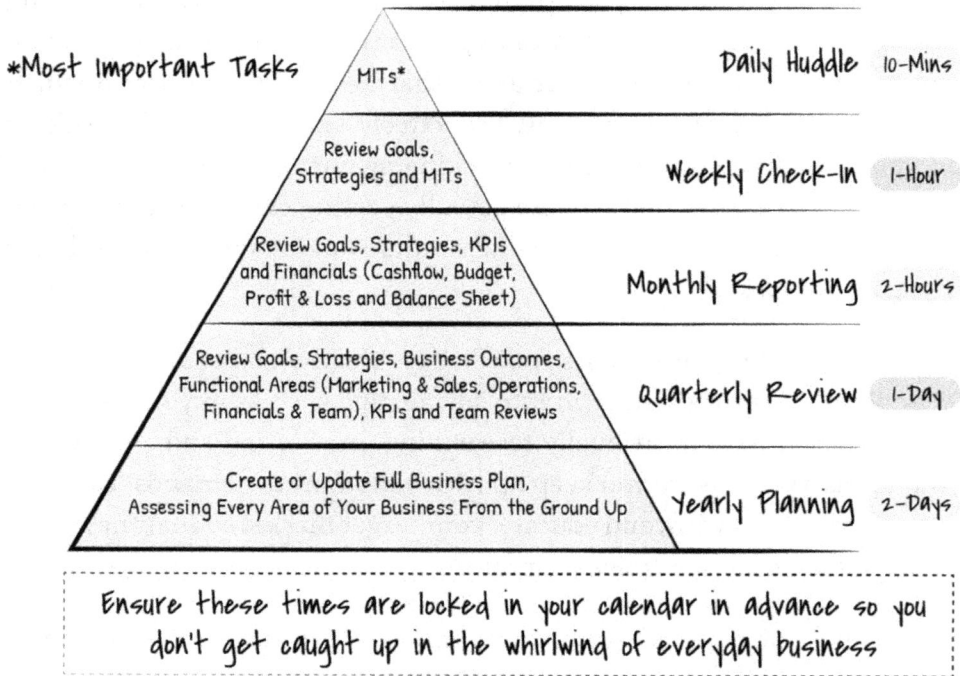

Most Important Tasks — MITs	Daily Huddle	10-Mins
Review Goals, Strategies and MITs	Weekly Check-In	1-Hour
Review Goals, Strategies, KPIs and Financials (Cashflow, Budget, Profit & Loss and Balance Sheet)	Monthly Reporting	2-Hours
Review Goals, Strategies, Business Outcomes, Functional Areas (Marketing & Sales, Operations, Financials & Team), KPIs and Team Reviews	Quarterly Review	1-Day
Create or Update Full Business Plan, Assessing Every Area of Your Business From the Ground Up	Yearly Planning	2-Days

Ensure these times are locked in your calendar in advance so you don't get caught up in the whirlwind of everyday business

Diagram 11.1

Chapter 11
Blue Ocean Thinking

☐ **Write a business plan in line with your vision and goals**

Write a comprehensive business plan that ties everything together.

Put time aside to review your goals monthly, quarterly and yearly.

☐ **Schedule monthly planning meetings**

Diarise monthly planning with your key team members, determine the strategies required to ensure you're on the right track and assess your financial reports.

☐ **Check in regularly**

Review your goals and strategies on a weekly basis, starting each day with a quick huddle to determine your most important tasks for that day.

"Your hardest times often lead to the greatest moments of your life. Keep going. Tough situations build strong people in the end."

Roy T. Bennett

CHAPTER TWELVE

Overcoming Adversity

Over the next few years, our big wealth creation plan was right on schedule. Property investing remained the main source of income for David and me. We were turning over two or three properties per year and putting any extra profits we'd made into an appropriately selected property for holding, as a long-term rental investment asset. The plan was simple, and we were delighted with how it was all progressing. By this stage, we had three *keeper properties* (houses with heaps of equity), securely rented which gave us added positive cashflow. We also had another eight or nine properties at different stages of development.

After about four or five years of property investing and developing, you could say we were flying. The property market in Western Australia was heating up rapidly; we made profits on all our deals for the first five years. We were on a high and felt that things just couldn't go wrong for us.

That was until the global financial crisis (GFC) hit in 2007 and began to seriously impact Australia in 2008. At this point, we experienced what is called a severe mid-course correction as we had managed to get *brains and a bull market* mixed up. We thought we were making money because we knew what we were doing, but that was not so. The reality was that we were making money because the market was rising so rapidly and property prices were following, so it would have been difficult for us to *not* make money on property!

As the GFC hit, house prices plummeted. We were forced to sell property after property at huge losses just to pay for the school fees, groceries and mortgage repayments. We couldn't sell the properties fast enough; the losses we were incurring in each property were enormous. To say we were running scared was an understatement. We even subdivided our own property and sold our backyard to bring in some income.

All the while, David had been focused tirelessly on being a successful trader for eight years, but unfortunately his unwavering dedication didn't translate into the success he'd intended. In fact, over that time we had invested close to one hundred and twenty thousand dollars into share trading without a return. With our losses in the property market and the lack of success in shares, it compounded our situation. In truth, we had created a massive drain on our family's financial security.

Still to this day, I'm sure David carries some hidden emotion around the losses we incurred. However, we acted as a team and created these circumstances together, so we would get ourselves out of our predicament the same way.

Beating the Demon Once and For All

At 52 years old, David announced out of the blue that he'd made the decision to stop drinking once and for all. He had decided that it was not serving him anymore, even though he had cut down his alcohol consumption considerably over the years. It was an amazing breakthrough; David never wavered on his resolve.

I think back to the countless times I had yearned to hear those words. Every birthday when I blew out the candles on my birthday cake, my friends and family would shout, "Make a wish, Suzzie." I'd always have the same wish each year; for David to stop drinking and for it to stop controlling our life. I lived in hope of that day, which I think my mum and friends prayed for too.

There were a few instrumental turning points which, over time, brought David to his ultimate decision to stop drinking. One of them was the effects, both visible and invisible, his drinking had on Hamish and Eve.

An example of this was when, at the age of ten, Eve wrote him a letter asking him in great detail, "Why don't you just stop drinking?" This was after he had taken her to a surf lifesaving event and got so drunk the night before that he was badly hungover, and fell asleep in the sand dunes during her events. He was still fast asleep when the day's activities finished, and all the parents were desperately looking for him, as little Eve was distraught and alone. She had lost her dad and had no one to take her home.

Eventually, they found David. He was embarrassed and poor Eve was so sad and confused. David still has that letter in his bedside table drawer as a reminder of where he has been with alcohol and where he wishes to never return.

On another occasion, when he was attempting to free himself from the grip of booze, he did a simple *test and measure* research project. He hung a yearly calendar beside his bed and marked an 'X' on any day that was totally wiped off due to an unnecessary hangover. This was excluding all the hangovers that he allowed himself because it was a special birthday celebration, wedding or a festive event such as Christmas or New Year. He made a commitment to undertaking this research project for a full 12 months. In the end his 'X' days equated to wiping a couple of months off the calendar each year. Over six years, he realised this equated to losing nearly a whole year every six years of his life. It was a huge wake up call for him.

David also finally gained the strength to begin a journey of discovery around his emotions, ego, self-belief and trust. Ultimately, this inner journey gave him the courage to stop drinking altogether. Even though this huge milestone was over a decade ago, I still wake up and pinch myself that my husband is no longer controlled by alcohol.

At that same point, David also noticed that his best friend from childhood, Stuart (not only his best mate, but also his drinking buddy), was drowning his sorrows in alcohol and drugs. Unfortunately, Stuart was not having the same realisations around his drinking as David. Stuart and David had known each other since the age of eight, when they were neighbours in Scotland. Stuart had even moved his whole life from

Scotland and immigrated to Western Australia just so he could still be within walking distance and living around the corner from his best friend.

David was desperate to help his long-time friend, and knew a heartfelt conversation was in order. He sat down with Stuart to explain how he had finally overcome his addiction, with support and some recommendations. He tried his hardest to help his friend overcome the battles that had consumed them both for much of their lives. Sadly, Stuart was too far gone and said he was not interested in changing his habits.

Devastatingly, just a year after David's sobriety began, he watched his best friend pass away from liver cancer. He was gone within a few weeks of being diagnosed with the illness. Stuart was only in his mid-50s and his daughter, Caley (our god-daughter) had not even graduated from high school. It was devastating for us to watch her graduate without her dad there. Additionally, as her mum had split from her dad when she was only a pre-schooler, and had only ever lived with her dad growing up, Caley decided to move in with us. She was already an extended part of our family, spending time with us most weekends (and her childhood holidays spent playing with Hamish and Eve), so it was a natural decision for her to live with us when her dad passed away. She stayed with us for the eight years that followed.

Seeing Caley every morning served as a daily reminder to David that alcohol was a serious poison he must refrain from for the rest of his life.

Starting Again

In the five years that followed the GFC, which rocked our world, we desperately tried to save some of our property portfolio. However, in the aftermath we had pretty much lost it all. We were left with a useless block and a debt of around 1.8 million dollars. Thankfully, we managed to keep our family home that we once owned outright, but now we had a massive debt secured against it. It was a challenging period in our lives, to say the least.

Eve and Caley were still full time at university and Hamish was at college. Eve's boyfriend, Dylan, (whom she had been dating for a couple of years) had also moved in with us. He had come up from the country to get a city job and to be closer to Eve, and couldn't find accommodation. With a household of six adults to feed and almost two million dollars of debt to service, I was not about to declare bankruptcy nor lose our family home.

We were in a daunting situation, but our house was filled with love and optimism which held us together. Despite our grave challenges, I was grateful that our house was still filled with loving individuals who were continuing to learn, live and grow together.

Sometimes with losses come incredible wins. I have come to discover that sometimes it's about how you look at a situation and how you can learn from it and better yourself, which makes all the difference.

With much of our wealth and livelihood lost, for the first time in our lives we had to seriously consider how we were going to re-build our wealth. We had to create a plan to lessen the huge debt that we had accrued. With David in his early 50s and being self-employed for the previous 20 years, it was going to be hard for him to get a full-time job.

We had tried and we had lost, so it was time to change things up. With our backs against the wall, I decided it was time to put that old saying to the test, "If it's going to be, it's up to me." There was no better time to give it my all and start my own business coaching practice.

Business Coaching

With failure not an option, I decided to back myself 100% and invested $100,000 to buy a business coaching licence, adding further debt on our overdraft. After three months of serious research, I decided to buy a Business Coaching franchise. This entailed flying across the country to Queensland to complete my due diligence, followed by ten days of gruelling training in Las Vegas, USA.

This commitment was going to add an extra financial weight to our already crippling monthly interest payments, which was unnerving, to say the least. However, with so many business owners struggling and going under due to lack of education, I knew I could make a difference with all I had learned. I was committed to my vision of helping others, and used this overarching passion to continue my path, despite what I had hanging on the line.

I decided on an ActionCOACH franchise because many years earlier, when David and I were running our business together, we had worked with a business coach who was part of the ActionCOACH team. We liked the simple frameworks and models they used as well as the fact that the founder of ActionCOACH, Brad Sugars, was an Australian who established the profession of business coaching back in the mid-1990s.

Funnily enough, we had seen Brad presenting on stage when we were only in our third year of business, and we loved what we saw so much that we got in contact with him a few years later to source our own business coach. When we went to Brad Sugars' event, we were still very 'green' and thought we knew it all. We assumed that we didn't need the help of a business coach at the time, so we were naïve and too full of ourselves to accept help.

How I wish I knew then, what I now know!

As soon as I got home from my ActionCOACH training, I was ready to open for business. I contacted everyone I knew in business and offered my services for free so I had some practice clients. I knew they would gain from the experience too, so it was beneficial for us both. I had a slow start, not taking on a paying client until five months after opening my doors. But I knew that change took time and I was giving it all I had.

I often felt overwhelmed, alone and scared with the new mountain in front of me which I had decided to climb. I frequently doubted myself and heard those horrible sabotaging voices in my head, but I simply told them to *be quiet* as I had well laid out plans that I was determined to accomplish.

An extremely powerful step I took early on in my coaching business was to join a Business Network International (BNI) group. Without a doubt, this was one of the best business decisions I have ever made. In 1985, the founder Ivan Misner started with one small group, with the goal of helping to support, refer and educate each other. Now, decades later, there are thousands of chapters globally. Each chapter is made up of local groups of positive, motivated businesses owners who meet weekly, often over breakfast or lunch. There is only one of each profession in the group, so there is no competition and each person has the opportunity to share their field of expertise.

For many new business owners, going out into the marketplace solo can be a lonely journey. I found the comfort of catching up with my business referral group each week to be invaluable for both my sanity and my business. My peers knew exactly the road I was traveling and were by my side to support my business, as I was theirs. Believing in the law of reciprocity, BNI's motto is, 'The Givers Gain'. This relates to recognising the power of giving without the expectation of receiving. I have continued to be part of a BNI group ever since.

After the slow start, my business steadily grew each year. I thrived on being able to help more and more business owners to increase their own success and achieve their dreams. As a coach, I always ask clients what they want to achieve from their life as well as their business. I considered it imperative that their business supported their life. A commonly repeating personal goal of my clients was that they wanted to "Get fit, lose weight and increase their energy." I kept having a niggling thought that, "I know it can be done; my husband has done it."

Suddenly, I had a *blinding flash of the obvious* moment. With everything David had been through, I knew he could help other people to transform their lives through mindset and health training. With loads of encouragement, I suggested David get his Personal Trainer qualification so he could help people do what he did.

Initially, David said, "Why would anyone want a burnt, old man as their personal trainer?"

I replied, "Lots of people would! Your story is amazing. You're not going to make anyone feel like they're too old or too fat or too injured. You have been there, done that, so I think you'd be just perfect. You can teach them how to turn their lives around."

Originally reluctant, David then got excited about the idea. He was ready to create a new career of his own, dedicated to helping people who were in the same position as he once was. So grateful to be out of that soul destroying and destructive place himself, he was inspired to go on a new path to help others.

Firstly, David transformed our home garage into a little private gym, and it was not long before he built a solid client base. David's motto is, "Your health is your wealth." We couldn't believe how seamlessly David's new business direction fitted in with my business coaching. In fact, our businesses aligned perfectly.

Aligning Our Business and Life

David and I have dedicated the last ten years to helping people positively transform their lives. We have achieved this beyond many of their, and our own, expectations.

David now helps people to transform their body and mindset, and I help with educating and motivating others to achieve greater business success. With our wealth of life experiences, we are able to support people to navigate their challenges and objectively help them to reach their potential. We're not about 'talking the talk'; we are truly dedicated to helping others to overcome the types of challenges we have faced ourselves. We know, first-hand, how disheartening and frightening it can be when even the best laid plans come up against unexpected challenges.

Looking back, all the dreams David and I wrote down almost 40 years ago, have paved the way for us to live out our wildest dreams. We have achieved almost all of what we set out to achieve in that list, plus so much more. We have started and run multiple businesses successfully, had two beautiful children, travelled the world, achieved many sporting accolades, bought a holiday house, owned our own home and became the fittest and healthiest versions of ourselves possible.

We are now both working our dream jobs, giving back to our community and globally, always striving to help more people. I am a proud ambassador of an amazing charity, Opportunity International, which supports the poorest of poor families around the world to break the poverty cycle. They provide micro business loans to help families set up their own small business, with coaching and support to help them escape the poverty loop. I love donating part of my income to help change business owners' lives around the globe. I see it as another way I can make a positive impact.

My previously overweight 118kg, alcoholic husband in his early 40s is now in his mid-60s and a lean 75kg. He is in the best physical and mental shape of his life. If David can be the fittest and strongest he's ever been, then anyone else can be too. My heart swells when I think of how David totally transformed his life by stopping drinking, looking after his body and mind in a way he had never done before. David has now completed well over a hundred triathlon races, over a dozen of these being 70.3 Ironman races (1.9 km swim, 90 km bike ride and 21.1 km run – the 70.3 represents the total distance in miles), one full Ironman event (double the distance of a 70.3 ironman race), over half a dozen full marathons (42.2km run) and represented Australia twice for his age in the ITU World Triathlon Championships. It is something we never imagined would be possible in our lives.

David has since gone on to become a yoga instructor too, after an accidental introduction to the practice. Four years into his fitness coaching journey, David needed a shoulder reconstruction due to spurs and bursitis that were causing him much pain. A fellow triathlete suggested that he try yoga before jumping into surgery, so David asked his surgeon what he thought.

"You can try it," his surgeon laughed. "It won't hurt, but I guarantee you will be back to get a shoulder reconstruction, as you'll be in pain and never have full movement of your shoulder without surgery."

After hearing this news, David actually cried in the car, ringing me to say how gutted he felt after his fitness career was really taking off. Later that day, David thought of everything he had overcome previously and decided to give yoga a try before he rushed into a shoulder reconstruction.

He joined a local Bikram Yoga studio and started practising yoga three to five times a week, determined to avoid going under the knife. The pain and stiffness lessened over time and, within a few years, the pain in his shoulder subsided considerably and he regained a huge degree of movement in his once rigid shoulder. He became a passionate and raving fan of yoga and never had to go back to the surgeon for that shoulder reconstruction.

With yoga and meditation a huge part of David's transformation, he travelled to India in 2014 to complete his Yoga Teacher's training and develop himself further spiritually. He lived in a Yoga Ashram in a village at the bottom of the Himalayas and acquired his Yoga Teacher certification. After living the yoga philosophy of *no harm* for a month in the ashram (which included not harming or eating animals), he decided to adopt the same vegan lifestyle when he came back to Australia. He said he had never felt so light, clear and energetic as he had on the vegan diet. Therefore, he chose to continue to live all the parts of the yogic philosophy back home.

Now a fully-fledged yoga teacher, the next on the list of transformations was our huge family room which David converted into a yoga studio. Once all the furniture was emptied out, the room was given a fresh coat of paint and new flooring, creating a perfect little yoga studio in our house filled with candles, inspiring décor and great energy.

Through his yoga, personal fitness, strength and transformational coaching, David inspires people every day to be pushed by their dreams, not pulled by their problems. He lives by the creed, "There's no such thing as *can't* – only *won't* – and if you believe you can change, you can."

Next time you think, *"I can't do that,"* just add the word 'yet' to the end of the sentence. You don't have to be unfit just because you are older. You also don't have to be sad, overweight, unsuccessful or broke.

David will tell you himself that he wasted a good part of 20 years of his life punishing his mind and body after the burns accident, not living to his true potential. If I was told 20 years ago that I'd be sitting in my family room doing a yoga class with another 20 people, led by my non-drinking, non-smoking, vegan living, yogi, personal trainer husband, I would've said you were crazy. Now, I am proud to say that I have been inspired and amazed by David's courage, realising that whatever age you are, you can change and strive to be your best. We know anything is possible.

Our Life Today

I feel an enormous sense of gratitude when I look back over my 35-year life journey with David. I love the work I do; I adore my husband and my family; we are still in peak physical condition. After close to 20 years of triathlon training and competition, I have represented my country at world championship level four times, completed well over a dozen 70.3 Ironman races, a couple of full Ironman races and multiple marathons. Much of this occurred after I was given just five years left to live.

Having been through the GFC, I never thought we'd recover to the position that we are now in. I am so incredibly proud to know that through our respective enlightening careers, we are helping others to change their own realities. At the same time, we have also been slowly repaying our close-to-2-million-dollar debt which once loomed so large in our lives, we thought we would never overcome it. We're not quite there yet, but we've paid off three-quarters of it and can see the light at the end of the tunnel.

Eve finished her degree in Human Resources (HR) and went on to complete her Masters in HR. She currently works with me in my business and is a great asset, helping to transform the culture of many businesses by improving employee engagement and bringing more happiness, commitment and harmony to the workplace. Dylan, her now husband, recently started his own roof plumbing business, which I thoroughly enjoy chatting enthusiastically about with him.

Caley completed two degrees, one in Interior Architecture and the other in Law, recently being admitted to the West Australian Bar. She moved out of our home a couple of years ago with her partner to buy their first house. Still very much part of our family, she exercises with David and Eve regularly in our home gym. She has always been treated as part of our family and it was beautiful to see her as one of Eve's bridesmaids as a touching tribute, showing the close-knit ties with which we are blessed.

Hamish, our first-born, secured a place working at the prestigious Kings Park in Perth, studying Horticulture. He was the first to leave home five years ago, when he followed his girlfriend to Melbourne. It was there that he discovered a new career in Real Estate, which he really enjoys. We still hope one day he will come back to Perth to live. However, until then, the bond is so strong that we still manage to see him every few months (with us visiting him in Melbourne or him visiting us). He was only recently in Perth for Eve and Dylan's wedding, carrying out the role of MC and one of Dylan's groomsmen.

Of Only recently, the last of our young bunch moved out, with Eve and Dylan moving into their first home which they have beautifully renovated. We also had the joy of having their son, Chet, with us in our family home for the first two years of his life. Having them all move out was bittersweet. Although sad at the thought of not sharing our house again, and adjusting to the new dynamics, we have so many exciting things in our lives. Our children are now on their own adventures, and we love being part of it all. I feel incredibly blessed; it could have been so very different. I am eternally grateful that we were able to overcome the obstacles we faced.

As I sit writing the finishing touches to this book, I am outside our tiny cabin at Rottnest Island, holidaying with my mum, daughter and grandson. It's my favourite place on Earth, and we've been coming here as a family tradition for the same week every year since I was three years old. Many of my dreams have taken seed here in the countless hours we've spent as a family on this beautiful island. So, it's a fitting place for me to complete the final chapter of this book as I feel immense gratitude for the opportunity to be with four generations of my family. Especially knowing once again, that my business is continuing to run just fine without me for the week.

In fact, Renee has worked tirelessly by my side for the past four years and shares the same passion and determination as I do – to help business owners to achieve their goals. She was chosen out of a few hundred applicants who applied for the same position, but as our passions and values were so aligned, she was the perfect fit. We are so in sync with each other that we often have the same thoughts, and Renee's generally one step ahead of me when I want something done. She has gone from strength to strength in her career pursuits and, together, we achieve more.

Renee has been by my side through a large process of writing this book and I don't know what I'd do without her. Since she came into my life, she has been like an angel by my side. I also know our clients are grateful for her ongoing support as she is an integral part of my team. I trust her with everything; she's like one of the family. I can't wait to see what else we can achieve together; the sky has no limits.

Reflecting on my path, I cannot explain how proud I am of what David and I have achieved together and how honoured we are to have touched so many lives. It has been an incredible journey of highs, lows, discovery and transformation.

So often in life, we think we can control what happens around us, either at work or with our partners, friends or our children. However, through experience I've come to realise that the only thing we can really control is ourselves, and it all starts with the thoughts inside our head. There are many people who join us along this journey of life – some for just a short time and some, like me, are lucky enough to have a person like David to share the path for a long time. Yet, I also know that all relationships eventually end and circumstances in life pass, so the only one thing you can control is you; your thoughts, decisions and actions.

Through our respective careers, David and I now both help people to realise that they are *not* their business or their career. We remind them that work is not the only thing they have to do in life; that they can change if they choose to. Their history does not define their future. We encourage others to understand that attitude is a choice and you can choose to have a positive or a negative one. I know which one makes for a better life and a better you.

It is a choice to master our lives, as we each have the power to determine how we think and how we run our lives. It takes courage, persistence and often the strength to get back up through the battles we each face, but it is possible to change your life for the better if you truly want it. For David and me, we're no longer solely focused on making money, but on making a difference.

David still battles the *black dog* on occasions (a metaphor referring to his lurking demons of depression in the background), only now it's just a brown dog and doesn't bark as loud as it used to. I, too, still have self-doubt and negative voices that creep in my head when I least expect it, but through all our learnings and the tools that we have acquired, we know what helps us to bounce back, so we can reach for those tools when we need them most.

As David and I recently celebrated our 35th wedding anniversary, we reflected on our amazing journey together. We find it hard to believe that one split decision decades ago could have changed everything. David chose to fight so we could pursue our dreams; he had the courage to take the hard road so we could follow the roadmap of what we'd planned for our life together. He could have easily given up, many times over; his trauma could have been avoided by choosing the easy option.

So, when life next presents you with a fork in the road, and you're tempted by the easy option, just remember that one decision was the difference between David and I having our journey together or not. If you give up every time things are tough, or the road ahead looks too hard to bear, you're never going to grow as much as you could. The hard road is where the learning happens, where you will be inspired to achieve greater things. It is a place where you can experience life and love on a deeper level. It is through adversity and challenges that we grow the most and you will become stronger, wiser, and more resilient on the other side of it.

It's up to you to decide the direction of your life. If there are things holding you back and not serving your dreams, take hold of what matters to you most and don't settle for less. Continue to dream, create and build the life and business that you want. Be rich in time, people and knowledge.

Always keep learning abundantly, be grateful for what you have right now and keep envisioning what else is possible in your business and life. Live your life to the fullest and make your business a reflection of who you are and the legacy you want to leave. Anything is possible. If you can dream it, you can plan it and learn it and do it.

I am often asked by business owners what the difference is between a business that's successful and one that's not. The difference that I see is that it all starts in the business owner's mind. Successful people are proactive, positive, have a motivated attitude with an openness to listen, learn, research and act with clarity. They don't have pre-conceived and limiting beliefs. Their ego is not at the forefront of their decisions and they treat all people with the same level of respect (regardless of whether they are talking to a major client, a friend, a customer or a team member). They are honest, vulnerable human beings who live life from the heart and are ready to learn. There is no such thing as *secrets to success*. It is the result of preparation, hard work and lifelong learning and planning. Living this way will change the way you run your business and life indefinitely.

By facing your fears and getting out of your comfort zone, you can take your life to whole new heights and transform it forever. If this is the one thing that you take away in your heart, after reading my story, then I'm so grateful that you took the time to read my book and happy that my aim of inspiring you has been achieved.

"Positivity is a superpower and optimism is the magic dust that helps push you through."

Pamela Jabbour

Eve and Dylan's wedding, 1 February 2020.

From left to right: Suzzanne Laidlaw, David Laidlaw, Hamish Laidlaw, Eve Laidlaw, Chet Kavanagh, Dylan Kavanagh, Caley Catto.

© Photography by Banks Bridal

"Some succeed because they are destined to, but most succeed because they are determined to."

Henry Van Dyke

How Can I Help?

On my website, www.suzzannelaidlaw.com.au, you can download many free templates that I have mentioned in this book, find out when my free webinars and upcoming events are scheduled and subscribe to my newsletter for updated content and more. You can also find bonus *What's Your Plan?* content and photographs that relate to my story.

The last five years have seen my focus expand from working with just a select few business owners to looking at ways to broaden my reach and impact. I continue to help a multitude of different businesses in varying ways; some through one-on-one coaching, helping to motivate and hold them accountable to following through with their strategies, some through business planning workshops to help them develop a solid and comprehensive business plan for success, and some through group education and accountability programs. I also do my part for the community and host free online educational webinars and small local seminars and events to help business owners to become educated on the opportunities available to them. I find it heart-warming to witness the amazing ripple effect that the positive changes I teach my clients have on their families, team members, friends and, of course, themselves. Having a successful business makes everyone's world brighter and happier.

I run regular business planning workshops where I take business owners through a two-day journey of creating their own business plan, which results in all the jigsaw pieces of their business being pulled out of their heads and written into a five year business plan. The journey is not so much about having the plan, it's about the learning and clarification that occurs whilst creating that plan. I've had businesses from the start-up phase right through to established multi-million dollar enterprises go through this process, and it's illuminating to everyone. After helping hundreds of business owners, I have never had anyone say they didn't gain huge clarity, learning, motivation and inspiration from creating their business plan. Additionally, using the online log-in portal provided, business owners can input all their data into a cloud-based platform, which integrates all their research, goals, milestones, financials and strategies into one place that is easily accessible to them and their team.

I then encourage them to regularly assess, adjust and fine-tune their plans along the way, based on what can be improved or what has changed. It becomes a huge paradigm shift, going from reactively running a business, constantly putting out bushfires and facing challenges every day, to proactively planning out a successful future and following the path to achieving those goals.

Because our time on Earth is finite, it's important to me to create a legacy that will remain after I'm gone. Ever since I was a teenager, I've heard people talk about becoming a *millionaire*, earning boundless amounts of money and living a lavish life, but one day I thought, "I can do more than that. I'd like to be a *millionaire of hearts* instead." So, rather than earning millions of dollars, I want to impact one million people by touching their hearts and inspiring them to live their best life possible. That goal is so much more powerful, meaningful and rewarding to me. I have been thinking over the last few years how I can reach more people in order to achieve this goal, so in publishing this book, I'm thankful to be one step closer to achieving my goal. Every time someone reads this book, I hope to have touched one more heart.

By now I trust you've taken away some knowledge and inspiration that you can act upon. The last thing I want is for you to be overwhelmed and I would never expect anyone to read this book and be able to implement everything I have gone through immediately. This book is about taking you *one step closer*. It's about bringing your awareness to all the things that you *didn't know that you didn't know*. Once you have read right through, I hope you have a clearer picture of what you want and a better understanding that anything is possible in your business and your life.

My suggestion, or should I say challenge, is for you to go back through one chapter of this book every month and identify any relevant actions, learnings and goals that you can implement to help your business prosper. In doing so, I am confident your business will grow dramatically. I challenge you to create your own plan for success over the next 12 months, by discovering and acting upon the things that scream at you the loudest from each chapter. By this time next year, with your consistency and follow through, your business will be very different to the one it is now, if you plan for success and follow through with those plans.

Similarly, if you're ready for a physical or mind transformation, I'd encourage you to seek help from a fitness and health coach. My husband, David, offers personal fitness, nutrition, health coaching, personal training and yoga classes, both locally at our home studio in Karrinyup, Western Australia, or virtually for anyone around the globe. Wherever you are in the world, you can contact David to find out what mentoring is available to you. You can reach him through his website, www.newuptyoga.com.au.

If you'd like greater business support and would like to be one of the million hearts that I empower in my life's journey, I'd love the opportunity to help you turn your dreams into a reality. Wherever you are on your journey, my advice is to start making positive changes now! Your business and your life is too important to wait. Here are some of the ways I can help you:

- **Business Planning Workshops**, where I facilitate my clients through the entire process of planning a successful business model from the ground up. We assess what works and what doesn't, and build a clear path to help you achieve your goals. Each person create their own business plan and, which can be regularly updated over time. The end document can be used for a multitude of pursuits; for bank finance, a grant application or even for selling the business. You'll have the option of printing your plan to PDF, or ordering a printed and bound copy if you want to hold it in your hands or send a hard copy to someone. I run these workshops live over one or two days, or, if you can't attend live, I also offer this workshop via an online platform, which includes recorded business planning sessions and a step-by-step guide to completing your business plan remotely. This way I can help to mentor business owners globally through each part of the business planning process.

- ***Group Business Planning and Entrepreneurial Sessions***, are perfect for those who prefer to speak or listen to a real person. I run regular events and programs, so you can receive live, professional, ongoing coaching support in the comfort of an inspiring business environment with the added benefit of brainstorming with other like-minded business owners. My group programs are a great way to accelerate your education, professional development, leadership skills and more, plus network with other business owners who are there for the same reason you are.

- ***One-On-One Executive or Business Coaching Programs***, are available for those business owners that have a solid business plan in place and require specific coaching, accountability and motivation to leverage their efforts. I coach business owners privately either face-to-face or via Zoom (if you're in a different state or country to me, or prefer remote coaching), to help create results where your business can run without you (if you choose). Ultimately, I want to help *give you a life*, rather than your business taking that away from you.

- ***Motivational Speaking***, across various platforms, both live and virtually, offers me the gratifying opportunity of inspiring and educating others. I speak regularly on motivational topics, including business planning, to groups all over the globe. You can find out where I'll be next or enquire about the opportunity of me speaking for your organisation, on my website.

Alongside this book, my '*What's Your Plan?* **Business Play Book**' is available for those who love putting pen to paper and enjoy writing, sketching and drawing their business goals. It's also for those who don't have reliable internet access for online planning; as anything you can do on a computer, you can do by hand. My *Play Book* includes activities and strategies to implement, based on the content of each chapter in this book, with examples and templates for you to fill out by hand. I want everyone in any position globally to be able to dream and plan their business, whichever way works for them.

If you're not sure where to start, I'm offering a complimentary *Business Needs Analysis* phone call to anyone who's keen to find out what the next step could be for them. Obligation free, I (or one of my team) can discuss your goals and challenges, point you in the right direction and help to discover the answer to my question, *"What's Your Plan?"*

Finally, I send you my heart-felt congratulations for making it to the end of my book! By reading this, you have succeeded in prioritising yourself and your business development and taking the first step in fast-tracking your success. I look forward to connecting with you again soon.

To your success.

Suzzanne Laidlaw

My Website

For resources, templates and picture gallery of the
stories in this book, visit

www.suzzannelaidlaw.com.au

David's Website

To find out how David can help you with your
health and fitness goals, visit

www.newuptyoga.com.au

Recommended Reading

Collins, Jim and Morten T. Hansen *"Great by Choice,"* Century Trade. USA 2011

Dweck, Dr Carol S. *"Mindset: The New Psychology of Success,"* Ballantine Books. USA 2007

Gerber, Michael E. *"The E Myth Revisited,"* HarperCollins Publishers. New York 1995

Covey, Sean. *"The 4 Disciplines of Execution: Achieving Your Wildly Important Goals,"* UK 2012

Johnson, Spencer. *"Who Moved My Cheese?"* Vermilion UK 1999

Olsen, Jeff. *"The Slight Edge,"* In House Publishing GOKO. USA 2016

Pape, Scott. *"The Barefoot Investor,"* Wiley. Australia 2019

Senik, Simon. *"Start with Why,"* Penguin Press. London UK 2011

Singer, Michael. *"The Surrender Experiment,"* Yellow Kite. 2015

Singer, Michael. *"The Untethered Soul,"* New Harbinger Publications. 2007

Sugars, Brad. *"Billionaire in Training,"* McGraw-Hill Education. Australia 2006

Sugars, Brad. *"Instant Cashflow,"* McGraw-Hill Education. Australia 2006

Tolle, Eckhart. *"The Power of Now,"* Hachette. Australia 2011

Warrillow, John. *"Built to Sell,"* Portfolio. USA 2011

Endnotes

[1] McAlaney, Clare. *"Inspirational WA Women, Their Story."* Creatavision Publishing Australia. 2016

[2] Talking Heads. *"Burning Down the House."* from the Album *"Speaking in Tongues."* Sire. 1983

[3] Mind Tools Content Team. *"The Conscious Competence Ladder"* Mind Tools. https://www.mindtools.com/pages/article/newISS_96.htm

[4] Dweck, Carol. Growth Mindset theory, popularized in her book, *"Mindset: The New Psychology of Success"* Ballantine Books. USA. 2007

[5] Image shared by Be One https://www.thebeone.com/post/fixed-vs-growth-mindset

[6] Oxford Learners Dictionaries. *Definition of Vision.* https://www.oxfordlearnersdictionaries.com/definition/english/vision?q=vision

[7] 2016 Deloitte Study *"Employee Engagement Disrupted"* Conducted by, Josh Bersin, Deloitte Principal. Further reading at Deloitte Insights https://www2.deloitte.com/us/en/insights/focus/human-capital-trends/2016/employee-engagement-and-retention.html

[8] *Collins, Jim and Morten T. Hansen* "Great by Choice," Century Trade. USA 2011https://www.jimcollins.com/books/great-by-choice.html

[9] Senik, Simon. Twitter Tweet https://twitter.com/simonsinek/status/456545886143643649?lang=en

[10] Senik, Simon. *"How Great Leaders Inspire Action."* TED Talk. 2009 https://www.ted.com/talks/simon_sinek_how_great_leaders_inspire_action?

[11] Lexico. *Definition of Key Performance Indicator* https://www.lexico.com/en/definition/key_performance_indicator

[12] The 'S.M.A.R.T' acronym first appeared in the November 1981 issue of *Management Review*, written by George Doran, Arthur Miller and James Cunningham. https://www.achieveit.com/resources/blog/the-history-and-evolution-of-smart-goals

[13] Matthews, Dr Gail. *"Written Goals Study,"* Goalband. UK. http://www.goalband.co.uk/uploads/1/0/6/5/10653372/gail_matthews_research_summary.pdf

[14] Lexico. *Definition of Reticular Formation* https://www.lexico.com/en/definition/reticular_formation

[15] ActionCOACH, *"The 5 Reasons Customers Leave,"* ServiceRICH Workshop. 2020

[16] IBIS World: Where Knowledge is Power Website https://www.ibisworld.com

[17] Legal information verified by Jeremy McKerracher (LLB, LLM), Juniper Legal

[18] Legal information verified by Jeremy McKerracher (LLB, LLM), Juniper Legal

[19] Legal information verified by Jeremy McKerracher (LLB, LLM), Juniper Legal

[20] Legal information verified by Jeremy McKerracher (LLB, LLM), Juniper Legal

[21] Data provided by Lance Toutountzis, Toutountzis Insurance & Investment Services, ABN: 57 009 323 915

[22] Data provided by Risk Management and Insurance Services Pty Ltd, AFSL 403727

[23] Pape, Scott. *"The Barefoot Investor,"* Wiley. Australia 2019 https://barefootinvestor.com/barefoot-steps/step-2-set-up-buckets/

[24] Collier, Robert. *"Success is the Sum of Small Efforts Repeated Day in and Day Out."* Independently Published. 2019 https://www.amazon.com/Success-small-efforts-repeated-out/dp/1095627341

[25] LinkedIn Learning. *34% of Salary Wasted* https://learning.linkedin.com/blog/engaging-your-workforce/how-to-calculate-the-cost-of-employee-disengagement

[26] Engage and Grow Global. *"Global Disengagement Statistics,"* AON PLC, 2018

[27] Alessandra, Dr Tony. *"DISC and Motivator Profile Assessments"* https://www.alessandra.com/

[28] National Geographic is the official magazine of the National Geographic Society. It has been published continuously since its first issue in 1888. https://www.nationalgeographic.com/magazine/

[29] Collins Dictionary. *"Definition of Policy."* www.collinsdictionary.com › dictionary › english › policy

[30] Lexico. *"Definition of Process."* https://www.lexico.com/en/definition/process

[31] Oxford Learners Dictionary. *Definition of Procedures."* https://www.oxfordlearnersdictionaries.com/definition/english/procedure

[32] *Singer, Michael. "The Surrender Experiment,"* Yellow Kite. 2015 https://untetheredsoul.com/surrender-experiment

[33] Mosley, Michael. *"The Brain: A Secret History, T.V Mini Series,"* IMDB. *UK 2011* https://www.imdb.com/title/tt7512880/

[34] Suzuki, Wendy. "The Brain Changing Benefits of Exercise," TED Talk. 2017 https://www.ted.com/talks/wendy_suzuki_the_brain_changing_benefits_of_exercise?language=en

[35] *Olsen, Jeff. "The Slight Edge,"* In House Publishing GOKO. USA 2016

About the Author

. . . .

Suzzanne Laidlaw is an internationally accredited and award-winning business coach, passionate about supporting business owners to achieve their dreams. Recognised as a global leader in business planning, Suzzanne has an established career in educating others on the importance of planning which has landed her the affectionate nickname, "The Business Planning Queen."

With her expertise in business planning, business coaching and team engagement, Suzzanne has seen and experienced the myriad of challenges people face in building, running and maintaining a happy, profitable business. Firmly believing that everyone has the ability to break free of their old habits and plan for greater success, Suzzanne's aim is to help business owners globally to overcome their setbacks and reach their true potential.

With over 25 years in key business management roles and as an elite athlete, Suzzanne knows what it takes to overcome adversity, and function at the top level to achieve extraordinary results.

Attributing her combined love of coaching and business with her drive to help others, Suzzanne's personal vision is to become a *Millionaire of Hearts*; that is, positively impact one million people on this Earth before she dies. Living by the law of reciprocity, she believes that sharing her knowledge has a way of empowering others, bettering the economy and the world in which we live.

It gives Suzzanne great pleasure to help mentor and coach other business owners to develop the necessary foundations to grow a sustainable and successful business that withholds all challenges.